ICTS 096 Basic Skills

Teacher Certification Exam

By: Sharon Wynne, M.S.

XAMonline, INC.

Boston

XAMonline, Inc.
25 First Street, Suite 106
Cambridge, MA 02141
Toll Free 1-800-509-4128
Email: info@xamonline.com
Web www.xamonline.com
Fax: 1-617-583-5552

Library of Congress Cataloging-in-Publication Data
Wynne, Sharon A.
ICTS: Basic Skills 096 Teacher Certification / Sharon A. Wynne.
ISBN: 978-1-58197-694-6
1. ICTS: Basic Skills 096 2. Study Guides. 3. ICTS 4. Teachers' Certification & Licensure. 5. Careers

Managing Editor	Dr. Harte Weiner, Ph. D.
Copy Editor	Eleanor Binnings, M.A.
Production Coordinator	David Aronson

Disclaimer:

The opinions expressed in this publication are the sole works of XAMonline and were created independently from the National Education Association, Educational Testing Service, and any State Department of Education, National Evaluation Systems or other testing affiliates. Between the time of publication and printing, state specific standards as well as testing formats and website information may change that is not included in part or in whole within this product. Sample test questions are developed by XAMonline and reflect similar content as on real tests; however, they are not former tests. XAMonline assembles content that aligns with state standards but makes no claims nor guarantees of teacher candidates achieving a passing score. Numerical scores are determined by testing companies such as NES or ETS and then are compared with individual state standards. A passing score varies from state to state.

Printed in the United States of America

ICTS: Basic Skills 096
ISBN: 978-1-58197-694-6

Table of Contents

SUBAREA I.   READING COMPREHENSION

COMPETENCY 1.0   DETERMINE THE MEANING OF WORDS AND PHRASES IN CONTEXT 1

Skill 1.1   Use context clues to determine the meaning of unfamiliar words or words with multiple meanings.. 1

Skill 1.2   Recognize the correct use of commonly misused pairs in a passage. 5

Skill 1.3   Determine the meaning of figurative or colloquial language in a passage. 9

Skill 1.4   Identify appropriate synonyms or antonyms for words in a passage 11

COMPETENCY 2.0   UNDERSTAND THE MAIN IDEA AND SUPPORTING DETAILS IN WRITTEN MATERIAL 12

Skill 2.1   Identify the stated main idea of a paragraph or passage.................. 12

Skill 2.2   Establish the sequence of events or steps presented in a passage. 13

Skill 2.3   Recognize information that supports, illustrates, or elaborates the main idea of a paragraph or a passage. 14

Skill 2.4   Identify the meaning of a figurative expression in a passage. 15

COMPETENCY 3.0   APPLY SKILLS OF INFERENCE AND INTERPRETATION OF A VARIETY OF WRITTEN MATERIALS 16

Skill 3.1   Recognize a writer's implied purpose for writing.............................. 16

Skill 3.2   Identify the statement that best expresses the implied main idea of a paragraph or passage 16

Skill 3.3   Recognize implied cause-and-effect relationships in a passage 17

Skill 3.4   Interpret the content, word choice, and phrasing of a passage to determine a writer's opinions, point of view, or position on an issue 18

COMPETENCY 4.0   ANALYZE RELATIONSHIPS AMONG IDEAS IN WRITTEN MATERIAL 20

Skill 4.1   Recognize similarities and differences among ideas in a passage..20

Skill 4.2   Analyze relationships between ideas in opposition 21

Skill 4.3   Select solutions to problems based on information presented in written material 22

Skill 4.4   Draw conclusions from information stated or implied in a passage..23

COMPETENCY 5.0   USE CRITICAL REASONING SKILLS TO EVALUATE WRITTEN MATERIAL 25

Skill 5.1   Recognize stated or implied assumptions upon which the validity of an argument depends...25

Skill 5.2   Determine the relevance of specific facts, examples, or graphic data to a writer's argument 26

Skill 5.3   Recognize fallacies in the logic of a writer's argument 27

Skill 5.4   Recognize qualifying language and distinguish between fact and opinion in written material..28

Skill 5.5   Assess the credibility, objectivity, or bias of the author of a passage or the author's sources 30

COMPETENCY 6.0   APPLY SKILLS FOR OUTLINING AND SUMMARIZING WRITTEN MATERIALS AND FOR INTERPRETING INFORMATION..33

Skill 6.1   Organize the main ideas in a passage into an outline or another form of graphic or tabular organization 33

Skill 6.2   Identify an accurate summary of a passage 34

Skill 6.3   Interpret information presented in charts, graphs, or tables 34

Sample Test: Reading **35**

Answer Key: Reading **45**

Rigor Table: Reading **46**

Rationales with Sample Questions: Reading **47**

SUBAREA II.   **LANGUAGE ARTS**

COMPETENCY 7.0   **DEMONSTRATE COMMAND OF STANDARD USAGE IN EDITED ENGLISH IN THE UNITED STATES** **67**

Skill 7.1   Understand the standard use of verbs 67

Skill 7.2   Identify and apply the standard use of pronouns 81

Skill 7.3   Recognize and apply the standard use of modifiers 91

COMPETENCY 8.0   **UNDERSTAND AND APPLY KNOWLEDGE OF MECHANICAL CONVENTIONS IN EDITED ENGLISH IN THE UNITED STATES** **95**

Skill 8.1   Recognize instances in which incorrect or extraneous punctuation has been used or necessary punctuation has been omitted 95

Skill 8.2   Identify standard initial capitalization and standard capitalization with proper words and titles 99

Skill 8.3   Recognize the standard spelling of words 104

COMPETENCY 9.0   **UNDERSTAND THE ROLE OF PURPOSE AND AUDIENCE IN WRITTEN COMMUNICATION** **110**

Skill 9.1   Assess the appropriateness of written material for a specific purpose or audience 110

Skill 9.2   Determine the likely effect on an audience of a writer's choice of a particular word or words 110

Skill 9.3   Identify persuasive techniques used by a writer in a passage 111

Skill 9.4   Demonstrate the ability to adapt forms, organizational strategies, and styles for different audiences and purposes 112

COMPETENCY 10.0 UNDERSTAND UNITY, FOCUS, DEVELOPMENT AND ORGANIZATION IN WRITING 113

Skill 10.1   Identify organizational methods used by the author of a passage 113

Skill 10.2   Distinguish between effective and ineffective thesis statements 114

Skill 10.3   Recognize unnecessary shifts in point of view or distracting details that impair development of the main idea in a passage 115

Skill 10.4   Select appropriate and effective supporting material 115

Skill 10.5   Recognize examples of focused, concise, and well-developed writing 116

COMPETENCY 11.0 UNDERSTAND AND APPLY EDITING AND REVISION STRATEGIES 118

Skill 11.1   Apply editing and revision strategies affecting diction, syntax, transitions, organization, clarity, coherence, and point of view 118

Skill 11.2   Make revisions that improve the unity and focus of a passage or that improve cohesion and the effective sequence of ideas 119

Skill 11.3   Improve the clarity and effectiveness of a passage through changes in word choice 120

Skill 11.4   Eliminate or replace unnecessary or imprecise words and phrases 125

Skill 11.5   Insert appropriate transitional words or phrases in a passage to convey the structure of the text and to help readers understand the sequence of a writer's ideas 125

COMPETENCY 12.0 RECOGNIZE SENTENCES AND PARAGRAPHS THAT EFFECTIVELY COMMUNICATE INTENDED MESSAGES 127

Skill 12.1   Demonstrate an understanding of unity within paragraphs and apply methods for enhancing paragraph organization and unity 127

Skill 12.2   Recognize effective topic sentences and distinguish between effective and ineffective development of ideas within a paragraph 127

Skill 12.3   Identify sentence fragments and run-on sentences 127

Skill 12.4   Recognize wordiness, redundancy, and ineffective repetition in sentences and paragraphs 135

Skill 12.5   Recognize inefficiency in sentence and paragraph construction 138

COMPETENCY 13.0 PREPARE AN ORGANIZED, DEVELOPED COMPOSITION IN EDITED ENGLISH AS USED IN THE UNITED STATES IN REPONSE TO INSTRUCTIONS REGARDING CONTENT, PURPOSE, AND AUDIENCE 141

Sample Test: Language Arts 155

Answer Key: Language Arts 167

Rigor Table: Language Arts 168

Rationales with Sample Questions: Language Arts 169

SUBAREA III.   **MATHEMATICS**

COMPETENCY 14.0 SOLVE PROBLEMS INVOLVING INTEGERS, FRACTIONS, DECIMALS AND UNITS OF MEASUREMENT 194

Skill 14.1   Solve problems involving integers, fractions, and decimals, including percentages 194

Skill 14.2   Solve problems involving ratios and proportions 212

Skill 14.3   Solve problems involving units of measurement, including U.S. customary and metric measurements and conversions, including scientific notation 215

Skill 14.4   Use estimation skills to solve problems 219

COMPETENCY 15.0 APPLY MATHEMATICAL REASONING SKILLS TO ANALYZE PATTERNS AND SOLVE PROBLEMS 221

Skill 15.1   Draw conclusions using inductive reasoning 221

Skill 15.2   Draw conclusions using deductive reasoning. 224

Skill 15.3   Identify errors in mathematical explanations 227

COMPETENCY 16.0 SOLVE PROBLEMS INVOLVING ALGEBRA AND GEOMETRY 228

Skill 16.1   Graph numbers or number relationships 228

Skill 16.2   Find the value of the unknown in a given one-variable equation 235

Skill 16.3   Express one variable in terms of a second variable in two-variable equations 236

Skill 16.4   Solve problems involving lines and angles 238

Skill 16.5   Solve problems involving two- and three-dimensional geometric figures 241

COMPETENCY 17.0 UNDERSTAND CONCEPTS AND PROCEDURES RELATED TO DATA ANALYSIS AND STATISTICS..........251

Skill 17.1   Interpret information from tables, line graphs, bar graphs, histograms, pictographs, and pie charts.............................251

Skill 17.2   Recognize appropriate representations of various data in graphic form (discrete and continuous).........................254

Skill 17.3   Demonstrate an understanding of fundamental statistical concepts..255

Skill 17.4   Interpret graphic and nongraphic representations of frequency distributions, percentiles, central tendency, variability, and correlation..256

COMPETENCY 18.0 SOLVE APPLIED PROBLEMS USING A COMBINATION OF MATHEMATICAL SKILLS 258

Skill 18.1   Apply combinations of mathematical skills to solve a series of related problems........................258

Skill 18.2   Identify an equation to solve word problems involving one and two variables........................258

Skill 18.3   Apply number concepts and geometric principles to solve practical problems........................262

Skill 18.4   Apply statistical principles to analyze patterns and trends in data.....262

Sample Test: Mathematics **264**

Answer Key: Mathematics **277**

Rigor Table: Mathematics **278**

Rationales with Sample Questions: Mathematics..**279**

Great Study and Testing Tips!

What to study in order to prepare for the subject assessments is the focus of this study guide, but equally important is *how* you study.

You can increase your chances of truly mastering the information by taking some simple but effective steps.

Study Tips:

1. Some foods aid the learning process. Foods such as milk, nuts, seeds, rice, and oats help your study efforts by releasing natural memory enhancers called CCKs (*cholecystokinin*) composed of *tryptophan*, *choline*, and *phenylalanine*. All of these chemicals enhance the neurotransmitters associated with memory. Before studying, try a light, protein-rich meal of eggs, turkey, and fish. All of these foods release the memory-enhancing chemicals. The better the connections, the more you comprehend.

Likewise, before you take a test, stick to a light snack of energy-boosting and relaxing foods. A glass of milk, a piece of fruit, or some peanuts all release various memory-boosting chemicals and help you to relax and focus on the subject at hand.

2. Learn to take great notes. A by-product of our modern culture is that we have grown accustomed to getting our information in short doses (i.e., TV news sound-bytes or *USA Today*-style newspaper articles.)

Consequently, we've subconsciously trained ourselves to assimilate information better in neat little packages. Scrawling notes all over the paper fragments the flow of the information. Strive for clarity. Newspapers use a standard format to achieve clarity. Your notes can be much clearer through use of proper formatting. A very effective format is called the *"Cornell Method."*

> Take a sheet of looseleaf, lined notebook paper and draw a line all the way down the paper about 2-½" from the left-hand edge.

> Draw another line across the width of the paper about 2" up from the bottom. Repeat this process on the reverse side of the page.

Look at the highly effective result. You have ample room for notes, a left-hand margin for emphasizing special items or for inserting supplementary data from the textbook, a large area at the bottom for a brief summary, and a little rectangular space for just about anything you want.

3. <u>Get the concept, then the details</u>. Too often we focus on the details and don't gather an understanding of the concept. However, if we simply memorize only dates, places, or names, we may well miss the whole point of the subject.

A key way to understand concepts is to put them in your own words. If you are working from a textbook, automatically summarize each paragraph in your mind. If you are outlining text, don't simply copy the author's words.

Rephrase the concepts in your own words. You remember your own thoughts and words much better than someone else's and subconsciously tend to associate the important details to the core concepts.

4. <u>Ask why.</u> Pull apart written material paragraph by paragraph, and remember to look at the captions under the illustrations. Then ask why.

Example: If the heading is "Stream Erosion", flip it around to read "Why do streams erode?" Then answer the question.

If you train your mind to think in a series of questions and answers, not only will you learn more, but this process will also help to lessen test anxiety because you are used to answering questions.

5. <u>Read for reinforcement and future needs</u>. Even if you only have ten minutes, put your notes or a book in your hand. Your mind is similar to a computer; you have to input data in order to have it processed. *By reading, you are creating the neural connections for future retrieval.* The more times you read a text, the more you reinforce the learning of its ideas.

Even if you don't fully understand something on the first pass, *your mind stores much of the material for later recall.*

6. <u>Relax to learn, so go into exile</u>. Our bodies respond to an inner clock called biorhythms. Burning the midnight oil works well for some people, but not everyone.

If possible, set aside a particular place to study that is free of distractions. Shut off the television, cell phone, and pager, and exile your friends and family during your study period.

If you really are bothered by silence, try background music. Light classical music at a low volume has been shown to aid in concentration over other types. Music that evokes pleasant emotions without lyrics is highly suggested. Anything by Mozart relaxes you.

7. <u>Use arrows, not highlighters</u>. At best, it's difficult to read a page full of yellow, pink, blue, and green streaks. Try staring at a neon sign for a while, and you'll soon see that the horde of colors obscures the message.

A quick note, a brief dash of color, an underline, and an arrow pointing to a particular passage are much clearer than a horde of highlighted words.

8. **Budget your study time.** Although you shouldn't ignore any of the material, *allocate your available study time in the same ratio that topics may appear on the test.*

Testing Tips:

1. <u>Get smart, play dumb</u>. Don't read anything into the question. Don't make an assumption that the writer of the test is looking for something else than what is asked. Stick to the question as written, and don't read extra things into it.

2. <u>Read the question and all the choices _twice_ before answering the question</u>. You may miss something by not carefully reading--and then re-reading--both the question and the answers.

If you really don't have a clue as to the right answer, don't answer the first time through. Go on to the other questions, which may provide a clue as to how to answer skipped questions.

If later on, you still can't answer the skipped ones . . . *Guess.* The only penalty for guessing is that you *might* get it wrong. Only one thing is certain: if you don't put anything down, you will get it wrong!

3. <u>Turn the question into a statement</u>. Look at the way the questions are worded. The syntax of the question usually provides a clue. Does it seem more familiar as a statement rather than as a question? Does it sound strange?

By turning a question into a statement, you may be able to spot if an answer sounds right, and it may also trigger memories of material you have read.

4. <u>Look for hidden clues</u>. It's actually very difficult to compose multiple- choice questions without giving away part of the answer in the options presented.

In most multiple-choice questions you can often readily eliminate one or two of the potential answers. This leaves you with only two real possibilities, and automatically your odds go to 50-50 for very little work.

5. <u>Trust your instincts</u>. For every fact you have read, you subconsciously retain something of that knowledge. On questions that you aren't really certain about, go with your basic instincts. **Your first impression on how to answer a question is usually correct.**

6. <u>Mark your answers directly on the test booklet</u>. Don't bother trying to fill in the optical scan sheet on the first pass through the test.

Be careful not to miss-mark your answers when you transcribe them to the scan sheet.

7. <u>Watch the clock</u>! You have a set amount of time to answer the questions. Don't get bogged down trying to answer a single question at the expense of ten questions you can more readily answer.

THIS PAGE BLANK

COMPETENCY 1.0   DETERMINE THE MEANING OF WORDS AND PHRASES IN CONTEXT

Skill 1.1   Use context clues to determine the meaning of unfamiliar words or words with multiple meanings.

Context clues help readers determine the meaning of words they are not familiar with. The context of a word is the sentence or sentences that surround the word.

Read the following sentences and attempt to determine the meanings of the words in bold print.

> The **luminosity** of the room was so incredible that there was no need for lights.

> If there was no need for lights then one must assume that the word luminosity has something to do with giving off light. The definition of luminosity is: the emission of light.

> Jamie could not understand Joe's feelings. His mood swings made understanding him somewhat of an **enigma.**

> The fact that he could not be understood made him somewhat of a puzzle. The definition of enigma is: a mystery or puzzle.

Familiarity with word roots (the basic elements of words) and with prefixes can also help one determine the meanings of unknown words.

Following is a partial list of roots and prefixes. It might be useful to review these.

Root	Meaning	Example
aqua	water	aqualung
astro	stars	astrology
bio	life	biology
carn	meat	carnivorous
circum	around	circumnavigate
geo	earth	geology
herb	plant	herbivorous
mal	bad	malicious
neo	new	neonatal
tele	distant	telescope

Prefix	Meaning	Example
un-	not	unnamed
re-	again	reenter
il-	not	illegible
pre-	before	preset
mis-	incorrectly	misstate
in-	not	informal
anti-	against	antiwar
de-	opposite	derail
post-	after	postwar
ir-	not	irresponsible

Word forms

Sometimes a very familiar word can appear as a different part of speech.

You may have heard that *fraud* involves a criminal misrepresentation, so when it appears in its adjective form *fraudulent* ("He was suspected of fraudulent activities."), you can make an educated guess.

You probably know that something out of date is *obsolete;* therefore, when you read about "built-in *obsolescence,*" you can detect the meaning of the unfamiliar word.

Practice Questions: Read the following sentences and attempt to determine the meanings of the underlined words.

1.	Farmer John got a two-horse plow and went to work. Straight <u>furrows</u> stretched out behind him.

	The word <u>furrows</u> means

	(A)	long cuts made by plow
	(B)	vast, open fields
	(C)	rows of corn
	(D)	pairs of hitched horses

2.	The survivors struggled ahead, <u>shambling</u> through the terrible cold, doing their best not to fall.

	The word <u>shambling</u> means

	(A)	frozen in place
	(B)	running
	(C)	shivering uncontrollably
	(D)	walking awkwardly

Answers:

1. (A) is the correct answer. The words "straight" and the expression "stretched out behind him" are your clues.

2. (D) is the correct answer. The words "ahead" and "through" are your clues.

*   *   *

The context for a word is the written passage that surrounds it. Sometimes the writer offers synonyms—words that have nearly the same meaning. Context clues can appear within the sentence itself, within the preceding and/or following sentence(s), or in the passage as a whole.

Sentence clues

Often, a writer will actually **define** a difficult or particularly important word for you the first time it appears in a passage. Phrases such as *that is, such as, which is,* or *is called* might announce the writer's intention to give just the definition you need. Occasionally, a writer will simply use a synonym (a word that means the same thing) or near-synonym joined by the word *or.* Look at the following examples:

> *The <u>credibility</u>, that is to say the believability, of the witness was called into question by evidence of previous perjury.*

> *Nothing would <u>assuage</u> or lessen the child's grief.*

Punctuation at the sentence level is often a clue to the meaning of a word. Commas, parentheses, quotation marks and dashes tell the reader that a definition is being offered by the writer.

> *A tendency toward <u>hyperbole,</u> extravagant exaggeration, is a common flaw among persuasive writers.*

> *Political <u>apathy</u>--lack of interest--can lead to the death of the state.*

A writer might simply give an **explanation** in different words that you can understand in the same sentence:

> *The <u>xenophobic</u> townspeople were suspicious of every foreigner.*

Writers also explain a word in terms of its opposite at the sentence level:

> *His <u>incarceration</u> was ended, and he was elated to be out of jail.*

Adjacent sentence clues

The context for a word goes beyond the sentence in which it appears. At times, the writer uses adjacent (adjoining) sentences to present an explanation or definition:

> *The 200 dollars for the car repair would have to come out of the <u>contingency</u> fund. Fortunately, Angela's father had taught her to keep some money set aside for just such emergencies.*

Analysis: The second sentence offers a clue to the definition of *contingency* as used in this sentence: "emergencies." Therefore, a fund for contingencies would be money tucked away for unforeseen and/or urgent events.

Entire passage clues

On occasion, you must look at an entire paragraph or passage to figure out the definition of a word or term. In the following paragraph, notice how the word *nostalgia* undergoes a form of extended definition throughout the selection rather than in just one sentence.

> *The word <u>nostalgia</u> links Greek words for "away from home" and "pain." If you're feeling <u>nostalgic</u>, then, you are probably in some physical distress or discomfort, suffering from a feeling of alienation and separation from loved ones or loved places. <u>Nostalgia</u> is that awful feeling you remember the first time you went away to camp or spent the weekend with a friend's family—homesickness or some condition even more painful than that. But in common use, <u>nostalgia</u> has come to have more sentimental associations. A few years back, for example, a <u>nostalgia</u> craze had to do with the 1950s. We resurrected poodle skirts and saddle shoes, built new restaurants to look like old ones, and tried to make chicken à la king just as mother probably never made it. In TV situation comedies, we recreated a pleasant world that probably never existed and relished our <u>nostalgia,</u> longing for a homey, comfortable, lost time.*

Skill 1.2   Recognize the correct use of commonly misused pairs (e.g., affect/effect) in a passage.

Students frequently encounter problems with homonyms—words that are spelled and pronounced the same as another but that have different meanings such as *mean*, a verb, "to intend"; *mean* an adjective, "unkind"; and *mean* a noun or adjective, "average." These words are actually both homonyms and homographs (written the same way).

A similar phenomenon that causes trouble is heteronyms (also sometimes called heterophones), words that are spelled the same but have different pronunciations and meanings. (In other words, they are homographs that differ in pronunciation or, technically, homographs that are not homophones). For example, the homographs *desert* (abandon) and *desert* (arid region) are heteronyms (pronounced differently); but *mean* (intend) and *mean* (average) are not. They are pronounced the same, or are homonyms.

Another similar occurrence in English is the capitonym, a word that is spelled the same but has different meanings when it is capitalized and may or may not have different pronunciations. Example: *polish* (to make shiny) and *Polish* (from Poland).

Some of the most troubling homonyms are those that are spelled differently but sound the same. Examples: *its* (third-person singular neuter pronoun) and *it's* ("it is"); *there*, *their* (third-person plural pronoun) and *they're* ("they are"); and *to, too,* and *two.*

Some homonyms/homographs are particularly complicated. *Fluke*, for instance, is a fish, a flatworm, the end parts of an anchor, the fins on a whale's tail, and a stroke of luck.

Common misused words:

Accept is a verb meaning to receive or to tolerate. **Except** is usually a preposition meaning excluding. Except is also a verb meaning to exclude.

Advice is a noun meaning recommendation. **Advise** is a verb meaning to recommend.

Affect is usually a verb meaning to influence. **Effect** is usually a noun meaning result. Effect can also be a verb meaning to bring about.

Allusion is an indirect reference. **Illusion** is a misconception or false impression.

Add is a verb meaning to put together. **Ad** is a noun abbreviating the word advertisement.

Ain't is a common nonstandard contraction for the contraction **aren't**.

Allot is a verb meaning to distribute. **A lot** can be an adverb that means often, or to a great degree. It can also be a noun meaning a large quantity.

Allowed is an adjective that means permitted. **Aloud** is an adverb that means audibly.

Bare is an adjective that means naked or exposed. It can also indicate a minimum. As a noun, **bear** is a large mammal. As a verb, **bear** means to carry a heavy burden.

Capital refers to a city; capitol refers to a building where lawmakers meet. **Capital** also refers to wealth or resources. As an adjective, **capital** means first and foremost.

A **chord** is a noun that refers to a group of musical notes. **Cord** is a noun meaning rope or a long electrical line.

Compliment is a noun meaning a praising or flattering remark. **Complement** is a noun that refers to something that completes or makes perfect.

Climactic is derived from climax, the point of greatest intensity in a series or progression of events. **Climatic** is derived from climate; it refers to meteorological conditions.

Discreet is an adjective that means tactful or diplomatic; **discrete** is an adjective that means separate or distinct.

Dye is a noun or verb used to indicate artificially coloring something. **Die** is a verb that means to pass away. **Die** is also a noun that means a cube-shaped game piece.

Effect is a noun that means outcome. **Affect** is a verb that means to produce an effect.

Elicit is a verb meaning to bring out or to evoke. **Illicit** is an adjective meaning unlawful.

Emigrate means to leave one country or region to settle in another. **Immigrate** means to enter another country and reside there.

Hoard is a verb that means to accumulate or store up. **Horde** is a noun that means a large group.

Lead is a verb that means to guide or serve as the head of. (**Led** is the past tense of **lead**.) **Lead** is also a noun that is a type of metal.

Medal is a noun that means an award. **Meddle** is a verb that means to involve oneself in a matter without right or invitation. **Metal** is an element such as silver or gold. **Mettle** is a noun meaning toughness or courage.

Morning is a noun indicating the time between midnight and midday. **Mourning** is a verb or noun pertaining to the period of grieving after a death.

Past is a noun meaning a time before now (past, present and future). **Passed** is past tense of the verb "to pass."

Piece is a noun meaning a portion. **Peace** is a noun meaning harmony or the opposite of war.

Peak is a noun meaning the tip or height or the highest point. **Peek** is a verb that means to take a brief look. **Pique** is a verb meaning to incite or raise interest.

Principal is a noun meaning the head of a school or an organization or a sum of money. As an adjective, it means most important. **Principle** is a noun meaning a basic truth or law.

Rite is a noun meaning a special ceremony. **Right** is an adjective meaning correct or direction. **Write** is a verb meaning to compose in writing.

Than is a conjunction used in comparisons; **then** is an adverb denoting time.

There is an adverb specifying place; it is also an expletive. (Expletive: <u>There</u> are two plums left.) **Their** is a possessive pronoun. **They're** is a contraction of they are.
To is a preposition; **too** is an adverb; **two** is a number.

Your is a possessive pronoun; **you're** is a contraction of *you are*.

Strategies to help students conquer these demons: Practice using them in sentences. Context is useful in understanding the difference. Drill is necessary to overcome the misuses.

To effectively teach language, it is necessary to understand that as human beings acquire language, they realize that words have denotative and connotative meanings. Generally, denotative words define, and connotative words deal with mental suggestions that the words convey. The word skunk has a denotative meaning if the speaker intends the word to identify the actual animal. Skunk has connotative meaning depending upon the tone of delivery, the socially acceptable attitudes about the animal, and the speaker's personal feelings about the animal.

Problem Phrases

Correct	Incorrect
Supposed to	Suppose to
Used to	Use to
Toward	Towards
Anyway	Anyways
Couldn't care less	Could care less
For all intents and purposes	For all intensive purposes
Come to see me	Come and see me
En route	In route
Regardless	Irregardless
Second, Third	Secondly, Thirdly

Other confusing words

Lie is an intransitive verb meaning to recline or rest on a surface. Its principal parts are lie, lay, lain. **Lay** is a transitive verb meaning to put or place. Its principal parts are lay, laid, laid.

> Birds lay eggs.
> I lie down for bed around 10 PM.

Set is a transitive verb meaning to put or to place. Its principal parts are set, set, set. **Sit** is an intransitive verb meaning to be seated. Its principal parts are sit, sat, sat.

> I set my backpack down near the front door.
> They sat in the park until the sun went down.

Among is a preposition to be used with three or more items. **Between** is to be used with two items.

> Between you and me, I cannot tell the difference among those three Johnson sisters.

As is a subordinating conjunction used to introduce a subordinating clause. **Like** is a preposition meaning "similar to" that is followed by a noun or a noun phrase.

> As I walked to the lab, I realized that the recent experiment findings were much like those we found last year.

Can is a verb that means to be able. **May** is a verb that means to have permission. They are only interchangeable in cases of possibility.

> I can lift 250 pounds.
> May I go to Alex's house?

Skill 1.3   Determine the meaning of figurative or colloquial language in a passage.

1. Simile: Direct comparison between two things. "My love is like a red-red rose."
2. Metaphor: Indirect comparison between two things. The use of a word or phrase denoting one kind of object or action in place of another to suggest a comparison between them. While poets use them extensively, they are also integral to everyday speech. For example, chairs are said to have "legs" and "arms" although we know that it's humans and other animals that have these appendages.
3. Parallelism: The arrangement of ideas in phrases, sentences, and paragraphs that balance one element with another of equal importance and similar wording. An example from Francis Bacon's *Of Studies:* "Reading maketh a full man, conference a ready man, and writing an exact man."
4. Personification: Human characteristics are attributed to an inanimate object, an abstract quality, or animal. Examples: John Bunyan wrote characters named Death, Knowledge, Giant Despair, Sloth, and Piety in his *Pilgrim's Progress*. The metaphor of the arm of a chair is a form of personification.
5. Euphemism: The substitution of an agreeable or inoffensive term for one that might offend or suggest something unpleasant. Many euphemisms are used to refer to death to avoid using the real word--such as "passed away," "crossed over," or "passed."
6. Hyperbole: Deliberate exaggeration for effect or comic effect. An example from Shakespeare's *The Merchant of Venice*:
   > Why, if two gods should play some heavenly match
   > And on the wager lay two earthly women,
   > And Portia one, there must be something else
   > Pawned with the other, for the poor rude world
   > Hath not her fellow.

7. Climax: A number of phrases or sentences are arranged in ascending order of rhetorical forcefulness. Example from Melville's *Moby Dick*:
"All that most maddens and torments; all that stirs up the lees of things; all truth with malice in it; all that cracks the sinews and cakes the brain; all the subtle demonisms of life and thought; all evil, to crazy Ahab, were visibly personified and made practically assailable in Moby Dick."

8. Bathos: A ludicrous attempt to portray pathos—that is, to evoke pity, sympathy, or sorrow. It may result from inappropriately dignifying the commonplace, using elevated language to describe something trivial, or demonstrating greatly exaggerated pathos.

9. Oxymoron: A contradiction in terms that is deliberately employed for effect. It is usually seen in a qualifying adjective whose meaning is contrary to that of the noun it modifies, such as "wise folly."

10. Irony: Expressing something other than and particularly opposite the literal meaning, such as words of praise when blame is intended. In poetry, it is often used as a sophisticated or resigned awareness of contrast between what is and what ought to be and expresses a controlled pathos without sentimentality. It is a form of indirection that avoids overt praise or censure. An early example: the Greek comic character Eiron, a clever underdog who by his wit repeatedly triumphs over the boastful character Alazon.

11. Alliteration: The deliberate repetition of consonant or vowel sounds in two or more neighboring words or syllables. In its simplest form, it reinforces one or two consonant sounds. Example: Shakespeare's Sonnet #12:
When I do count the clock that tells the time.
Some poets have used more complex patterns of alliteration by creating consonants both at the beginning of words and at the beginning of stressed syllables within words. Example: Shelley's "Stanzas Written in Dejection Near Naples"
The City's voice itself is soft like Solitude's

12. Onomatopoeia: The naming of a thing or action by a vocal imitation of the sound associated with it, such as "buzz" or "hiss" or the use of words whose sound suggests the sense. A good example: from "The Brook" by Tennyson:
I chatter over stony ways,
In little sharps and trebles,
I bubble into eddying bays,
I babble on the pebbles.

Skill 1.4   **Identify appropriate synonyms or antonyms for words in a passage.**

Synonyms are words with similar meanings. Sometimes, synonyms can be used in place of another word to make a draft more appealing or descriptive. Teachers should encourage their students to utilize appropriate synonyms when drafting or revising their work to expand a written work's interest and imagery. The thesaurus is helpful in incorporating synonyms into one's writing.

> Examples of synonyms:
> Happy – gay, joyful, ecstatic, content, cheerful
> Angry – irritated, fuming, livid, irate, annoyed
> Beautiful - gorgeous, attractive, striking

However, teachers should also alert students that sometimes one word cannot be simply replaced by another just because it was listed as a synonym. Sometimes the meaning or the connotation will vary somewhat. For example, in the sentence "Harold was <u>angry</u> when his brother spilled fingerpaint on his book report." Replacing "angry" with "fuming" might be a better choice than "annoyed" as the words describe the situation a little differently. As teachers work with students, they can help students expand their vocabularies so students know which synonyms to use.

Antonyms are words that have opposite meanings. Like with synonyms, a thesaurus will help students identify words that are antonyms.

> Examples of antonyms:
> Sad – cheerful, delighted
> Angry - calm, content
> Beautiful – ugly, repulsive, hideous

COMPETENCY 2.0 UNDERSTAND THE MAIN IDEA AND SUPPORTING DETAILS IN WRITTEN MATERIAL

Skill 2.1 Identify the stated main idea of a paragraph or passage.

The main idea of a passage or paragraph is the basic message, idea, point, concept, or meaning that the author wants to convey to the reader. Understanding the main idea of a passage or paragraph is the key to understanding the more subtle components of the author's message. The main idea is what is being said about a topic or subject. Once you have identified the basic message, you will have an easier time answering other questions that test critical skills.

Main ideas are either *stated* or *implied*. A *stated main idea* is explicit. It is directly expressed in a sentence or two in the paragraph or passage. An *implied main idea* is suggested by the overall reading selection. In the first case, you need not pull information from various points in the paragraph or passage in order to form the main idea because it is already stated by the author. If a main idea is implied, however, you must formulate, in your own words, a main idea statement by condensing the overall message contained in the material itself.

Practice Question: Read the following passage and select an answer

Sometimes too much of a good thing can become a very bad thing indeed. In an earnest attempt to consume a healthy diet, dietary supplement enthusiasts have been known to overdose. Vitamin C, for example, long thought to help people ward off cold viruses, is currently being studied for its possible role in warding off cancer and other diseases that cause tissue degeneration. Unfortunately, an overdose of vitamin C —more than 10,000 mg—on a daily basis can cause nausea and diarrhea. Calcium supplements, commonly taken by women, are helpful in warding off osteoporosis. More than just a few grams a day, however, can lead to stomach upset and even kidney and bladder stones. Niacin, proven useful in reducing cholesterol levels, can be dangerous in large doses to those who suffer from heart problems, asthma, or ulcers.

The main idea expressed in this paragraph is:

A. supplements taken in excess can be a bad thing indeed
B. dietary supplement enthusiasts have been known to overdose
C. vitamins can cause nausea, diarrhea, and kidney or bladder stones.
D. people who take supplements are preoccupied with their health.

Answer: Answer A is a paraphrase of the first sentence and provides a general framework for the rest of the paragraph: excess supplement intake is bad. The rest of the paragraph discusses the consequences of taking too many vitamins. Options B and C refer to major details, and Option D introduces the idea of preoccupation, which is not included in this paragraph.

Skill 2.2   Establish the sequence of events or steps presented in a passage.

The ability to organize events or steps provided in a passage (especially when presented in random order) serves a useful purpose, and it encourages the development of logical thinking and the processes of analysis and evaluation.

Working through and discussing with your students examples like the one below help students to gain valuable practice in sequencing events. In the example below, identify the proper order of events or steps:

Example:
1. Matt tied a knot in his shoelace.
2. Matt put on his green socks because they were clean and complemented the brown slacks he was wearing.
3. Matt took a bath and trimmed his toenails.
4. Matt put on his brown slacks.

Answers: The proper order of events is: 3, 4, 2, and 1

Students need to be aware of their audience and how their writing comes across to their audience in order to write clearly and in a logical sequence. As with events or steps (discussed in Skill 3.1), the ability to organize a set of instructions into the proper sequence (especially when presented in random order) serves a useful purpose, and it encourages the development of logical thinking and the processes of analysis and evaluation.

Skill 2.3   Recognize information that supports, illustrates, or elaborates the main idea of a paragraph or a passage.

Supporting details are examples, facts, ideas, illustrations, cases and anecdotes used by a writer to explain, expand on, and develop the general main idea. A writer's choice of supporting materials is determined by the nature of the topic being covered. Supporting details are specifics that relate directly to the main idea. Writers select and shape material according to their purposes. An advertisement writer seeking to persuade the reader to buy a particular running shoe, for instance, will emphasize only the positive characteristics of the shoe for advertisement copy. A columnist for a running magazine, on the other hand, might list the good and bad points about the same shoe in an article recommending appropriate shoes for different kind of runners. Both major details (those that directly support the main idea) and minor details (those that provide interesting, but not always essential, information) help create a well-written and fluid passage.

In the following paragraph, the sentences in **bold print** provide a skeleton of a paragraph on the benefits of recycling. The sentences in bold are generalizations that by themselves do not explain the need to recycle. The sentences in *italics* add details to SHOW the general points in bold. Notice how the supporting details help you understand the necessity for recycling.

While one day recycling may become mandatory in all states, right now it is voluntary in many communities. *Those of us who participate in recycling are amazed by how much material is recycled.* **For many communities, the blue-box recycling program has had an immediate effect.** *By just recycling glass, aluminum cans, and plastic bottles, we have reduced the volume of disposable trash by one-third, thus extending the useful life of local landfills by over a decade. Imagine the difference if those dramatic results were achieved nationwide.* **The amount of reusable items we thoughtlessly dispose of is staggering.** *For example, Americans dispose of enough steel every day to supply Detroit car manufacturers for three months. Additionally, we dispose of enough aluminum annually to rebuild the nation's air fleet. These statistics, available from the Environmental Protection Agency (EPA), should encourage all of us to watch what we throw away.* **Clearly, recycling in our homes and in our communities directly improves the environment.**

Notice how the author's supporting examples enhance the message of the paragraph and relate to the author's thesis. If you read only the bold-face sentences, you have a glimpse of the topic. This, however, is developed through numerous details creating specific images: *reduced the volume of disposable trash by one-third; extended the useful life of local landfills by over a decade; enough steel every day to supply Detroit car manufacturers for three months; enough aluminum to rebuild the nation's air fleet.* If the writer had merely written a few general sentences, as those shown in bold face, you would not fully understand the vast amount of trash involved in recycling nor the positive results of current recycling efforts.

Skill 2.4 Identify the meaning of a figurative expression in a passage.

See Skill 1.3.

COMPETENCY 3.0   APPLY SKILLS OF INFERENCE AND INTERPRETATION TO A VARIETY OF WRITTEN MATERIALS.

Skill 3.1   Recognize a writer's implied purpose for writing (e.g., to persuade, to describe).

An essay is an extended discussion of a writer's point of view about a particular topic. This point of view may be supported by using such writing modes as examples, argument and persuasion, analysis or comparison/contrast. In any case, a good essay is clear, coherent, well-organized, and fully developed.

When an author sets out to write a passage, he/she usually has a purpose for doing so. That purpose may be to simply give information that might be interesting or useful to a reader; it may be to persuade the reader of a point of view or to move the reader to act in a particular way; it may be to tell a story; or it may be to describe something in such a way that an experience becomes available to the reader through the five senses. Following are the primary devices for expressing a particular purpose in a piece of writing:

- **Basic expository writing** simply gives information not previously known about a topic or is used to explain or define a topic. Facts, examples, statistics, cause and effect, direct tone, objective rather than subjective delivery, and non-emotional information are presented in a formal manner.
- **Descriptive writing** centers on person, place, or object, using concrete and sensory words to create a mood or impression, arranging details in a chronological or spatial sequence.
- **Narrative writing** is developed using an incident or anecdote or related series of events. Chronology, the 5 Ws (who, what, where, when, why), topic sentence, and conclusion are essential ingredients.
- **Persuasive writing** implies the writer's ability to select vocabulary and arrange facts and opinions in such a way as to direct the actions of the listener/reader. Persuasive writing may incorporate exposition and narration to illustrate the main idea.
- **Journalistic writing** is theoretically free of author bias. It is essential when relaying information about an event, person, or thing that it be factual and objective. Provide students with an opportunity to examine newspapers and create their own newspaper. Many newspapers have educational programs that are offered free to schools.

Skill 3.2   Identify the statement that best expresses the implied main idea of a paragraph or passage.

See Skill 2.1

Skill 3.3   Recognize implied cause-and-effect relationships in a passage.

A cause is the necessary source of a particular outcome. If a writer were addressing the question "How will the new tax laws affect small businesses?" or "Why has there been such political unrest in Somalia?", he or she would use cause and effect as an organizational pattern to structure the response. In the first case, the writer would emphasize effects of the tax legislation as they apply to owners of small businesses. In the second, the writer would focus on causes for the current political situation in Somalia.

Some word clues that identify a cause-effect passage are: *accordingly, as a result, therefore, because, consequently, hence, in short, thus, then, due to.*
Sample passage:
Simply put, inflation is an increase in price levels. It happens when a government prints more currency than is already in circulation, and there is, consequently, *additional money available for the same amount of goods or services. There might be multiple* reasons *for a government to crank up the printing presses. A war, for instance, could* cause *an immediate need for steel. A national disaster might create a sudden need for social services. To get the money it needs, a government can raise taxes, borrow, or print more currency. However, raising taxes and borrowing are not always plausible options.*

Analysis: The paragraph starts with a definition and proceeds to examine a causal chain. The words *consequently, reasons* and *cause* provide the clues.

Explicit Cause and Effect

General Hooker failed to anticipate General Lee's bold flanking maneuver. As a result, *Hooker's army was nearly routed by a smaller force.*

Mindy forgot to bring the lunch her father had packed for her. Consequently, *she had to borrow money from her friends at school during lunch period.*

Implicit Cause and Effect

The engine in Lisa's airplane began to sputter. She quickly looked below for a field in which to land.

Luther ate the creamed shrimp that had been sitting in the sun for hours. Later that night, he was so sick he had to be rushed to the hospital.

Skill 3.4 **Interpret the content, word choice, and phrasing of a passage to determine a writer's opinions, point of view, or position on an issue.**

The **tone** of a written passage is the author's attitude toward the subject matter. The tone (mood, feeling) is revealed through the qualities of the writing itself and is a direct product of such stylistic elements as language and sentence structure. The tone of the written passage is much like a speaker's voice; instead of being spoken, however, it is the product of words on a page.

Often, writers have an emotional stake in the subject, and their purpose, either explicitly or implicitly, is to convey those feelings to the reader. In such cases, the writing is generally subjective: that is, it stems from opinions, judgments, values, ideas, and feelings. Both sentence structure (syntax) and word choice (diction) are instrumental tools in creating tone.

Tone may be thought of generally as positive, negative, or neutral. Below is a statement about snakes that demonstrates this.

> *Many species of snakes live in Florida. Some of those species, both poisonous and non-poisonous, have habitats that coexist with those of human residents of the state.*

The voice of the writer in this statement is neutral. The sentences are declarative (not exclamations or fragments or questions). The adjectives are few and nondescript—*many, some, poisonous* (balanced with *non -poisonous*). Nothing much in this brief paragraph would alert the reader to the feelings of the writer about snakes. The paragraph has a neutral, objective, detached, impartial tone.

Then again, if the writer's attitude toward snakes involves admiration or even affection the tone would generally be positive:

> *Florida's snakes are a tenacious bunch. When they find their habitats invaded by humans, they cling to their home territories as long as they can, as if vainly attempting to fight off the onslaught of the human hordes.*

An additional message emerges in this paragraph: The writer quite clearly favors snakes over people. The writer uses adjectives such as *tenacious* to describe his/her feelings about snakes. The writer also humanizes the reptiles, making them brave, beleaguered creatures. Obviously the writer is more sympathetic to snakes than to people in this paragraph.

If the writer's attitude toward snakes involves active dislike and fear, then the tone would also reflect that attitude by being negative:

> *Countless species of snakes, some more dangerous than others, still lurk on the urban fringes of Florida's towns and cities. They will often invade domestic spaces, terrorizing people and their pets.*

Here, obviously, the snakes are the villains. They *lurk,* they *invade,* and they *terrorize.* The tone of this paragraph might be said to be distressed about snakes.

In the same manner, a writer can use language to portray characters as good or bad. A writer uses positive and negative adjectives, as seen above, to convey the manner of a character.

COMPETENCY 4.0   ANALYZE RELATIONSHIPS AMONG IDEAS IN WRITTEN MATERIAL.

Skill 4.1   Recognize similarities and differences among ideas in a passage.

To **compare** ideas or information presented in different sections of a reading selection or from different sources is to point out the similarities in such ideas or information. To **contrast** these ideas or the information is to point out the differences in them.

Keeping track of how the different sections of a reading selection or how different sources present similar ideas or information (comparing) reinforces those ideas or that information for the reader. Keeping track of how the different sections of a reading selection or how different sources present differing ideas or information on some topic (contrasting) alerts readers that there is some degree of controversy operative in the discussion. It might even reveal weaknesses, errors or inconsistencies in the author's or authors' presentation(s).   Both activities, comparing and contrasting, are active reading skills. This means that they require readers to engage with text beyond merely decoding the words in the immediate context. Both activities promote better understanding of the text(s) and longer retention of the information.

Using **graphic organizers** to track comparisons and contrasts can help readers gain a clearer understanding of the points that the author has in mind. Venn diagrams are graphic organizers particularly suited to track comparisons and contrasts. A Venn diagram has two circles. Each circle represents ideas or information from a particular section of a reading selection or from a particular source, and these circles are drawn so that there is an overlap area common to both. Similarities (comparisons) between the ideas or information from the two sections or sources are recorded in the overlap area of the Venn diagram, and differences (contrasts) are recorded in the other areas of the two circles.

As an example of how to apply comparison and contrast skills, consider Edgar Allan Poe's short story, "The Tell-Tale Heart." In it, Poe employed first- person narration to describe a bizarre murder and its after-effects on the narrator, the guilty party. At the beginning of the story, the narrator states that his purpose in describing the events is to establish that he is not crazy because he can describe them impassively. As he nears the story's end, his descriptions become far from impassive.

By contrasting his promise to tell the story impassively with his later wild description of events, readers can gain the insight needed to conclude that even by his own minimal standards, the narrator is truly crazy.

Another useful application of these skills to the same story could be to compare how nearly every paragraph of the story includes at least one revelation by the narrator that would tend to establish that he is crazy no matter how calmly he can tell the story. Both applications allow readers to gain insight into the story's real point.

Skill 4.2   Analyze relationships between ideas in opposition (e.g., pro and con).

Whenever there are two ideas in opposition, there is the ghost of an "either/or" conceptual basis lurking invisibly in the background of the "pro/con" setting.

For example, one person may argue that automobiles are a safer mode of transportation than are motorcycles and support that contention with statistics showing that fatalities are more frequent per accident in motorcycle crashes than in car crashes.

The opposition to this argument may counter that while fatalities are more frequent per accident in motorcycle accidents, it is erroneous to over generalize from that statistic that motorcycles are "therefore more dangerous."

Thus, each participant in the argument has assumed a position of "either/or," that is to say, the automobile is "either" safer than the motorcycle, or it is not (or the motorcycle is "either" safer than the automobile or it is not). With the argument thus formulated, a conclusion acceptable to both sides is not likely to happen.

Here is a short essay showing how to avoid this deadlock.

Which is safer? The car or the motorcycle?

Most experienced drivers would agree that while it is more exhilarating to drive a motorcycle than to drive an automobile, it is illogical to therefore conclude that this exhilaration leads to careless driving and, therefore, to more accidents, deaths, and injuries to motorcycle drivers than to car drivers. The critical concept to be understood here is not the exhilaration of driving a motorcycle, which is a given, but how the exhilaration comes about and causes serious injury and death to motorcycle riders.

There is safe and unsafe thrill-seeking. "Exhilaration" is defined as the "state of being stimulated, refreshed, or elated." An example of safe exhilaration is the excitement of sledding downhill, which results in the sled-rider feeling stimulated, refreshed, and/or elated.

Unsafe exhilaration, which is usually the consequence of reckless thrill-seeking, is, therefore, a state of being over-stimulated, frightened, and depressed by terror.

Which then causes more dangerous exhilaration, the car or the motorcycle? The answer is that the two forms of exhilaration are the consequences not of the motorcycle or the automobile per se, but of the operation of the respective vehicles. Without an operator, both vehicles are metal entities, sitting in space, neither threatening nor harmful to anyone.

Therefore, neither the motorcycle nor the car is more or less dangerous than one another: it is the attitude of their operators that creates the danger, death, and dismemberment resulting from accidents.

Notice how the writer has avoided the logical trap of the "either/or" construction built into the "pro con" argument by defining the key term "exhilaration" to clarify the issue (and shift the focus to the operator) and resolve the either/or dilemma by arguing that it is the operators of the vehicles who are responsible for negative consequences, not the vehicles themselves.

Skill 4.3   Select solutions to problems based on information presented in written material.

Within the assessment of reading, working with more than one selection is important in deciding if students can make generalizations. Sometimes this may involve problems specifically identified within what was read. For example, the characters in the story may be having a specific problem, such as a lack of money. Then as the passage continues, the characters in the story are hired for a new job, which allows them to earn more money. Using the information read, students can identify the problem (a lack of money) and the solution (a new job).

In other cases, generalizations will need to be made across multiple selections. In those cases, selecting problems and solutions may be more evasive. Problems and solutions across texts will require broader thinking. The problems and solutions will not be as clearly spelled out in the text. It will involve thinking on a different level about how the two passages relate. Connecting texts to other texts and finding common elements within them allows drawing out the common problems and solutions. Working through multiple selections requires more complex thinking skills as well as thinking of problems and solutions in other terms. Perhaps thinking of the challenge or issue that is faced in the text and then how that issue is overcome will help to broaden the scope and understanding of identifying the common problem—and, therefore, the solution.

Skill 4.4 Draw conclusions from information stated or implied in a passage.

An **inference** is sometimes called an "educated guess" because it requires that you go beyond the strictly obvious to create additional meaning by taking the text one logical step further. Inferences and conclusions are based on the content of the passage–that is, on what the passage says or how the writer says it–and inferences are derived by reasoning.

Inference is an essential and automatic component of most reading. It involves making educated guesses about the meaning of unknown words, the author's main idea, or the author's biases.. You use your own ability to reason in order to figure out what the writer implies. As a reader, then, you must often logically extend meaning to what is only implied.

Consider the following example. Assume you are an employer, and you are reading over the letters of reference submitted by a prospective employee for the position of clerk/typist in your real estate office. The position requires the applicant to be neat, careful, trustworthy, and punctual. You come across this letter of reference submitted by an applicant:

To Whom It May Concern:

Todd Finley has asked me to write a letter of reference for him. I am well qualified to do so because he worked for me for three months last year. His duties included answering the phone, greeting the public, and producing some simple memos and notices on the computer. Although Todd initially had few computer skills and little knowledge of telephone etiquette, he did acquire some during his stay with us. Todd's manner of speaking, both on the telephone and with the clients who came to my establishment, could be described as casual. He was particularly effective when communicating with peers. Please contact me by telephone if you wish to have further information about my experience with Todd Finley.

Here the writer implies rather than openly states the main idea. This letter calls attention to itself because of its tone. A truly positive letter would say something like "I have distinct honor to recommend Todd Finley." Here, however, the letter simply verifies that Todd worked in the office. Second, the praise is obviously lukewarm. For example, the writer says that Todd "was particularly effective when communicating with peers." And educated guess translates that statement into a nice way of saying Todd was not serious about his communication with clients.

In order to draw **inferences** and make **conclusions**, a reader must use prior knowledge and apply it to the current situation. A conclusion or inference is never stated. You must rely on your common sense.

Practice Questions: Read the following passages and select an answer

1. The Smith family waited patiently around carousel number 7 for their luggage to arrive. They were exhausted after their five-hour trip and were eager to get to their hotel. After about an hour, they realized that they no longer recognized any of the other passengers' faces. Mrs. Smith asked the person who appeared to be in charge if they were at the right carousel. The man replied, "Yes, this is it, but we finished unloading that baggage almost half an hour ago."

    From the man's response we can infer that:
    (A) The Smiths were ready to go to their hotel.
    (B) The Smith's luggage was lost.
    (C) The man had their luggage.
    (D) They were at the wrong carousel.

2. Tim Sullivan had just turned 15. As a birthday present, his parents had given him a guitar and a certificate for ten guitar lessons. He had always shown a love of music and a desire to learn an instrument. Tim began his lessons, and before long, he was making up his own songs. At the music studio, Tim met Josh who played the piano, and Roger who played the saxophone. They all shared the same dream, to start a band, and each was praised by his teacher as having real talent.

    From this passage one can infer that
    (A) Tim, Roger & Josh are going to start their own band.
    (B) Tim is going to give up his guitar lessons.
    (C) Tim, Josh & Roger will no longer be friends.
    (D) Josh & Roger are going to start their own band.

Answers:

1. Since the Smiths were still waiting for their luggage, we know that they were not yet ready to go to their hotel. From the man's response, we know that they were not at the wrong carousel and that he did not have their luggage. Therefore, though not directly stated, it appears that their luggage was lost. Choice (B) is the correct answer.

2. (A) is the correct choice. Given the fact that Tim wanted to be a musician and start his own band, after meeting others who shared the same dreams, we can infer that they joined together in an attempt to make their dreams become a reality.

COMPETENCY 5.0   USE CRITICAL REASONING SKILLS TO EVALUATE WRITTEN MATERIAL.

Skill 5.1   **Recognize stated or implied assumptions on which the validity of an argument depends.**

On the test, the terms **valid** and **invalid** have special meaning. If an argument is valid, it is reasonable. It is objective (not biased) and can be supported by evidence. If an argument is invalid, it is not reasonable. It is not objective. In other words, one can find evidence of bias.

Practice Questions: Read the following passages and select answers:

1.   Most dentists agree that Bright Smile Toothpaste is the best for fighting cavities. It tastes good and leaves your mouth minty fresh.

     Is this a valid or invalid argument?

     (A) valid
     (B) invalid

2.   It is difficult to decide who will make the best presidential candidate, Senator Johnson or Senator Keeley. They have both been involved in scandals and have both gone through messy divorces while in office.

     Is this argument valid or invalid?

     (A) valid
     (B) invalid

Answers:

1. (B) is the correct choice. It mentions that "most" dentists agree. What about those who do not agree? The author is clearly exhibiting bias in leaving those who disagree out. Thus the argument is invalid.

2. (A) is the correct choice. The author appears to be listing facts. He does not seem to favor one candidate over the other. Thus the argument is valid.

Skill 5.2   **Determine the relevance of specific facts, examples, or graphic data to a writer's argument.**

The main idea of a passage may contain a wide variety of supporting information, but it is important that each sentence be related to the main idea. When a sentence contains information that bears little or no connection to the main idea it is said to be **irrelevant**.

The following passage has several irrelevant sentences that are highlighted in bold.

The New City Planning Committee is proposing a new capitol building to represent the multicultural face of New City. **The current mayor is a Democrat.** The new capitol building will be on 10th Street across from the grocery store and next to the recreational center. It will be within walking distance to the subway and bus depot, as the designers want to emphasize the importance of public transportation. Aesthetically, the building will have a contemporary design featuring a brushed-steel exterior and large, floor-to-ceiling windows. **It is important for employees to have a connection with the outside world even when they are in their offices.** Inside the building, the walls will be moveable. This will not only facilitate a multitude of creative floor plans, but it will also create a focus on open communication and flow of information. **It sounds a bit gimmicky to me.** Finally, the capitol building will feature a large outdoor courtyard full of lush greenery and serene fountains. **Work will now seem like Club Med to those who work at the New City capitol building!**

Skill 5.3   Recognize fallacies in the logic of a writer's argument.

An argument is a generalization that is proven or supported with facts. If the facts are not accurate, the generalization remains unproven. Using inaccurate "facts" to support an argument is called a *fallacy* in reasoning. Some factors to consider when judging whether the facts used to support an argument are accurate are as follows:

1. Are the facts current or are they out of date? For example, if the proposition is "Birth defects in babies born to drug-using mothers are increasing," then the data must include the latest that is available.
2. Another important factor to consider in judging the accuracy of a fact is its source. Where was the data obtained, and is that source reliable?
3. The calculations on which the facts are based may be unreliable. It's a good idea to run one's own calculations before using derived information.

Even facts that are true and have a sharp impact on the argument may not be relevant to the case at hand.

1. Health statistics from an entire state may have no relevance, or little relevance, to a particular county or zip code. Statistics from an entire country cannot be used to prove very much about a particular state or county.
2. An analogy can be useful in making a point, but the comparison must match up in all characteristics or it will not be relevant. Analogy should be used very carefully. It is often just as likely to destroy an argument as it is to strengthen it.

The importance or significance of a fact may not be sufficient to strengthen an argument. For example, of the millions of immigrants in the U.S., using a single family to support a solution to the immigration problem will not make much difference overall even though those single-example arguments are often used to support one approach or another. They may achieve a positive reaction, but they will not prove that one solution is better than another. If enough cases were cited from a variety of geographical locations, the information might be significant.

How much is enough? Generally speaking, three strong supporting facts are sufficient to establish the thesis of an argument. For example:

Conclusion: All green apples are sour.

- When I was a child, I bit into a green apple from my grandfather's orchard, and it was sour.
- I once bought green apples from a roadside vendor, and when I bit into one, it was sour.
- My grocery store had a sale on green Granny Smith apples last week, and I bought several only to find that they were sour when I bit into one.

The fallacy in the above argument is that the sample is insufficient. A more exhaustive search of literature, tasting, etc., will probably turn up some green apples that are not sour.

Sometimes more than three arguments are too many. On the other hand, it's not unusual to hear public speakers, particularly politicians, cite a long litany of facts to support their positions.

A very good example of the omission of facts in an argument is the résumé of an applicant for a job. The applicant is arguing that he/she should be chosen to be awarded a particular job. The application form will ask for information about past employment, and unfavorable dismissals from jobs in the past may just be omitted. Employers are usually suspicious of periods of time when the applicant has not listed an employer.

A writer makes choices about which facts will be used and which will be discarded in developing an argument. Those choices may exclude anything that is not supportive of the point of view the arguer is taking. It's always a good idea for the reader to do some research to spot the omissions and to ask whether they have impact on acceptance of the point of view presented in the argument.

No judgment is either black or white. If the argument seems too neat or too compelling, there are probably facts that might be relevant that have not been included.

Skill 5.4 Recognize qualifying language and distinguish between fact and opinion in written material.

Facts are statements that are verifiable. Opinions are statements that must be supported in order to be accepted such as beliefs, values, judgments or feelings. Facts are objective statements used to support subjective opinions. For example, "Jane is a bad girl" is an opinion. However, "Jane hit her sister with a baseball bat" is a *fact* upon which the opinion is based. Judgments are opinions—decisions or declarations based on observation or reasoning that express approval or disapproval. Facts report what has happened or exists and come from observation, measurement, or calculation. Facts can be tested and verified whereas opinions and judgments cannot..

Most statements cannot be so clearly distinguished. "I believe that Jane is a bad girl" is a fact. The speaker knows what he/she believes. However, it obviously includes a judgment that could be disputed by another person who might believe otherwise. Judgments are not usually so firm. Rather, they are plausible opinions that provoke thought or lead to factual development.

Joe DiMaggio, a Yankees' center-fielder, was replaced by Mickey Mantle in 1952.

This is a fact. If necessary, evidence can be produced to support this.

First-year players are more ambitious than seasoned players.

This is an opinion. There is no proof to support that everyone feels this way

Practice Questions: Decide if the statement is fact or opinion

1. The Inca were a group of Indians who ruled an empire in South America.

   (A) fact
   (B) opinion

2. The Inca were clever.

   (A) fact
   (B) opinion

3. The Inca built very complex systems of bridges.

   (A) fact
   (B) opinion

Answers:

1. (A) is the correct answer. Research can prove this to be true.
2. (B) is the correct answer. It is doubtful that all people who have studied the Inca agree with this statement. Therefore, no proof is available.
3. (A) is the correct answer. As with question number one, research can prove this to be true.

Skill 5.5 **Assess the credibility, objectivity, or bias of the author of a passage and/or the author's sources.**

Bias is defined as an opinion, feeling or influence that strongly favors one side in an argument. A statement or passage is biased if an author attempts to convince a reader of something.

Practice Questions: Read the following statement.

1.   Using a calculator cannot help a student understand the process of graphing, so its use is a waste of time.

Is there evidence of bias in the above statement?

(A) yes
(B) no

2.   Some teachers feel that computer programs are quite helpful in helping students grasp certain math concepts. Other teachers disagree with this feeling. It is up to each individual math teacher to decide if computer programs benefit his/her particular group of students.

Is there evidence of bias in this paragraph?

(A) yes
(B) no

Answers:

1. Since the author makes it perfectly clear that he does not favor the use of the calculator in graphing problem, the answer is (A). He has included his opinion in this statement.

2. (B) is the correct answer. The author seems to state both sides of the argument without favoring a particular side.

The sky is blue." "The sky looks like rain." One is a fact; the other, an opinion. This is because one is **readily provable by objective empirical data**, while the other is a **subjective evaluation based upon personal bias**. This means that facts are things that can be proved by the usual means of study and experimentation. We can look and see the color of the sky. Since the shade we are observing is expressed as the color blue and is an accepted norm, the observation that the sky is blue is therefore a fact. (Of course, this depends on other external factors such as time and weather conditions).

This brings us to our next idea: that it looks like rain. This is a subjective observation in that an individual's perception will differ from another. What looks like rain to one person will not necessarily look like that to another person. The question thus remains as to how to differentiate fact from opinion. The best and only way is to ask oneself if what is being stated can be proved from other sources, by other methods, or by the simple process of **reasoning**.

Primary and secondary sources

The resources used to support a piece of writing can be divided into two major groups: primary sources and secondary sources.

Primary sources are the basic materials that provide raw data and information. Secondary sources are the works that contain the explications of--and judgments on--this primary material.

Primary sources include the following kinds of materials:

- Documents that reflect the immediate, everyday concerns of people: memoranda, bills, deeds, charters, newspaper reports, pamphlets, graffiti, popular writings, journals or diaries, records of decision-making bodies, letters, receipts, snapshots, etc.
- Theoretical writings which reflect care and consideration in composition and an attempt to convince or persuade. The topic will generally be deeper and more pervasive values than is the case with "immediate" documents. These may include newspaper or magazine editorials, sermons, political speeches, philosophical writings, etc.
- Narrative accounts of experiments, events, ideas, trends, etc. written with intentionality by someone contemporary with the events described.
- Statistical data, although statistics may be misleading.
- Literature and nonverbal materials, novels, stories, poetry and essays from the period, as well as coins, archaeological artifacts, and art produced during the period.

Secondary sources include the following kinds of materials:

- Books or articles written on the basis of primary materials.

- Books or articles written on the basis of primary materials about persons who played a major role in the events under consideration.
- Books and articles written on the basis of primary materials about the culture, the social norms, the language, and the values of the period.
- Quotations from primary sources.
- Statistical data on the period.
- The conclusions and inferences of other historians.
- Multiple interpretations of the ethos of the time.

Guidelines for the use of secondary sources:

1. Do not rely upon only a single secondary source.
2. Check facts and interpretations against primary sources whenever possible.
3. Do not accept the conclusions of historians uncritically.
4. Place greatest reliance on secondary sources created by the best and most respected scholars.
5. Do not use the inferences of other scholars as if they were facts.
6. Ensure that you recognize any bias the writer brings to his/her interpretation of history.
7. Understand the primary point of the book or article as a basis for evaluating the value of the material presented with regard to your questions.

COMPETENCY 6.0   APPLY SKILLS FOR OUTLINING AND SUMMARIZING MATERIALS AND INTERPRETING INFORMATION PRESENTED IN GRAPHS OR TABLES

Skill 6.1   Organize the main ideas in a passage into an outline or another form of graphic or tabular organization.

Sample Passage

Chile peppers may turn out to be the wonder drug of the decade. The fiery fruit comes in many sizes, shapes, and colors, all of which grow on plants that are genetic descendants of the tepin plant, originally native to the Americas. Connoisseurs of the regional cuisines of the Southwest and Louisiana are already well aware that food flavored with chiles can cause a good sweat, but medical researchers are learning more every day about the medical power of capsaicin, the ingredient in the peppers that produces the heat.

Capsaicin as a pain medication has been a part of folk medicine for centuries. It is, in fact, the active ingredient in several currently available over-the-counter liniments for sore muscles. Recent research has been examining the value of the compound for the treatment of other painful conditions. Capsaicin shows some promise in the treatment of phantom limb syndrome, shingles, and some types of headaches. Additional research focuses upon the use of capsaicin to relieve pain in post-surgical patients. Scientists speculate that application of the compound to the skin causes the body to release endorphins–natural pain relievers manufactured by the body itself. An alternative theory holds that capsaicin somehow interferes with the transmission of signals along the nerve fibers, thus reducing the sensation of pain.

In addition to its well-documented history as a painkiller, capsaicin has recently received attention as a phytochemical, one of the naturally occurring compounds from foods that show cancer-fighting qualities. Like the phytochemical sulfoaphane found in broccoli, capsaicin might turn out to be an agent capable of short-circuiting the actions of carcinogens at the cell level before they cause cancer.

Summary: Chile peppers contain a chemical called capsaicin which has proved useful for treating a variety of ailments. Recent research reveals that capsaicin is a phytochemical, a natural compound that may help fight cancer.

Outline: -Chile peppers could be the wonder drug of the decade
-Chile peppers contains capsaicin
-Capsaicin can be used as a pain medication
-Capsaicin is a phytochemical
-Phytochemicals show cancer-fighting qualities
-Capsaicin might be able to short-circuit the effects of carcinogens

Skill 6.2   Identify an accurate summary of a passage.

See Skill 6.1.

Skill 6.3   Interpret information presented in charts, graphs, or tables.

Many educational disciplines require the ability to recognize representations of written information in graphic or tabular form. Tables help condense and organize written data, and graphs help reveal and emphasize comparisons and trends.

Example: A survey asked five elementary school students to list the number and type of pets they had at home. The first student had three dogs and three fish. The second student had two cats and one dog. The third student had three fish and two dogs. The fourth student had one rabbit, two cats, and one dog. The fifth student had no pets.

Construct a data table and line graph that represents the survey information.

Solution: The following is a table that appropriately represents the data.

Student #	# of Dogs	# of Cats	# of Fish	# of Rabbits	Total # of Pets
1	3	0	3	0	6
2	1	2	0	0	3
3	2	0	3	0	5
4	1	2	0	1	4
5	0	0	0	0	0

The following is a line graph that appropriately represents the total number of pets each student has.

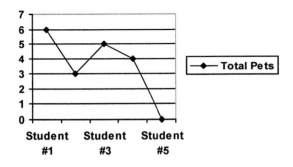

See also Skill 17.1.

Sample Test: Reading

Read the passages and answer the questions that follow.

This writer has often been asked to tutor hospitalized children with cystic fibrosis. While undergoing all the precautionary measures to see these children (i.e. scrubbing thoroughly and donning sterilized protective gear- for the child's protection), she has often wondered why their parents subject these children to the pressures of schooling and trying to catch up on what they have missed because of hospitalization, which is a normal part of cystic fibrosis patients' lives. These children undergo so many tortuous treatments a day that it seems cruel to expect them to learn as normal children do, especially with their life expectancies being as short as they are.

1. **What is meant by the word "precautionary" in the second sentence?**
   (Average Rigor) (Skill 1.1)

   A. Careful

   B. Protective

   C. Medical

   D. Sterilizing

2. **What is the main idea of this passage?**
   (Average Rigor) (Skill 1.1)

   A. There is a lot of preparation involved in visiting a patient of cystic fibrosis.

   B. Children with cystic fibrosis are incapable of living normal lives.

   C. Certain concessions should be made for children with cystic fibrosis.

   D. Children with cystic fibrosis die young.

3. **What is the author's purpose?**
   (Rigorous) (Skill 3.1)

   A. To inform

   B. To entertain

   C. To describe

   D. To narrate

4. **How is the author so familiar with the procedures used when visiting a child with cystic fibrosis?**
   (Easy) (Skill 5.5)

   A. She has read about it.

   B. She works in a hospital.

   C. She is the parent of one.

   D. She often tutors them.

5. **Is there evidence of bias in this paragraph?**
    (Rigorous) (Skill 5.5)

    A. Yes

    B. No

6. **What type of organizational pattern is the author using?**
    (Rigorous) (Skill 8.1)

    A. Classification

    B. Explanation

    C. Comparison and contrast

    D. Cause and effect

7. **What kind of relationship is found within the last sentence which starts with "These children undergo..." and ends with "...as short as they are"?**
    (Rigorous) (Skill 8.1)

    A. Addition

    B. Explanation

    C. Generalization

    D. Classification

8. **What is the author's tone?**
    (Average Rigor) (Skill 9.2)

    A. Sympathetic

    B. Cruel

    C. Disbelieving

    D. Cheerful

9. **The author states that it is "cruel" to expect children with cystic fibrosis to learn as "normal" children do. Is this a fact or an opinion?**
    (Average Rigor) (Skill 9.3)

    A. Fact

    B. Opinion

10. **Does the author present an argument that is valid or invalid concerning the schooling of children with cystic fibrosis?**
    (Rigorous) (Skill 9.3)

    A. Valid

    B. Invalid

Disciplinary practices have been found to affect diverse areas of child development such as the acquisition of moral values, obedience to authority, and performance at school. Even though the dictionary has a specific definition of the word "discipline," it is still open to interpretation by people of different cultures.

There are four types of disciplinary styles: assertion of power, withdrawal of love, reasoning, and permissiveness. Assertion of power involves the use of force to discourage unwanted behavior. Withdrawal of love involves making the love of a parent conditional on a child's good behavior. Reasoning involves persuading the child to behave one way rather than another. Permissiveness involves allowing the child to do as he or she pleases and face the consequences of his/her actions.

11. **What is the meaning of the word "diverse" in the first sentence?**
(Easy) (Skill 1.1)

A. Many

B. Related to children

C. Disciplinary

D. Moral

12. **What is the main idea of this passage?**
(Average Rigor) (Skill 2.1)

A. Different people have different ideas of what discipline is.

B. Permissiveness is the most widely used disciplinary style.

C. Most people agree on their definition of discipline.

D. There are four disciplinary styles.

13. **Name the four types of disciplinary styles.**
(Easy) (Skill 2.3)

A. Reasoning, power assertion, morality, and permissiveness.

B. Morality, reasoning, permissiveness, and withdrawal of love.

C. Withdrawal of love, permissiveness, assertion of power, and reasoning.

D. Permissiveness, morality, reasoning, and power assertion.

14. **What is the author's purpose in writing this?**
(Easy) (Skill 3.1)

A. To describe

B. To narrate

C. To entertain

D. To inform

15. **From reading this passage we can conclude that**
(Rigorous) (Skill 4.4)

A. The author is a teacher.

B. The author has many children.

C. The author has written a book about discipline.

D. The author has done a lot of research on discipline.

16. **What does the technique of reasoning involve?**
(Easy) (Skill 5.1)

A. Persuading the child to behave in a certain way.

B. Allowing the child to do as he/she pleases.

C. Using force to discourage unwanted behavior.

D. Making love conditional on good behavior.

17. **The author states that "assertion of power involves the use of force to discourage unwanted behavior." Is this a fact or an opinion?**
(Average Rigor) (Skill 5.4)

A. Fact

B. Opinion

18. **Is this passage biased?**
(Rigorous) (Skill 5.5)

A. Yes

B. No

19. **What organizational structure is used in the first sentence of the second paragraph?**
(Rigorous) (Skill 8.1)

A. Addition

B. Explanation

C. Definition

D. Simple listing

20. **What is the author's tone?**
    (Average Rigor) (Skill 9.2)

    A. Disbelieving

    B. Angry

    C. Informative

    D. Optimistic

21. **What is the overall organizational pattern of this passage?**
    (Rigorous) (Skill 11.5)

    A. Generalization

    B. Cause and effect

    C. Addition

    D. Summary

One of the most difficult problems plaguing American education is the assessment of teachers. No one denies that teachers ought to be answerable for what they do, but what exactly does that mean? The Oxford American Dictionary defines accountability as: the obligation to give a reckoning or explanation for one's actions.

Does a student have to learn for teaching to have taken place? Historically, teaching has not been defined in this restrictive manner; the teacher was thought to be responsible for the quantity and quality of material covered and the way in which it was presented. However, some definitions of teaching now imply that students must learn in order for teaching to have taken place.

As a teacher who tries my best to keep current on all the latest teaching strategies, I believe that those teachers who do not bother even to pick up an educational journal every once in a while should be kept under close watch. There are many teachers out there who have been teaching for decades and refuse to change their ways even if research has proven that their methods are outdated and ineffective. There is no place in the profession of teaching for these types of individuals. It is time that the American educational system clean house, for the sake of our children.

22. **What is the meaning of the word "reckoning" in the third sentence?**
    (Average Rigor) (Skill 1.1)

    A. Thought

    B. Answer

    C. Obligation

    D. Explanation

23. **What is meant by the word "plaguing" in the first sentence?**
    (Easy) (Skill 1.1)

    A. Causing problems

    B. Causing illness

    C. Causing anger

    D. Causing failure

24. **Where does the author get her definition of "accountability?"**
    (Easy) (Skill 1.1)

    A. Webster's Dictionary

    B. Encyclopedia Britannica

    C. Oxford Dictionary

    D. World Book Encyclopedia

25. **The author states that teacher assessment is a problem for**
    (Easy) (Skill 2.1)

    A. Elementary schools

    B. Secondary schools

    C. American education

    D. Families

26. **What is the main idea of the passage?**
    (Average Rigor) (Skill 2.3)

    A. Teachers should not be answerable for what they do.

    B. Teachers who do not do their job should be fired.

    C. The author is a good teacher.

    D. Assessment of teachers is a serious problem in society today.

27. **What is the author's purpose in writing this?**
    (Average Rigor) (Skill 3.1)

    A. To entertain

    B. To narrate

    C. To describe

    D. To persuade

28. **From the passage, one can infer that**
(Rigorous) (Skill 4.4)

 A. The author considers herself a good teacher.

 B. Poor teachers will be fired.

 C. Students have to learn for teaching to take place.

 D. The author will be fired.

29. **Is this a valid argument?**
(Rigorous) (Skill 5.3)

 A. Yes

 B. No

30. **Teachers who do not keep current on educational trends should be fired. Is this a fact or an opinion?**
(Average Rigor) (Skill 5.4)

 A. Fact

 B. Opinion

31. **Is there evidence of bias in this passage?**
(Rigorous) (Skill 5.5)

 A. Yes

 B. No

32. **What is the organizational pattern of the second paragraph?**
(Rigorous) (Skill 8.1)

 A. Cause and effect

 B. Classification

 C. Addition

 D. Explanation

33. **What is the author's overall organizational pattern?**
(Rigorous) (Skill 8.1)

 A. Classification

 B. Cause and effect

 C. Definition

 D. Comparison and contrast

34. **The author's tone is one of**
(Average Rigor) (Skill 9.2)

 A. Disbelief

 B. Excitement

 C. Support

 D. Concern

Mr. Smith gave instructions for the painting to be hung on the wall. And then it leaped forth before his eyes: the little cottages on the river, the white clouds floating over the valley and the green of the towering mountain ranges which were seen in the distance. The painting was so vivid that it seemed almost real. Mr. Smith was now absolutely certain that the painting had been worth money.

35. **What is the meaning of the word "vivid" in the third sentence?**
(Average Rigor) (Skill 1.1)

A. Lifelike

B. Dark

C. Expensive

D. Big

36. **From the last sentence, one can infer that**
(Rigorous) (Skill 2.1)

A. The painting was expensive.

B. The painting was cheap.

C. Mr. Smith was considering Purchasing the painting.

D. Mr. Smith thought the painting was too expensive and decided not to purchase it.

37. **The author's purpose is to**
(Rigorous) (Skill 2.1)

A. Inform

B. Entertain

C. Persuade

D. Narrate

38. **What is the main idea of this passage?**
(Average Rigor) (Skill 2.1)

A. The painting that Mr. Smith purchased is expensive.

B. Mr. Smith purchased a painting.

C. Mr. Smith was pleased with the quality of the painting he had purchased.

D. The painting depicted cottages and valleys.

39. **What does the author mean by the expression "it leaped forth before his eyes"?** *(Average Rigor) (Skill 2.4)*

A. The painting fell off the wall.

B. The painting appeared so real it was almost three-dimensional.

C. The painting struck Mr. Smith in the face.

D. Mr. Smith was hallucinating.

40. **Is this passage biased?** *(Rigorous) (Skill 5.5)*

A. Yes

B. No

Chili peppers may turn out to be the wonder drug of the decade. the fiery fruit comes in many sizes, shapes and colors, all of which grow on plants that are genetic descendants of the tepin plant, originally native to the Americas. Connoisseurs of the regional cuisines of the South west and Louisiana are already well aware that food flavored with chilies can cause a good sweat, but medical researchers are learning more every day about the medical power of capsaicin, the ingredient in the peppers that produces the heat.

Capsaicin as a pain medication has been a part of fold medicine for centuries. It is, in fact, the active ingredient in several currently available over-the-counter liniments for sore muscles. Recent research has been examining the value of the compound for the treatment of other painful conditions. Capsaicin shows some promise in the treatment of phantom limb syndrome, as well as shingles, and some types of headaches. Additional research focuses upon the use of capsaicin to relieve pain in post-surgical patients. Scientists speculate that application of the compound to the skin cause the body to release endorphins – natural pain relievers manufactured by the body itself. An alternative theory holds that capsaicin somehow interferes with t transmission of signals along the nerve fibers, thus reducing the sensation of pain.

In addition to its well-documented history as a pain killer, capsaicin has recently received attention as a phytochemical, one of the naturally occurring compounds from foods that show cancer-fighting qualities. Like the phytochemical sulforaphane found in broccoli, capsaicin might turn out to be an agent capable of short-circuiting the actions of carcinogens at the cell level before they can cause cancer.

41.   The author's primary purpose is to:

(Average Rigor) (Skill 2.1)

A. entertain the reader with unusual stories about chilies.

B. narrate the story of the discovery of capsaicin.

C. describe the medicinal properties of the tepin plant.

D. inform the reader of the medical research about capsaicin.

42.   All of the following medical problems have been treated using capsaicin EXCEPT:
(Average Rigor) (Skill 2.3)

A. cancer.

B. shingles.

C. sore muscles.

D. headache.

43.   The statement "Chili peppers may turn out to be the wonder drug of the decade," is a statement of:

(Average Rigor) (Skill 5.4)

A. fact.

B. opinion.

Answer Key: Reading

1. B
2. C
3. C
4. D
5. A
6. B
7. B
8. A
9. B
10. B
11. A
12. A
13. C
14. D
15. D
16. D̶A̶
17. A
18. B
19. D
20. C
21. C
22. D
23. A
24. C
25. C
26. D
27. D
28. A
29. B
30. B
31. A
32. D
33. C
34. D
35. A
36. A
37. D
38. C
39. B
40. B
41. D
42. A
43. B

Rigor Table: Reading

	Easy 20%	Average 40%	Rigorous 40%
Questions (43)	4, 11, 13, 14, 16, 23, 24, 25	1, 2, 8, 9, 12, 17, 20, 22, 26, 27, 30, 34, 35, 38, 39, 41, 42, 43	3, 5, 6, 7, 10, 15, 18, 19, 21, 28, 29, 31, 32, 33, 36, 37, 40
TOTALS	8 (18.6%)	18 (41.8%)	17 (39.5%)

Rationales with Sample Questions: Reading

Read the passages and answer the questions that follow.

This writer has often been asked to tutor hospitalized children with cystic fibrosis. While undergoing all the precautionary measures to see these children (i.e. scrubbing thoroughly and donning sterilized protective gear- for the child's protection), she has often wondered why their parents subject these children to the pressures of schooling and trying to catch up on what they have missed because of hospitalization, which is a normal part of cystic fibrosis patients' lives. These children undergo so many tortuous treatments a day that it seems cruel to expect them to learn as normal children do, especially with their life expectancies being as short as they are.

1.   **What is meant by the word "precautionary" in the second sentence? *(Average Rigor) (Skill 1.1)***

   A. Careful

   B. Protective

   C. Medical

   D. Sterilizing

Answer B: Protective

The writer uses expressions such as "protective gear" and "child's protection" to emphasize this.

2.   **What is the main idea of this passage?**
     (Average Rigor) (Skill 1.1)

    A. There is a lot of preparation involved in visiting a patient of cystic fibrosis.

    B. Children with cystic fibrosis are incapable of living normal lives.

    C. Certain concessions should be made for children with cystic fibrosis.

    D. Children with cystic fibrosis die young.

Answer C: Certain concessions should be made for children with cystic fibrosis.

The author states that she wonders "why parents subject these children to the pressures of schooling" and that "it seems cruel to expect them to learn as normal children do." In making these statements she appears to be expressing the belief that these children should not have to do what "normal" children do. They have enough to deal with – their illness itself.

3.   **What is the author's purpose?**
     (Rigorous) (Skill 3.1)

    A. To inform

    B. To entertain

    C. To describe

    D. To narrate

Answer C: To describe

The author is simply describing her experience in working with children with cystic fibrosis.

4. **How is the author so familiar with the procedures used when visiting a child with cystic fibrosis?**
(Easy) (Skill 5.5)

 A. She has read about it.

 B. She works in a hospital.

 C. She is the parent of one.

 D. She often tutors them.

Answer D: She often tutors them.

The writer states this fact in the opening sentence.

5. **Is there evidence of bias in this paragraph?**
(Rigorous) (Skill 5.5)

 A. Yes

 B. No

Answer A: Yes

The writer clearly feels sorry for these children and gears her writing in that direction.

6. **What type of organizational pattern is the author using?**
(Rigorous) (Skill 8.1)

 A. Classification

 B. Explanation

 C. Comparison and contrast

 D. Cause and effect

Answer B: Explanation

The author mentions tutoring children with cystic fibrosis in her opening sentence and goes on to "explain" some of these issues that are involved with her job.

7.   **What kind of relationship is found within the last sentence which starts with "These children undergo..." and ends with "...as short as they are"?**
     (Rigorous) (Skill 8.1)

     A. Addition

     B. Explanation

     C. Generalization

     D. Classification

Answer B: Explanation

In mentioning that their life expectancies are short, she is explaining by giving one reason why it is cruel to expect them to learn as normal children do.

8.   **What is the author's tone?**
     (Average Rigor) (Skill 9.2)

     A. Sympathetic

     B. Cruel

     C. Disbelieving

     D. Cheerful

Answer A: Sympathetic

The author states that "it seems cruel to expect them to learn as normal children do," thereby indicating that she feels sorry for them.

9. **The author states that it is "cruel" to expect children with cystic fibrosis to learn as "normal" children do. Is this a fact or an opinion?**
   (Average Rigor) (Skill 9.3)

   A. Fact

   B. Opinion

Answer B: Opinion

The fact that she states that it "seems" cruel indicates there is no evidence to support this belief.

10. **Does the author present an argument that is valid or invalid concerning the schooling of children with cystic fibrosis?**
   (Rigorous) (Skill 9.3)

   A. Valid

   B. Invalid

Answer B: Invalid

Even though to most readers, the writer's argument makes good sense, it is biased and lacks real evidence.

Disciplinary practices have been found to affect diverse areas of child development such as the acquisition of moral values, obedience to authority, and performance at school. Even though the dictionary has a specific definition of the word "discipline," it is still open to interpretation by people of different cultures.

There are four types of disciplinary styles: assertion of power, withdrawal of love, reasoning, and permissiveness. Assertion of power involves the use of force to discourage unwanted behavior. Withdrawal of love involves making the love of a parent conditional on a child's good behavior. Reasoning involves persuading the child to behave one way rather than another. Permissiveness involves allowing the child to do as he or she pleases and face the consequences of his/her actions.

11. **What is the meaning of the word "diverse" in the first sentence? (Easy) (Skill 1.1)**

    A. Many

    B. Related to children

    C. Disciplinary

    D. Moral

Answer A: Many

Any of the other choices would be redundant in this sentence.

12. **What is the main idea of this passage? (Average Rigor) (Skill 2.1)**

    A. Different people have different ideas of what discipline is.

    B. Permissiveness is the most widely used disciplinary style.

    C. Most people agree on their definition of discipline.

    D. There are four disciplinary styles.

Answer A: Different people have different ideas of what discipline is.

Choice C is not true; the opposite is stated in the passage. Choice B could be true, but we have no evidence of this. Choice D is just one of the many facts listed in the passage.

13. **Name the four types of disciplinary styles.**
    (Easy) (Skill 2.3)

    A. Reasoning, power assertion, morality, and permissiveness.

    B. Morality, reasoning, permissiveness, and withdrawal of love.

    C. Withdrawal of love, permissiveness, assertion of power, and reasoning.

    D. Permissiveness, morality, reasoning, and power assertion.

Answer C: Withdrawal of love, permissiveness, assertion of power, and reasoning.

This is directly stated in the second paragraph.

14. **What is the author's purpose in writing this?**
    (Easy) (Skill 3.1)

    A. To describe

    B. To narrate

    C. To entertain

    D. To inform

Answer D: To inform

The author is providing the reader with information about disciplinary practices.

15. **From reading this passage we can conclude that**
(Rigorous) (Skill 4.4)

A. The author is a teacher.

B. The author has many children.

C. The author has written a book about discipline.

D. The author has done a lot of research on discipline.

Answer D: The author has done a lot of research on discipline.

Given all the facts mentioned in the passage, this is the only inference one can make.

16. **What does the technique of reasoning involve?**
(Easy) (Skill 5.1)

A. Persuading the child to behave in a certain way.

B. Allowing the child to do as he/she pleases.

C. Using force to discourage unwanted behavior.

D. Making love conditional on good behavior.

Answer D: Making love conditional on good behavior.

Given all the facts mentioned in the passage, this is the only inference one can make.

17. **The author states that "assertion of power involves the use of force to discourage unwanted behavior." Is this a fact or an opinion?**
(Average Rigor) (Skill 5.4)

A. Fact

B. Opinion

Answer A: Fact

The author appears to have done extensive research on this subject.

18.   **Is this passage biased?**
        (Rigorous) (Skill 5.5)

        A. Yes

        B. No

Answer B: No

If the reader were so inclined, he could research discipline and find this information.

19.   **What organizational structure is used in the first sentence of the second paragraph?**
        (Rigorous) (Skill 8.1)

        A. Addition

        B. Explanation

        C. Definition

        D. Simple listing

Answer D: Simple Listing

The author simply states the types of disciplinary styles.

20.   **What is the author's tone?**
        (Average Rigor) (Skill 9.2)

        A. Disbelieving

        B. Angry

        C. Informative

        D. Optimistic

Answer C: Informative

The author appears to simply be stating the facts.

21. **What is the overall organizational pattern of this passage?** *(Rigorous) (Skill 11.5)*

   A. Generalization

   B. Cause and effect

   C. Addition

   D. Summary

Answer C: Addition

The author has taken a subject, in this case discipline, and developed it point by point.

One of the most difficult problems plaguing American education is the assessment of teachers. No one denies that teachers ought to be answerable for what they do, but what exactly does that mean? The Oxford American Dictionary defines accountability as: the obligation to give a reckoning or explanation for one's actions.

Does a student have to learn for teaching to have taken place? Historically, teaching has not been defined in this restrictive manner; the teacher was thought to be responsible for the quantity and quality of material covered and the way in which it was presented. However, some definitions of teaching now imply that students must learn in order for teaching to have taken place.

As a teacher who tries my best to keep current on all the latest teaching strategies, I believe that those teachers who do not bother even to pick up an educational journal every once in a while should be kept under close watch. There are many teachers out there who have been teaching for decades and refuse to change their ways even if research has proven that their methods are outdated and ineffective. There is no place in the profession of teaching for these types of individuals. It is time that the American educational system clean house, for the sake of our children.

22. **What is the meaning of the word "reckoning" in the third sentence? (Average Rigor) (Skill 1.1)**

   A. Thought

   B. Answer

   C. Obligation

   D. Explanation

Answer D: Explanation

The meaning of this word is directly stated in the same sentence.

23. **What is meant by the word "plaguing" in the first sentence?**
   (Easy) (Skill 1.1)

   A. Causing problems

   B. Causing illness

   C. Causing anger

   D. Causing failure

Answer A: Causing problems

The first paragraph makes this definition clear.

24. **Where does the author get her definition of "accountability?"**
   (Easy) (Skill 1.1)

   A. Webster's Dictionary

   B. Encyclopedia Britannica

   C. Oxford Dictionary

   D. World Book Encyclopedia

Answer C: Oxford Dictionary

This is directly stated in the third sentence of the first paragraph.

25. **The author states that teacher assessment is a problem for**
   (Easy) (Skill 2.1)

   A. Elementary schools

   B. Secondary schools

   C. American education

   D. Families

Answer C: American education

This fact is directly stated in the first paragraph.

26. **What is the main idea of the passage?**
(Average Rigor) (Skill 2.3)

   A. Teachers should not be answerable for what they do.

   B. Teachers who do not do their job should be fired.

   C. The author is a good teacher.

   D. Assessment of teachers is a serious problem in society today.

Answer D: Assessment of teachers is a serious problem in society today.

Most of the passage is dedicated to elaborating on why teacher assessment is such a problem.

27. **What is the author's purpose in writing this?**
(Average Rigor) (Skill 3.1)

   A. To entertain

   B. To narrate

   C. To describe

   D. To persuade

Answer D: To persuade

The author does some describing, but the majority of her statements seemed geared towards convincing the reader that teachers who are lazy or who do not keep current should be fired.

28. **From the passage, one can infer that**
(Rigorous) (Skill 4.4)

    A. The author considers herself a good teacher.

    B. Poor teachers will be fired.

    C. Students have to learn for teaching to take place.

    D. The author will be fired.

Answer A: The author considers herself a good teacher.

The first sentence of the third paragraph alludes to this.

29. **Is this a valid argument?**
(Rigorous) (Skill 5.3)

    A. Yes

    B. No

Answer B: No

In the third paragraph, the author appears to be resentful of lazy teachers.

30. **Teachers who do not keep current on educational trends should be fired. Is this a fact or an opinion?**
(Average Rigor) (Skill 5.4)

    A. Fact

    B. Opinion

Answer B: Opinion

There may be those who feel they can be good teachers by using old methods.

31.   **Is there evidence of bias in this passage?**
      (Rigorous) (Skill 5.5)

      A. Yes

      B. No

Answer A: Yes

The entire third paragraph is the author's opinion on the matter.

32.   **What is the organizational pattern of the second paragraph?**
      (Rigorous) (Skill 8.1)

      A. Cause and effect

      B. Classification

      C. Addition

      D. Explanation

Answer D: Explanation

The author goes on to further explain what she meant by"...what exactly does that mean?" in the first paragraph.

33.   **What is the author's overall organizational pattern?**
      (Rigorous) (Skill 8.1)

      A. Classification

      B. Cause and effect

      C. Definition

      D. Comparison and contrast

Answer C: Definition

The author identifies teacher assessment as a problem and spends the rest of the passage defining why it is considered a problem.

34. **The author's tone is one of**
    (Average Rigor) (Skill 9.2)

    A. Disbelief

    B. Excitement

    C. Support

    D. Concern

Answer D: Concern

The author appears concerned with the future of education.

Mr. Smith gave instructions for the painting to be hung on the wall. And then it leaped forth before his eyes: the little cottages on the river, the white clouds floating over the valley and the green of the towering mountain ranges which were seen in the distance. The painting was so vivid that it seemed almost real. Mr. Smith was now absolutely certain that the painting had been worth money.

35. **What is the meaning of the word "vivid" in the third sentence?**
    (Average Rigor) (Skill 1.1)

    A. Lifelike

    B. Dark

    C. Expensive

    D. Big

Answer A: Lifelike

This is reinforced by the second half of the same sentence.

36. **From the last sentence, one can infer that**
    (Rigorous) (Skill 2.1)

    A. The painting was expensive.

    B. The painting was cheap.

    C. Mr. Smith was considering Purchasing the painting.

    D. Mr. Smith thought the painting was too expensive and decided not to purchase it.

Answer A: The painting was expensive.

Choice B is incorrect because, had the painting been cheap, chances are that Mr. Smith would no have considered his purchase. Choices C and D are ruled out by the fact that the painting had already been purchased. The author makes this clear when she says, "...the painting had been worth the money."

37. **The author's purpose is to**
    (Rigorous) (Skill 2.1)

    A. Inform

    B. Entertain

    C. Persuade

    D. Narrate

Answer D: Narrate

The author is simply narrating or telling the story of Mr. Smith and his painting.

38. **What is the main idea of this passage?**
    (Average Rigor) (Skill 2.1)

    A. The painting that Mr. Smith purchased expensive.

    B. Mr. Smith purchased a painting.

    C. Mr. Smith was pleased with the quality of the painting he had purchased.

    D. The painting depicted cottages and valleys.

Answer C: Mr. Smith was pleased with the quality of the painting he had purchased.

Every sentence in the paragraph alludes to this fact.

39. **What does the author mean by the expression "it leaped forth before his eyes"?**
    (Average Rigor) (Skill 2.4)

    A. The painting fell off the wall.

    B. The painting appeared so real it was almost three-dimensional.

    C. The painting struck Mr. Smith in the face.

    D. Mr. Smith was hallucinating.

Answer B: The painting appeared so real it was almost three-dimensional.

This is almost directly stated in the third sentence.

40. **Is this passage biased?**
    (Rigorous) (Skill 5.5)

    A. Yes

    B. No

Answer B: No

The author appears to just be telling what happened when Mr. Smith had his new painting hung on the wall.

Chili peppers may turn out to be the wonder drug of the decade. the fiery fruit comes in many sizes, shapes and colors, all of which grow on plants that are genetic descendants of the tepin plant, originally native to the Americas. Connoisseurs of the regional cuisines of the South west and Louisiana are already well aware that food flavored with chilies can cause a good sweat, but medical researchers are learning more every day about the medical power of capsaicin, the ingredient in the peppers that produces the heat.

Capsaicin as a pain medication has been a part of fold medicine for centuries. It is, in fact, the active ingredient in several currently available over-the-counter liniments for sore muscles. Recent research has been examining the value of the compound for the treatment of other painful conditions. Capsaicin shows some promise in the treatment of phantom limb syndrome, as well as shingles, and some types of headaches. Additional research focuses upon the use of capsaicin to relieve pain in post-surgical patients. Scientists speculate that application of the compound to the skin cause the body to release endorphins – natural pain relievers manufactured by the body itself. An alternative theory holds that capsaicin somehow interferes with t transmission of signals along the nerve fibers, thus reducing the sensation of pain.

In addition to its well-documented history as a pain killer, capsaicin has recently received attention as a phytochemical, one of the naturally occurring compounds from foods that show cancer-fighting qualities. Like the phytochemical sulforaphane found in broccoli, capsaicin might turn out to be an agent capable of short-circuiting the actions of carcinogens at the cell level before they can cause cancer.

41.   **The author's primary purpose is to:**

(Average Rigor) (Skill 2.1)

A. entertain the reader with unusual stories about chilies.

B. narrate the story of the discovery of capsaicin.

C. describe the medicinal properties of the tepin plant.

D. inform the reader of the medical research about capsaicin.

Answer D: inform the reader of the medical research about capsaicin.

This purpose is conveyed in the last sentence of paragraph one.

42. **All of the following medical problems have been treated using capsaicin EXCEPT:** *(Average Rigor) (Skill 2.3)*

   A. cancer.

   B. shingles.

   C. sore muscles.

   D. headache.

Answer A: cancer.

Choice A is the exception. The passage states that capsaicin "might turn out to be" effective in fighting cancer, but actual cancer treatments with the drug are not mentioned.

43. **The statement "Chili peppers may turn out to be the wonder drug of the decade," is a statement of:**

   (Average Rigor) (Skill 5.4)

   A. fact.

   B. opinion.

Answer B: opinion.

This sentence reflects an idea of the author which is not based on fact and cannot be proven. It is an opinion.

SUBAREA II LANGUAGE ARTS

COMPETENCY 7.0 DEMONSTRATE COMMAND OF STANDARD USAGE IN EDITED ENGLISH IN THE UNITED STATES.

Skill 7.1 Understand the standard use of verbs (e.g., subject-verb agreement, verb tense, consistency of tense).

Past tense and past participles
Both regular and irregular verbs must appear in their standard forms for each tense. Note: the ed or d ending is added to regular verbs in the past tense and for past participles.

Infinitive	Past Tense	Past Participle
Bake	Baked	Baked

Irregular Verb Forms

Infinitive	Past Tense	Past Participle
Be	Was, were	Been
Become	Became	Become
Break	Broke	Broken
Bring	Brought	Brought
Choose	Chose	Chosen
Come	Came	Come
Do	Did	Done
Draw	Drew	Drawn
Eat	Ate	Eaten
Fall	Fell	Fallen
Forget	Forgot	Forgotten
Freeze	Froze	Frozen
Give	Gave	Given
Go	Went	Gone
Grow	Grew	Grown
Have/has	Had	Had
Hide	Hid	Hidden
Know	Knew	Known
Lay	Laid	Laid
Lie	Lay	Lain
Ride	Rode	Ridden
Rise	Rose	Risen
Run	Ran	Run
See	Saw	Seen
Steal	Stole	Stolen
Take	Took	Taken
Tell	Told	Told
Throw	Threw	Thrown
Wear	Wore	Worn
Write	Wrote	Written

Error: She should have went to her doctor's appointment at the scheduled time.

Problem: The past participle of the verb *to go* is *gone*. *Went* expresses the simple past tense.

Correction: *She should have gone to her doctor's appointment at the scheduled time.*

Error: My train is suppose to arrive before two o'clock.

Problem: The verb following *train* is a present tense passive Construction, which requires the present tense verb *to be* and the past participle.

Correction: *My train is supposed to arrive before two o'clock.*

Error: Linda should of known that the car wouldn't start after leaving it out in the cold all night.

Problem: *Should of* is a nonstandard expression. *Of is* not a verb.

Correction: *Linda should have known that the car wouldn't start after leaving it out in the cold all night.*

PRACTICE EXERCISE – STANDARD VERB FORMS

Choose the option that corrects an error in the underlined portion(s). If no error exists, choose "No change is necessary."

1) My professor had knew all along that we would pass his course.

   A. know
   B. had known
   C. knowing
   D. No change is necessary

2) Kevin was asked to erase the vulgar words he had wrote.

   A. writes
   B. has write
   C. had written
   D. No change is necessary

3) Melanie had forget to tell her parents that she left the cat in the closet.

   A. had forgotten
   B. forgot
   C. forget
   D. No change is necessary

4) Craig always leave the house a mess when his parents aren't there.

   A. left
   B. leaves
   C. leaving
   D. No change is necessary

5) The store manager accused Kathy of having stole more than five hundred dollars from the safe.

   A. has stolen
   B. having stolen
   C. stole
   D. No change is necessary

ANSWER KEY : PRACTICE EXERCISE FOR STANDARD VERB FORMS

1. B   Option B is correct because the past participle needs the helping verb *had*. Option A is incorrect because *it* is in the infinitive tense. Option C incorrectly uses the present participle.

2. C   Option C is correct because the past participle follows the helping verb *had*. Option A uses the verb in the present tense. Option B is an incorrect use of the verb.

3. A   Option A is correct because the past participle uses the helping verb *had*. Option B uses the wrong form of the verb. Option C uses the wrong form of the verb.

4. B   Option B correctly uses the past tense of the verb. Option A uses the verb in an incorrect way. Option C uses the verb without a helping verb like *is*.

5. B   Option B is correct because it is the past participle. Option A and C use the verb incorrectly.

Past tense and past participles

Both regular and irregular verbs must appear in their standard forms for each tense. Note: the ed or d ending is added to regular verbs in the past tense and for past participles.

Infinitive	Past Tense	Past Participle
Bake	Baked	Baked

Irregular Verb Forms

Infinitive	Past Tense	Past Participle
Be	Was, were	Been
Become	Became	Become
Break	Broke	Broken
Bring	Brought	Brought
Choose	Chose	Chosen
Come	Came	Come
Do	Did	Done
Draw	Drew	Drawn
Eat	Ate	Eaten
Fall	Fell	Fallen
Forget	Forgot	Forgotten
Freeze	Froze	Frozen
Give	Gave	Given
Go	Went	Gone
Grow	Grew	Grown
Have/has	Had	Had
Hide	Hid	Hidden
Know	Knew	Known
Lay	Laid	Laid
Lie	Lay	Lain
Ride	Rode	Ridden
Rise	Rose	Risen
Run	Ran	Run
See	Saw	Seen
Steal	Stole	Stolen
Take	Took	Taken
Tell	Told	Told
Throw	Threw	Thrown
Wear	Wore	Worn
Write	Wrote	Written

Error: She should have went to her doctor's appointment at the scheduled time.

Problem: The past participle of the verb *to go* is *gone. Went* expresses the simple past tense.

Correction: *She should have gone to her doctor's appointment at the scheduled time.*

Error: My train is suppose to arrive before two o'clock.

Problem: The verb following *train* is a present tense passive construction which requires the present tense verb *to be* and the past participle.

Correction: *My train is supposed to arrive before two o'clock.*

Error: Linda should of known that the car wouldn't start after leaving it out in the cold all night.

Problem: *Should of* is a nonstandard expression. *Of is* not a verb.

Correction: *Linda should have known that the car wouldn't start after leaving it out in the cold all night.*

PRACTICE EXERCISE – STANDARD VERB FORMS

Choose the option that corrects an error in the underlined portion(s). If no error exists, choose "No change is necessary."

1)   My professor _had knew_ all along that we would pass his course.

      A. know
      B. had known
      C. knowing
      D. No change is necessary

2)   Kevin was asked to erase the vulgar words he _had wrote._

      A. writes
      B. has write
      C. had written
      D. No change is necessary

3)   Melanie _had forget_ to tell her parents that she left the cat in the closet.

      A. had forgotten
      B. forgot
      C. forget
      D. No change is necessary

4)   Craig always _leave_ the house a mess when his parents aren't there.

      A. left
      B. leaves
      C. leaving
      D. No change is necessary

5)   The store manager accused Kathy of _having stole_ more than five hundred dollars from the safe.

      A. has stolen
      B. having stolen
      C. stole
      D. No change is necessary

ANSWER KEY : PRACTICE EXERCISE FOR STANDARD VERB FORMS

1. B   Option B is correct because the past participle needs the helping verb *had*. Option A is incorrect because *know* is in the infinitive tense. Option C incorrectly uses the present participle.

2. C   Option C is correct because the past participle follows the helping verb *had*. Option A uses the verb in the present tense. Option B is an incorrect use of the verb.

3. A   Option A is correct because the past participle uses the helping verb *had*. Option B uses the wrong form of the verb. Option C uses the wrong form of the verb.

4. B   Option B correctly uses the past tense of the verb. Option A uses the verb in an incorrect way. Option C uses the verb without a helping verb such as *is*.

5. B   Option B is correct because it is the past participle. Option A and C use the verb incorrectly.

Inappropriate shifts in verb tense

Verb tenses must refer to the same time period consistently, unless a change in time is required.

Error: Despite the increased number of students in the school this year, overall attendance is higher last year at the sporting events.

Problem: The verb *is* represents an inconsistent shift to the present tense when the action refers to a past occurrence.

Correction: *Despite the increased number of students in the school this year, overall attendance was higher last year at sporting events.*

Error: My friend Lou, who just competed in the marathon, ran since he was twelve years old.

Problem: Because Lou continues to run, the present perfect tense is needed.

Correction: *My friend Lou, who just competed in the marathon, has run since he was twelve years old.*

Error: The Mayor congratulated Wallace Mangham, who renovates the City Hall last year.

Problem: Although the speaker is talking in the present, the action of renovating the City Hall was in the past.

Correction: *The Mayor congratulated Wallace Mangham, who renovated the City Hall last year.*

PRACTICE EXERCISE – SHIFTS IN TENSE

Choose the option that corrects an error in the underlined portion(s).
If no error exists, choose "No change is necessary".

1)   After we <u>washed</u> the fruit that had <u>growing</u> in the garden, we knew
       there <u>was</u> a store that would buy them.

       A) washing
       B) grown
       C) is
       D) No change is necessary.

2)   The tourists <u>used</u> to visit the Atlantic City boardwalk whenever they
       <u>vacationed</u> during the summer. Unfortunately, their numbers have
       <u>diminished</u> every year.

       A) use
       B) vacation
       C) diminish
       D) No change is necessary.

3)   When the temperature <u>drops</u> to below thirty-two degrees Fahrenheit,
       the water on the lake <u>freezes</u>, which <u>allowed</u> children to skate across it.

       A) dropped
       B) froze
       C) allows
       D) No change is necessary.

4)   The artists were <u>hired</u> to <u>create</u> a monument that would pay tribute to
       the men who were <u>killed</u> in World War Two.

       A) hiring
       B) created
       C) killing
       D) No change is necessary.

5)   Emergency medical personnel rushed to the scene of the shooting,
       where many injured people <u>waiting</u> for treatment.

       A) wait
       B) waited
       C) waits
       D) No change is necessary.

ANSWER KEY : PRACTICE EXERCISE FOR SHIFTS IN TENSE

1) B   The past participle *grown* is needed instead of *growing* which is the progressive tense. Option A is incorrect because the past participle *washed* takes the *ed*. Option C incorrectly replaces the past participle *was* with the present tense *is*.

2) D   Option A is incorrect because *use* is the present tense. Option B incorrectly uses the noun *vacation*. Option C incorrectly uses the present tense *diminish* instead of the past tense *diminished*.

3) C   The present tense *allows* is necessary in the context of the sentence. Option A is incorrect because *dropped* is a past participle. Option B is incorrect because *froze* is also a past participle.

4) D   Option A is incorrect because *hiring* is the present tense. Option B is incorrect because *created* is a past participle. In Option C, *killing* doesn't fit into the context of the sentence.

5) B   In Option B, *waited*, corresponds with the past tense *rushed*. In Option A, *wait*, is incorrect because it is present tense. In Option C, *waits*, is incorrect because the noun *people* is plural and requires the singular form of the verb.

Agreement between subject and verb

A verb must correspond in the singular or plural form with the simple subject; it is not affected by any interfering elements. NOTE: A simple subject is never found in a prepositional phrase (a phrase beginning with a word such as *of, by, over, through, until*).

Present Tense Verb Form

	Singular	Plural
1st person (talking about oneself)	I do	We do
2nd person (talking to another)	You do	You do
3rd person (talking about someone or something)	He She does It	They do

Error: Sally, as well as her sister, plan to go into nursing.

Problem: The subject in the sentence is *Sally* alone, not the word *sister*. Therefore, the verb must be singular.

Correction: *Sally, as well as her sister, plans to go into nursing.*

Error: There has been many car accidents lately on that street.

Problem: The subject *accidents* in this sentence is plural; the verb must be plural also--even though it comes before the subject.

Correction: *There have been many car accidents lately on that street.*

Error: Every one of us have a reason to attend the school musical.

Problem: The simple subject is *every one*, not the *us* in the prepositional phrase. Therefore, the verb must be singular also.

Correction: *Every one of us has a reason to attend the school musical.*

Error: Either the police captain or his officers is going to the convention.

Problem: In either/or and neither/nor constructions, the verb agrees with the subject closer to it.

Correction: *Either the police captain or his officers are going to the convention.*

PRACTICE EXERCISE – SUBJECT-VERB AGREEMENT

Choose the option that corrects an error in the underlined portion(s).
If no error exists, choose "No change is necessary."

1)   Every year ,the store <u>stays</u> open late when shoppers desperately <u>try</u> to purchase Christmas presents as they <u>prepare</u> for the holiday.

   A. stay
   B. tries
   C. prepared
   D. No change is necessary.

2)   Paul McCartney, together with George Harrison and Ringo Starr,<u>sing</u> classic Beatles songs on a special greatest-hits CD.

   A. singing
   B. sings
   C. sung
   D. No change is necessary.

3)   My friend's cocker spaniel, while <u>chasing</u> cats across the street, always <u>manages</u> to <u>knock</u> over the trash cans.

   A. chased
   B. manage
   C. knocks
   D. No change is necessary.

4)   Some of the ice on the driveway <u>have melted.</u>

   A. having melted
   B. has melted
   C. has melt.
   D. No change is necessary.

5)   Neither the criminal forensics expert nor the DNA blood evidence <u>provide</u> enough support for that verdict.

   A. provides
   B. were providing
   C. are providing
   D. No change is necessary.

ANSWER KEY: PRACTICE EXERCISE FOR SUBJECT-VERB AGREEMENT

1) D   Option D is correct because *store* is third person singular and requires the third person singular verbs *stays*. Option B is incorrect because the plural noun *shoppers* requires a plural verb *try*. In Option C, there is no reason to shift to the past tense *prepared*.

2) B   Option B is correct because the subject, *Paul McCartney,* is singular and requires the singular verb *sings*. Option A is incorrect because the present participle *singing* does not stand alone as a verb. Option C is incorrect because the past participle *sung* alone cannot function as the verb in this sentence.

3) D   Option D is the correct answer because the subject *cocker spaniel* is singular and requires the singular verb *manages*. Options A,B, and C do not work structurally with the sentence.

4) B   The subject of the sentence is *some*, which requires a third person singular verb, *has melted*. Option A incorrectly uses the present participle *having*, which does not act as a helping verb. Option C does not work structurally with the sentence.

5) A   Option A because the singular subject *evidence* is closer to the verb and thus requires the singular in the neither/nor construction. Both Options B and C are plural forms with the helping verb and the present participle.

Skill 7.2   **Identify and apply the standard use of pronouns (e.g., pronoun-antecedent agreement, standard pronoun case, use of possessive pronouns, standard use of relative and demonstrative pronouns).**

Agreements between pronoun and antecedent

A pronoun must correspond to its antecedent in number (singular or plural), person (first, second or third person) and gender (male, female or neutral). A pronoun must refer clearly to a single word, not to a complete idea.

A **pronoun shift** is a grammatical error in which the author starts a sentence, paragraph, or section of a paper using one particular type of pronoun and then suddenly shifts to another. This often confuses the reader.

Error: A teacher should treat all their students fairly.

Problem: Since *teacher* is singular, the pronoun referring to it must also be singular. Otherwise, the noun has to be made plural.

Correction: *Teachers should treat all their students fairly.*
                            OR
                  A teacher should treat all his or her students fairly.

Error: When an actor is rehearsing for a play, it often helps if you can memorize the lines in advance.

Problem: *Actor* is a third-person word; that is, the writer is talking about the subject. The pronoun *you* is in the second person, which means the writer is talking to the subject.

Correction: *When actors are rehearsing for plays, it helps if they can memorize the lines in advance.*
                            OR
                  When an actor is rehearsing for a play, it often helps if he or she can memorize the lines in advance.

Error: The workers in the factory were upset when his or her paychecks didn't arrive on time.

Problem: *Workers* is a plural form, while *his or her* refers to one person.

Correction: *The workers in the factory were upset when their paychecks didn't arrive on time.*

Error: The charity auction was highly successful, which pleased everyone.

Problem: In this sentence the pronoun *which* refers to the idea of the auction's success. In fact, *which* has no antecedent in the sentence; the word success is not stated.

Correction: *Everyone was pleased at the success of the auction.*

Error: Lana told Melanie that she would like aerobics.

Problem: The person that she refers to is unclear; it could be either Lana or Melanie.

Correction: *Lana said that Melanie would like aerobics.*

OR

Lana told Melanie that she, Melanie, would like aerobics.

Error: I dislike accounting, even though my brother is one.

Problem: A person's occupation is not the same as a field, and the pronoun *one* is thus incorrect. Note that the word *accountant* is not used in the sentence, so *one* has no antecedent.

Correction: *I dislike accounting, even though my brother is an accountant.*

PRACTICE EXERCISE – PRONOUN/ANTECEDENT AGREEMENT

Choose the option that corrects an error in the underlined portion(s).
If no error exists, choose "No change is necessary."

1)   You can get to Martha's Vineyard by driving from Boston to Woods
      Hole. Once there, you can travel over on a ship, but you may find
      traveling by airplane to be an exciting experience.
      A. They
      B. Visitors
      C. It
      D. No change is necessary.

2)   Both the city leader and the journalist are worried about the new
      Interstate; she fears the new roadway will destroy precious farmland.
      A. journalist herself
      B. they fear
      C. it
      D. No change is necessary.

3)   When hunters are looking for deer in the woods, you must remain
      quiet for long periods of time.
      A. they
      B. it
      C. we
      D. No change is necessary.

4)   Florida's strong economy is based on the importance of the citrus
      industry. Producing orange juice for most of the country.
      A. They produce
      B. Who produce
      C. Farmers there produce
      D. No change is necessary.

5)   Dr. Kennedy told Paul Elliot, his assistant, that he would have to
      finish grading the tests before going home, no matter how long it
      took.
      A. their
      B. he, Paul
      C. they
      D. No change is necessary.

ANSWER KEY: PRACTICE EXERCISE FOR PRONOUN AGREEMENT

1) D   Pronouns must be consistent. As *you* is used throughout the sentence, the shift to *visitors* is incorrect. Option A, *They*, is vague and unclear. Option C, *it*, is also unclear.

2) B   The plural pronoun *they* is necessary to agree with the two nouns *leader* and *journalist*. There is no need for the reflexive pronoun *herself* in Option A. Option C, *it*, is vague.

3) A   The shift to *you* is unnecessary. The plural pronoun *they* is necessary to agree with the noun *hunters*. The word *we* in Option C is vague; the reader does not know who the word *we* might refer to. Option B, *it*, has no antecedent.

4) C   The noun *farmers* is needed for clarification because *producing* is vague. Option A is incorrect because *they produce* is vague. Option B is incorrect because *who* has no antecedent and creates a fragment.

5) B   The repetition of the name *Paul* is necessary to clarify who the pronoun *he* is referring to. (It could be Dr. Kennedy.) Option A is incorrect because the singular pronoun *his* is needed, not the plural pronoun *their*. Option C is incorrect because the pronoun *it* refers to the plural noun *tests*.

Clear pronoun references.

Rules for clearly identifying pronoun reference.

Make sure that the antecedent reference is clear and cannot refer to something else.

A "distant relative" is a relative pronoun or a relative clause that has been placed too far away from the antecedent to which it refers. It is a common error to place a verb between the relative pronoun and its antecedent.

Error: Return the books to the library that are overdue.

Problem: The relative clause "that are overdue" refers to the "books" and should be placed immediately after the antecedent.

Correction: Return the books that are overdue to the library.

OR

Return the overdue books to the library.

A pronoun should not refer to adjectives or possessive nouns.

Adjectives, nouns, and possessive pronouns should not be used as antecedents. This will create ambiguity in sentences.

Error: In Todd's letter he told his mom he'd broken the priceless vase.

Problem: In this sentence the pronoun "he" seems to refer to the noun phrase "Todd's letter" though it was probably meant to refer to the possessive noun "Todd's."

Correction: In his letter, Todd told his mom that he had broken the priceless vase.

A pronoun should not refer to an implied idea.

A pronoun must refer to a specific antecedent rather than an implied antecedent. When an antecedent is not stated specifically, the reader has to guess or assume the meaning of a sentence. Pronouns that do not have antecedents are called expletives. "It" and "there" are the most common expletives, though other pronouns can also become expletives.. In informal conversation, expletives allow for casual presentation of ideas without supporting evidence. However, in more formal writing, it is best to be precise.

Error: She said that it is important to floss every day.

Problem: The pronoun "it" refers to an implied idea.

Correction: She said that flossing every day is important.

Error: They returned the book because there were missing pages.

Problem: The pronouns "they" and "there" do not refer to the antecedent.

Correction: The customer returned the book with missing pages.

Using Who, Whom, Whose, That, and Which.

Who, whom and **whose** refer to human beings and can either introduce essential or nonessential clauses. **That** refers to things other than humans and is used to introduce essential clauses. **Which** refers to things other than humans and is used to introduce nonessential clauses.

Error: The doctor that performed the surgery said the man would be fully recovered.

Problem: Since the relative pronoun is referring to a human, *who* should be used.

Correction: The doctor who performed the surgery said the man would be fully recovered.

Error: That ice cream cone that you just ate looked really delicious.

Problem: *That* has already been used so you must use *which* to introduce the next clause, whether it is essential or nonessential.

Correction: That ice cream cone, which you just ate, looked really delicious.

Proper case forms

Pronouns, unlike nouns, change case forms. Pronouns must be in the subjective, objective, or possessive form according to their function in the sentence.

Personal Pronouns

Subjective (Nominative)		Possessive		Objective	
	Singular	Plural	Singular	Plural	Singular	Plural
1st person	I	We	My	Our	Me	Us
2nd person	You	You	Your	Your	You	You
3rd person	He She It	They	His Her Its	Their	Him Her It	them

Relative Pronouns
Who	Subjective/Nominative
Whom	Objective
Whose	Possessive

Error: Tom and me have reserved seats for next week's baseball game.

Problem: The pronoun *me* is the subject of the verb *have reserved* and should be in the subjective form.

Correction: *Tom and I have reserved seats for next week's baseball game.*

Error: Mr. Green showed all of we students how to make paper hats.

Problem: The pronoun *we* is the object of the preposition *of*. It should be in the objective form, *us*.

Correction: Mr. Green showed all of us students how to make paper hats.

Error: Who's coat is this?

Problem: The interrogative possessive pronoun is *whose*; *who's* is the contraction for *who is*.

Correction: Whose coat is this?

Error: The voters will choose the candidate whom has the best qualifications for the job.

Problem: The case of the relative pronoun *who* or *whom* is determined by the pronoun's function in the clause in which it appears. The word *who* is in the subjective case, and *whom* is in the objective. Analyze how the pronoun is being used within the sentence.

Correction: The voters will choose the candidate who has the best qualifications for the job.

PRACTICE EXERCISE – PRONOUN CASE

Choose the option that corrects an error in the underlined portion(s).
If no error exists, choose "No change is necessary".

1) Even though Sheila and <u>he</u> had planned to be alone at the diner,
<u>they</u> were joined by three friends of <u>their's</u> instead.

    A) him
    B) him and her
    C) theirs
    D) No change is necessary.

2) Uncle Walter promised to give his car to <u>whomever</u> will guarantee
to drive it safely.

    A) whom
    B) whoever
    C) them
    D) No change is necessary.

3) Eddie and <u>him</u> gently laid <u>the body</u> on the ground next to <u>the sign</u>.

    A) he
    B) them
    C) it
    D) No change is necessary.

4) Mary, <u>who</u> is competing in the chess tournament, is a better player
than <u>me</u>.

    A) whose
    B) whom
    C) I
    D) No change is necessary.

5) <u>We, ourselves,</u> have decided not to buy property in that development;
however, our friends have already bought <u>their selves</u> some land.

    A) We, ourself,
    B) themselves
    C) their self
    D) No change is necessary.

ANSWER KEY : PRACTICE EXERCISE FOR PRONOUN CASE

1) C   The possessive pronoun *theirs* doesn't need an apostrophe. Option A is incorrect because the subjective pronoun *he* is needed in this sentence. Option B is incorrect because the subjective pronoun *they*, not the objective pronouns *him* and *her*, is needed.

2) B   The subjective case *whoever*--not the objective case *whomever* --is the subject of the relative clause *whoever will guarantee to drive it safely*. Option A is incorrect because *whom* is an objective pronoun. Option C is incorrect because *car* is singular and takes the pronoun *it*.

3) A   The subjective pronoun *he* is needed as the subject of the verb *laid*. Option B is incorrect because *them* is vague; the noun *body* is needed to clarify *it*. Option C is incorrect because *it* is vague, and the noun *sign* is necessary for clarification.

4) C   The subjective pronoun *I* is needed because the comparison is understood. Option A incorrectly uses the possessive *whose*. Option B is incorrect because the subjective pronoun *who*, and not the objective *whom*, is needed.

5) B   The reflexive pronoun *themselves* refers to the plural *friends*. Option A is incorrect because the plural *we* requires the reflexive *ourselves*. Option C is incorrect because the possessive pronoun *their* is never joined with either *self* or *selves*.

Skill 7.3   **Recognize and apply the standard use of modifiers (e.g., adverbs, adjectives, prepositional phrases).**

Correct use of adjectives and adverbs

Adjectives are words that modify or describe nouns or pronouns. Adjectives usually precede the words they modify, but not always; for example, an adjective can occur *after* a linking verb.

Adverbs are words that modify verbs, adjectives, or other adverbs. They cannot modify nouns. Adverbs answer such questions as how, why, when, where, how much, or how often something is done. Many adverbs are formed by adding *ly*.

Error: The birthday cake tasted sweetly.

Problem: *Tasted* is a linking verb; the modifier that follows should be an adjective, not an adverb.

Correction: *The birthday cake tasted sweet.*

Error: You have done good with this project.

Problem: *Good* is an adjective and cannot be used to modify a verb phrase such as have done.

Correction: *You have done well with this project.*

Error: The coach was positive happy about the team's chance of winning.

Problem: The adjective *positive* cannot be used to modify another adjective, *happy*. An adverb is needed instead.

Correction: *The coach was positively happy about the team's chance of winning.*

Error: The fireman acted quick and brave to save the child from the burning building.

Problem: *Quick and brave* are adjectives and cannot be used to describe a verb. Adverbs are needed instead.

Correction: *The fireman acted quickly and bravely to save the child from the burning building.*

PRACTICE EXERCISE – ADJECTIVES AND ADVERBS

Choose the option that corrects an error in the underlined portion(s).
If no error exists, choose "No change is necessary."

1)   Moving <u>quick</u> throughout the house, the burglar <u>removed</u> several priceless antiques before <u>carelessly</u> dropping his wallet.

   A) quickly
   B) remove
   C) careless
   D) No change is necessary.

2)   The car <u>crashed loudly</u> into the retaining wall before spinning <u>wildly</u> on the sidewalk.

   A) crashes
   B) loudly
   C) wild
   D) No change is necessary.

3)   The airplane <u>landed safe</u> on the runway after <u>nearly</u> colliding with a helicopter.

   A) land
   B) safely
   C) near
   D) No change is necessary.

4)   The <u>horribly bad</u> special effects in the movie disappointed us <u>great</u>.

   A) horrible
   B) badly
   C) greatly
   D) No change is necessary.

5)   The man promised to <u>faithfully</u> obey the rules of the social club.

   A) faithful
   B) faithfulness
   C) faith
   D) No change is necessary.

ANSWER KEY: PRACTICE EXERCISE FOR ADJECTIVES AND ADVERBS

1) A   The adverb *quickly* is needed to modify *moving*. Option B is incorrect because it uses the wrong form of the verb. Option C is incorrect because the adverb *carelessly* is needed before the verb *dropping*, not the adjective *careless*.

2) D   The sentence is correct as it is written. Adverbs *loudly* and *wildly* are needed to modify *crashed* and *spinning*. Option A incorrectly uses the verb *crashes* instead of the participle *crashing*, which acts as an adjective.

3) B   The adverb *safely* is needed to modify the verb *landed*. Option A is incorrect because *land* is a noun. Option C is incorrect because *near* is an adjective, not an adverb.

4) C   The adverb *greatly* is needed to modify the verb *disappointed*. Option A is incorrect because *horrible* is an adjective, not an adverb. Option B is incorrect because *bad* needs to modify the adverb *horribly*.

5) D   The adverb *faithfully* is the correct modifier of the verb *promised*. Option A is an adjective used to modify nouns. Neither Option B nor Option C, which are both nouns, is a modifier.

COMPETENCY 8.0 UNDERSTAND AND APPLY KNOWLEDGE OF MECHANICAL CONVENTIONS IN EDITED ENGLISH IN THE UNITED STATES.

Skill 8.1 Recognize instances in which incorrect or extraneous punctuation has been used or necessary punctuation has been omitted.

Commas indicate a brief pause. They are used to set off dependent clauses and long introductory word groups, to separate words in a series, to set off unimportant material that interrupts the flow of the sentence, and to separate independent clauses joined by conjunctions.

Error: After I finish my master's thesis I plan to work in Chicago.

Problem: A comma is needed after an introductory dependent word-group containing a subject and verb.

Correction: *After I finish my master's thesis, I plan to work in Chicago.*

Error: I washed waxed and vacuumed my car today.

Problem: Nouns, phrases, or clauses in a list, as well as two or more coordinate adjectives that modify one word should be separated by commas. Although the word *and* is sometimes considered optional, it is often necessary to clarify the meaning.

Correction: *I washed, waxed, and vacuumed my car today.*

Error: She was a talented dancer but she is mostly remembered for her singing ability.

Problem: A comma is needed before a conjunction that joins two independent clauses (complete sentences).

Correction: *She was a talented dancer, but she is mostly remembered for her singing ability.*

Error: This incident is I think typical of what can happen when the community remains so divided.

Problem: Commas are needed between nonessential words or words that interrupt the main clause.

Correction: *This incident is, I think, typical of what can happen when the community remains so divided.*

Semicolons are needed to separate two or more closely related independent clauses when the second clause is introduced by a transitional adverb. (These clauses may also be written as separate sentences, preferably by placing the adverb within the second sentence).

Colons are used to introduce lists and to emphasize what follows.

Error:	I climbed to the top of the mountain, it took me three hours.
Problem:	A comma alone cannot separate two independent clauses. Instead a semicolon is needed to separate two related sentences.
Correction:	*I climbed to the top of the mountain; it took me three hours.*

Error:	In the movie, asteroids destroyed Dallas, Texas, Kansas City, Missouri, and Boston, Massachusetts.
Problem:	Semicolons are needed to separate items in a series that already contains internal punctuation.
Correction:	*In the movie, asteroids destroyed Dallas, Texas; Kansas City, Missouri; and Boston, Massachusetts.*

Error:	Essays will receive the following grades, A for excellent, B for good, C for average, and D for unsatisfactory.
Problem:	A colon is needed to emphasize the information or list that follows.
Correction:	*Essays will receive the following grades: A for excellent, B for good, C for average, and D for unsatisfactory.*

Error:	The school carnival included: amusement rides, clowns, food booths, and a variety of games.
Problem:	The material preceding the colon and the list that follows is not a complete sentence. Do not separate a verb (or preposition) from the object.
Correction:	*The school carnival included amusement rides ,clowns, food booths, and a variety of games.*

Apostrophes are used to show either contractions or possession.

Error: She shouldnt be permitted to smoke cigarettes in the building.

Problem: An apostrophe is needed in a contraction in place of the missing letter.

Correction: *She shouldn't be permitted to smoke cigarettes in the building.*

Error: My cousins motorcycle was stolen from his driveway.

Problem: An apostrophe is needed to show possession.

Correction: *My cousin's motorcycle was stolen from his driveway.* (Note: The use of the apostrophe before the letter "s" means that there is just one cousin. The plural form would read the following way: My cousins' motorcycle was stolen from their driveway.)

Error: The childrens new kindergarten teacher was also a singer.

Problem: An apostrophe is needed to show possession.

Correction: *The children's new kindergarten teacher was also a singer.*

Error: Children screams could be heard for miles.

Problem: An apostrophe and the letter *s* are needed in the sentence to show whose screams it is.

Correction: *Children's screams could be heard for miles.*

Quotation marks

In a quoted statement that is either declarative or imperative, place the period inside the closing quotation marks.

"The airplane crashed on the runway during takeoff."

If the quotation is followed by other words in the sentence, place a comma inside the closing quotations marks and a period at the end of the sentence.

"The airplane crashed on the runway during takeoff," said the announcer.

In most instances, when a quoted title or expression occurs at the end of a sentence, the period is placed before either the single or double quotation marks.

"The middle school readers were unprepared to understand Bryant's poem 'Thanatopsis.'"

Early book-length adventure stories like *Don Quixote* and *The Three Musketeers* are known as "picaresque novels."

There is an instance in which the final quotation mark will precede the period—if the content of the sentence is about a speech or quote so that understanding the meaning would be confused by the placement of the period.

The first thing out of his mouth was "Hi, I'm home."
but
The first line of his speech began "I arrived home to an empty house".

In interrogatory or exclamatory sentences, the question mark or exclamation point should be positioned outside the closing quotation marks if the quote itself is a statement, command, or cited title.

Who decided to lead us in the recitation of the "Pledge of Allegiance"?

Why was Tillie shaking as she began her recitation, "Once upon a midnight dreary . . ."?

I was embarrassed when Mrs. White said, "Your slip is showing"!

In declarative sentences, when the quotation is a question or an exclamation, place the question mark or exclamation point *inside* the quotation marks.

> The hall monitor yelled, "Fire! Fire!"

> "Fire! Fire!" yelled the hall monitor.

> Cory shrieked, "Is there a mouse in the room?" (In this instance, the question supersedes the exclamation.)

Quotations - Words, phrases, or clauses should be punctuated according to the rules of the grammatical function they serve in the sentence.

> The works of Shakespeare, "the bard of Avon," have been contested as originating with other authors.

> "You'll get my money," the old man warned, "when 'Hell freezes over'."

> Sheila cited the passage that began "Fourscore and seven years ago . . . ." (Note the ellipsis followed by an enclosed period.)

> "Old Ironsides" inspired the preservation of the *U.S.S. Constitution*.

Use quotation marks to enclose the titles of shorter works: songs, short poems, short stories, essays, and chapters of books. (See "Using Italics" for punctuating longer titles.)

> "The Tell-Tale Heart"   "Casey at the Bat"   "America the Beautiful"

Dashes and Italics

Place **dashes** to denote sudden breaks in thought.

> Some periods in literature-- the Romantic Age, for example-- spanned different time periods in different countries.

Use dashes instead of commas for amplification or explanation if commas are already used elsewhere in the sentence..

> The Fireside Poets included four Brahmans--James Russell Lowell, Henry David Wadsworth, Oliver Wendell Holmes, and John Greenleaf Whittier.

Use **italics** to punctuate the titles of long works of literature, names of periodical publications, musical scores, works of art, and motion picture, television, and radio programs. (When unable to write in italics, students should be instructed to underline in their own writing where italics would be appropriate.)

> *The Idylls of the King*   *Hiawatha*   *The Sound and the Fury*
> *Mary Poppins*   *Newsweek*   *The Nutcracker Suite*

Skill 8.2   Identify standard initial capitalization and standard capitalization with proper words and titles.

Capitalize all proper names of persons (including specific organizations or agencies of government); places (countries, states, cities, parks, and specific geographical areas); and things (political parties, structures, historical and cultural terms, and calendar and time designations); and religious terms (any deity, revered person or group, sacred writings).

> Percy Bysshe Shelley, Argentina, Mount Rainier National Park, Grand Canyon, League of Nations, the Sears Tower, Birmingham, Lyric Theater, Americans, Midwesterners, Democrats, Renaissance, Boy Scouts of America, Easter, God, Bible, Dead Sea Scrolls, Koran

Capitalize proper adjectives and titles used with proper names.

California Gold Rush, President John Adams, French fries, Homeric epic, Romanesque architecture, Senator John Glenn

Note: Some words that represent titles and offices are not capitalized unless used with a proper name.

Capitalized	Not Capitalized
Congressman McKay	the congressman from Florida
Commander Alger	commander of the Pacific Fleet
Queen Elizabeth	the queen of England

Capitalize all main words in titles of works of literature, art, and music.

Error: Emma went to Dr. Peters for treatment since her own Doctor was on vacation.

Problem: The use of capital letters with Emma and Dr .Peters is correct since they are specific (proper) names; the title Dr. is also capitalized. However, the word doctor is not a specific name and should not be capitalized.

Correction: *Emma went to Dr. Peters for treatment since her own doctor was on vacation.*

Error: Our Winter Break does not start until next wednesday.

Problem: Days of the week are capitalized, but seasons are not capitalized.

Correction: *Our winter break does not start until next Wednesday.*

Error: The exchange student from israel who came to study biochemistry spoke spanish very well.

Problem: Languages and the names of countries are always capitalized. Courses are also capitalized when they refer to a specific course; they are not capitalized when they refer to courses in general.

Correction: *The exchange student from Israel who came to study biochemistry spoke Spanish very well.*

PRACTICE EXERCISE – CAPITALIZATION AND PUNCTUALIZATION

Choose the option that corrects an error in the underlined portion(s). If no error exists, choose "No change is necessary".

1)   Greenpeace is an Organization that works to preserve the world's environment.

    A) greenpeace
    B) organization
    C) worlds
    D) No change is necessary

2)   When our class travels to France next year, we will see the country's many famous landmarks.

    A) france
    B) year; we
    C) countries
    D) No change is necessary

3)   New York City, the heaviest populated city in America has more than eight million people living there Every Day.

    A) new york city
    B) in America, has
    C) every day
    D) No change is necessary

4)   The television show *The X-Files* has gained a huge following because it focuses on paranormal phenomena, extraterrestrial life, and the oddities of human existence.

    A) Television
    B) following, because
    C) Human existence
    D) No change is necessary

5) Being a <u>Policeman</u> requires having many <u>qualities:</u> physical <u>agility,</u> good reflexes, and the ability to make quick decisions.

A) policeman
B) qualities;
C) agility:
D) No change is necessary

6) <u>"Better to have loved and lost than never to have loved at all,"</u> says the <u>writer, who</u> demonstrates the value of love in a <u>mans</u> life.

A) Better to have loved and lost, than never to have loved at all
B) writer who
C) man's
D) No change is necessary

7) The <u>Florida Marlins</u> won the <u>world Series</u> championship by defeating the New York Mets in <u>October 1996</u>.

A) Florida marlins
B) World Series
C) October,1996
D) No change is necessary

ANSWER KEY: PRACTICE EXERCISE FOR CAPITALIZATION AND PUNCTUATION

1. B   In the sentence, the word organization does not need to be capitalized since it is a general noun. In Option A, the name of the organization should be capitalized. In Option C, the apostrophe is used to show that one world is being protected, not more than one.

2. D   In Option A, France is capitalized because it is the name of a country. In Option B, the comma, not the semi-colon, should separate a dependent clause from the main clause. In Option C, the use of an apostrophe and an *s* indicates only one country is being visited.

3. B   In Option A, New York City is capitalized because it is the name of a place. In Option B, a comma is needed to separate the noun America, from the verb has. In Option C, the noun *every day* needs no capitalization.

4. D   In Option A, television does not need to be capitalized because it is a noun. In Option B, a comma is necessary to separate an independent clause from the main clause. In Option C, human existence is a general term that does not need capitalization.

5. A   In Option A, policeman does not need capitalization because it is a general noun. In Option B, a colon, not a semi-colon, is needed because the rest of the sentence is related to the main clause. In Option C, a comma, not a colon, is needed to separate the adjectives.

6. C   In Option A, a comma is needed to break the quote into distinct parts that give it a greater clarity. In Option B, a comma is needed to separate the subject of the sentence from his action. In Option C, an apostrophe is needed to show possession.

7. B   In Option A, Florida Marlins must be capitalized because it is the name of a team. In Option B, World Series needs to be capitalized because it is the title of a sporting event. In Option C, no comma is needed because month and year need no distinction; they are general terms.

Skill 8.3   Recognize the standard spelling of words.

Spelling correctly is not always easy, because English not only utilizes an often inconsistent spelling system but also uses many words derived from other languages. Good spelling is important because incorrect spelling damages the physical appearance of writing and may puzzle your reader.

The following list of words are misspelled the most often.

1. commitment
2. succeed
3. necessary
4. connected
5. opportunity
6. embarrassed
7. occasionally
8. receive
9. their
10. accelerate
11. patience
12. obstinate
13. achievement
14. responsibility
15. prejudice
16. familiar
17. hindrance
18. controversial
19. publicity
20. prescription
21. possession
22. accumulate
23. hospitality
24. judgment
25. conscious

26. height
27. leisurely
28. shield
29. foreign
30. innovative
31. similar
32. proceed
33. contemporary
34. beneficial
35. attachment
36. guarantee
37. tropical
38. misfortune
39. particular
40. yield

Spelling plurals and possessives

The multiplicity and complexity of spelling rules based on phonics, letter doubling, and exceptions to rules--not mastered by adulthood-- should be replaced by a good dictionary. As spelling mastery is also difficult for adolescents, our recommendation is the same. Learning the use of a dictionary and thesaurus will be a rewarding use of time.

Most plurals of nouns that end in hard consonants or hard consonant sounds followed by a silent *e* are made by adding *s*. Some words ending in vowels only add *s*.

   fingers, numerals, banks, bugs, riots, homes, gates, radios, bananas

Nouns that end in soft consonant sounds *s, j, x, z, ch,* and *sh,* add *es.* Some nouns ending in *o* add es.

   dresses, waxes, churches, brushes, tomatoes, potatoes

Nouns ending in *y* preceded by a vowel just add *s*.

   boys, alleys

Nouns ending in *y* preceded by a consonant change the *y* to *i* and add *es.*

   babies, corollaries, frugalities, poppies

Some nouns plurals are formed irregularly or remain the same.

   sheep, deer, children, leaves, oxen

Some nouns derived from foreign words, especially Latin, may make their plurals in two different ways--one of them Anglicized. Sometimes, the meanings are the same; other times, the two plurals are used in slightly different contexts. It is always wise to consult the dictionary.

   appendices, appendixes   criterion, criteria
   indexes, indices   crisis, crises

Make the plurals of closed (solid) compound words in the usual way except for words ending in *ful* which make their plurals on the root word.

   timelines, hairpins, cupsful

Make the plurals of open or hyphenated compounds by adding the change in inflection to the word that changes in number.

fathers-in-law, courts-martial, masters of art, doctors of medicine

Make the plurals of letters, numbers, and abbreviations by adding *s*.

Fives and tens, IBMs, 1990s, *p*s and *q*s (Note that letters are italicized.)

I before E

i before e	grieve, fiend, niece, friend
except after c	receive, conceive, receipt
or when sounded like "a"	as in reindeer and weight, and reign
Exceptions:	weird, foreign, seize, leisure

Test on ei/ie words

Circle the correct spelling of the word in each parenthesis.

1. The (shield, shield) protected the gladiator from serious injury.
2. Tony (received, recieved) an award for his science project.
3. Our (neighbors, nieghbors), the Thomsons, are in the Witness Protection Program.
4. Janet's (friend, freind), Olivia, broke her leg while running the marathon.
5. She was unable to (conceive, concieve) a child after her miscarriage.
6. "Rudolph the Red-Nosed (Riendeer, Reindeer)" is my favorite Christmas song.
7. The farmer spent all day plowing his (feild, field).
8. Kat's (wieght, weight) -loss plan failed, and she gained twenty pounds!
9. They couldn't (beleive, believe) how many people showed up for the concert.
10. Ruby's (niece, neice) was disappointed when the movie was sold out.

ANSWER KEY: EI/IE WORDS

1. shield
2. received
3. neighbors
4. friend
5. conceive
6. reindeer
7. field
8. weight
9. believe
10. niece

PRACTICE EXERCISE – SPELLING RULES

Add suffixes to the following words and write the correct spelling form in the blanks.

1) swing + ing = _____

2) use + able = _____

3) choke + ing = _____

4) furnish + ed = _____

5) punish + ment = _____

6) duty + ful = _____

7) bereave + ment = _____

8) shovel + ing = _____

9) argue + ment = _____

10) connect + ed = _____

11) remember + ed = _____

12) treat + able = _____

13) marry + s = _____

14) recycle + able = _____

15) waste + ful = _____

16) pray + ing = _____

17) reconstruct + ing = _____

18) outrage + ous = _____

ANSWER KEY: SPELLING RULES PRACTICE

1) swinging
2) useable
3) choking
4) furnished
5) punishment
6) dutiful
7) bereavement
8) shoveling
9) argument
10) connected
11) remembered
12) treatable
13) marries
14) recyclable
15) wasteful
16) praying
17) reconstructing
18) outrageous

COMPETENCY 9.0 UNDERSTAND THE ROLE OF PURPOSE AND AUDIENCE IN WRITTEN COMMUNICATION

Skill 9.1 **Assess the appropriateness of written material for a specific purpose or audience (e.g., a business letter, a communication to parents).**

See Skill 3.1

Skill 9.2 **Determine the likely effect on an audience of a writer's choice of a particular word or words (e.g., to evoke sympathy, to raise questions about an opposing point of view).**

Tailoring language for a particular **audience** is an important skill. Writing to be read by a business associate will surely sound different from writing to be read by a younger sibling. Not only are the vocabularies different, but the formality/informality of the discourse will need to be adjusted.

The things to be aware of in determining what the language should be for a particular audience hinges on two things: **word choice** and **formality/informality**. The most formal language does not use contractions or slang. The most informal language will probably feature a more casual use of common sayings and anecdotes. Formal language will use longer sentences and will not sound like a conversation. The most informal language will use shorter sentences—not necessarily simple sentences—but shorter constructions, and it may sound like a conversation.

In both formal and informal writing, there exists a **tone**, the writer's attitude toward the material and/or readers. Tone may be playful, formal, intimate, angry, serious, ironic, outraged, baffled, tender, serene, depressed, etc. The overall tone of a piece of writing is dictated by both the subject matter and the audience. Tone is also related to the actual words making up the document because we attach affective meanings to words, called **connotations**. Gaining this conscious control over language makes it possible to use language appropriately in various situations and to evaluate its uses in literature and other forms of communication. By evoking the proper responses from readers/listeners, we can prompt them to take action.

The following questions are an excellent way to assess the audience and tone of a given piece of writing.

1. Who is your audience(friend, teacher, business person, someone else)?
2. How much does this person know about you and/or your topic?
3. What is your purpose (to prove an argument, to persuade, to amuse, to register a complaint, to ask for a raise, etc)?
4. What emotions do you have about the topic (nervous, happy, confident, angry, sad, no feelings at all)?
5. What emotions do you want to register with your audience (anger, nervousness, happiness, boredom, interest)?
6. What persona do you need to create in order to achieve your purpose?
7. What choice of language is best suited to achieving your purpose with your particular subject (slang, friendly but respectful, formal)?
8. What emotional quality do you want to transmit to achieve your purpose (matter of fact, informative, authoritative, inquisitive, sympathetic, angry), and to what degree do you want to express this tone?

Skill 9.3   Identify persuasive techniques used by a writer in a passage.

Persuasive writing features facts and opinions that are used to get the reader to agree with something the author believes. Persuasive writing may have as its purpose getting its audience to change its mind, take a position on an issue, perform an action, or judge an event. Of course, there are many different ways to accomplish this goal. Authors may be straightforward and objective, in which case they will marshal a number of facts in support of a position. Alternatively, authors may use emotional words, and in so doing, reveal their personal preferences, biases, or strongly held opinions. While news articles have as their purpose to inform, other commonly read material such as editorials, reviews, and letters generally contain an element of persuasion.

Sample Passage and Analysis
Recent scientific research indicates that individuals who wish to lead long, healthy lives should switch from a meat-based to a vegetarian diet. The medical basis for this switch is irrefutable. One clinical study, published in Cancer Research, *found that meat-eaters are twice as likely to die from cancer as vegetarians. Moreover, changing to a low-fat, high-fiber vegetarian lifestyle incorporating healthy exercise and stress reduction techniques has been shown to reverse hardening of the arteries and lower blood pressure in patients suffering from heart disease. Other medical benefits may include the prevention of diabetes, gallstones, and osteoporosis, as well as reductions in the severity and frequency of asthma attacks.*

Though the paragraph uses unemotional words and facts to support the position that vegetarianism is preferable to a meat-based diet, close reading reveals why the writer's purpose is to persuade. First, the statement "that the medical basis for this switch is irrefutable" indicates an absolute commitment to a position and to the belief that the audience ought to agree with that position. But while one clinical study is solid support for he author's belief, it is hardly irrefutable. Second, though the author doesn't specifically tell the audience to change to a vegetarian diet, the first sentence makes it clear that he or she thinks the reader should do so. In fact, that sentence contains the main idea, which is supported with persuasive reasoning and supporting details. Because the author implicitly invites the audience to change behavior, this paragraph is classified as persuasive.

Skill 9.4   Demonstrate the ability to adapt forms, organizational strategies, and styles for different audiences and purposes.

See Skill 9.2.

COMPETENCY 10.0 UNDERSTAND UNITY, FOCUS, DEVELOPMENT, AND ORGANIZATION IN WRITING.

Skill 10.1   Identify organizational methods used by the author of a passage.

The **organization** of a written work includes two factors: the order the writer chooses to present the different parts of the discussion or argument and the relationships he or she constructs between these parts.

Written ideas need to be presented in a **logical order** so that a reader can follow the information easily and quickly. There are many different ways to order a series of ideas, but they all share one thing in common: to lead the reader along a desired path--avoiding backtracking and skipping around--to give a clear, strong presentation of the writer's main idea. Some ways a paragraph may be organized are:

Sequence of events – In this type of organization, the details are presented in the order they have occurred. Paragraphs that describe a process or procedure, give directions, or outline a given period of time (such as a day or a month) are often arranged chronologically.

Statement support – In this type of organization, the main idea is stated and the rest of the paragraph explains or proves it. This is referred to as *relative importance*. Four ways that this type of order is organized include: most to least, least to most, most-least-most, and least-most-least.

Comparison-Contrast – In this type of organization, the compare-contrast pattern is used when a paragraph describes the differences or similarities of two or more ideas, actions, events, or things. Usually the topic sentence describes the basic relationship between the ideas or items, and the rest of the paragraph explains this relationship.

Classification – In this type of organization, the paragraph presents grouped information about a topic. The topic sentence usually states the general category, and the rest of the sentences show how various elements of the category have a common base--and also how they differ from the common base.

Cause and Effect – This organizational pattern describes how two or more events are connected. The main sentence usually states the primary cause(s) and the primary effect(s) and how they are basically connected. The rest of the sentences explain the connection–how one event caused the next.

Spatial/Place – In this type of organization, certain descriptions are organized according to the location of items in relation to each other and in relation to a larger context.

Skill 10.2   Distinguish between effective and ineffective thesis statements.

Guidelines for Writing Thesis Statements

The following guidelines are not a formula for writing thesis statements but rather are general strategies for making your thesis statement clearer and more effective.

1.   State a *particular point* of *view* about the topic with both a *subject* and an *assertion*. The thesis should give the essay purpose and scope and thus provide the reader a guide. If the thesis is vague, your essay may be undeveloped because you do not have an idea to assert or a point to explain. Weak thesis statements are often framed as facts, questions or announcements:

   a.   Avoid a fact statement as a thesis. While a fact statement may provide a subject, it generally does not include a point of view about the subject that provides the basis for an extended discussion. Example: *Recycling saved our community over $10,000 last year.* This fact statement provides a detail, *not* a point of view. Such a detail might be found within an essay, but it does not state a point of view.

   b.   Avoid framing the thesis as a vague question. In many cases, rhetorical questions do not provide a clear point of view for an extended essay. Example: *How do people recycle?* This question neither asserts a point of view nor helpfully guides the reader to understand the essay's purpose and scope.

   c.   Avoid the "announcer" topic sentence that merely states the topic you will discuss
Example: I *will discuss ways to recycle.* This sentence states the subject but the scope of the essay is only suggested. Again, this statement does not assert a viewpoint that guides the essay's purpose. It merely "announces" that the writer will write about the topic.

2.   Start with a workable thesis. You might revise your thesis as you begin writing and discover your own point of view.

3.   If feasible and appropriate, perhaps state the thesis in multi-point form, expressing the scope of the essay. By stating the points in parallel form, you clearly lay out the essay's plan for the reader.
Example: *To improve the environment, we can recycle our trash, elect politicians who see the environment as a priority, and support lobbying groups who work for environmental protection.*

4.   Because of the exam time limit, place your thesis in the first paragraph to key the reader to the essay's main idea.

Skill 10.3   **Recognize unnecessary shifts in point of view (e.g., shifts from first to third person) or distracting details that impair development of the main idea in a passage.**

Point of view defines the focus a writer assumes in relation to a given topic. It is extremely important to maintain a consistent point of view in order to create coherent paragraphs. Point of view is related to matters of person, tense, tone, and number.

Person – A shift in the form which indicates whether a person is speaking (first), is being spoken to (second) or is being spoken about (third) can disrupt continuity of a passage. In your essay, it is recommended that you write in the third person, as it is often considered to be the most formal of the modes of person. If you do decide to use the more informal first (I, we) or second person (you) in your essay, be careful not to shift between first, second, and third persons (he, she, they) from sentence to sentence or paragraph to paragraph.

Tense – Verbs tenses indicate the time of an action or state of being – the past, present, or future. It is important to largely adhere to a selected tense, though this may not always be the case. For instance, in an essay about the history of environmental protection, it might be necessary to include a paragraph about the future benefits or consequences of protecting the earth.

Tone – The tone of an essay varies greatly with the purpose, subject and audience. It is best to assume a formal tone for this essay. (See Domain II, Skill 2.3).

Number – Words change when their meanings are singular or plural. Make sure that you do not shift number needlessly; if a meaning is singular in one sentence, do not make it plural in the subsequent sentence.

Skill 10.4   **Select appropriate and effective supporting material.**

See Skill 2.3.

Skill 10.5 Recognize examples of focused, concise, and well-developed writing.

The following example shows good logical order and transitions

No one really knows how Valentine's Day started. There are several legends, however, which are often told. The first attributes Valentine's Day to a Christian priest who lived in Rome during the third century, under the rule of Emperor Claudius. Rome was at war, and apparently Claudius felt that married men didn't fight as well as bachelors. Consequently, Claudius banned marriage for the duration of the war. But Valentinus, the priest, risked his life to secretly marry couples in violation of Claudius' law. The second legend is even more romantic. In this story, Valentinus is a prisoner, having been condemned to death for refusing to worship pagan deities. While in jail, he fell in love with his jailer's daughter, who happened to be blind. Daily he prayed for her sight to return, and miraculously it did. On February 14, the day that he was condemned to die, he was allowed to write the young woman a note. In this farewell letter he promised eternal love, and signed at the bottom of the page the now famous words, "Your Valentine."

Sample Prompt and Well-Written Response:

Written on July 15, 1944, three weeks before the Frank family was arrested by the Nazis, Anne's diary entry explains her worldview and future hopes.

It's difficult in times like these: ideals, dreams and cherished hopes rise within us, only to be crushed by grim reality. It's a wonder I haven't abandoned all my ideals;, they seem so absurd and impractical. Yet I cling to them because I still believe, in spite of everything, that people are truly good at heart.

It's utterly impossible for me to build my life on a foundation of chaos, suffering, and death. I see the world being slowly transformed into a wilderness, I hear the approaching thunder that, one day, will destroy us, too, I feel the suffering of millions, and yet, when I look up at the sky, I somehow feel that everything will change for the better, that this cruelty too shall end, that peace and tranquility will return once more. In the meantime, I must hold on to my ideals. Perhaps the day will come when I will be able to realize them!

Using your knowledge of literature, write a response in which you:

- Compare and contrast Anne's ideals with her awareness of the conditions in which she lives; and
- Discuss how the structure of Anne's writing—her sentences and paragraphs—emphasize the above contrast.

Sample Response

This excerpt from The Diary of Anne Frank reveals the inner strength of a young girl who refuses, despite the wartime violence and danger surrounding her, to let her idealism be overcome by hatred and mass killing. This idealism is reflected, in part, by her emphases on universal human hopes such as peace, tranquility, and goodwill. But Anne Frank is no dreamy Pollyanna. Reflecting on her idealism in the context of the war raging around her, she matter-of-factly writes: "my dreams, they seem so absurd and impractical."

This indicates Anne Frank's awareness of not only her own predicament but of human miseries that extend beyond the immediate circumstances of her life. For elsewhere she writes in a similar vein, "In times like these... I see the world being slowly transformed into a wilderness"; despite her own suffering she can "feel the suffering of millions."

And yet Anne Frank believes, "in spite of everything, that people are truly good at heart." This statement epitomizes the stark existential contrast of her worldview with the wartime reality that ultimately claimed her life.

The statement also exemplifies how Anne's literary form—her syntax and diction—mirror thematic content and contrasts. "In spite of everything," she still believes in people. She can "hear the approaching thunder...yet, when I look up at the sky, I somehow feel that everything will change for the better." At numerous points in this diary entry, first-hand knowledge of violent tragedy stands side-by-side with belief in humanity and human progress.

"I must hold on to my ideals," Anne concludes. "Perhaps the day will come when I'll be able to realize them!" In her diary she has done so, and more.

COMPETENCY 11.0 UNDERSTAND AND APPLY EDITING AND REVIONS STRATEGIES

Skill 11.1   Apply editing and revision strategies affecting diction, syntax, transitions, organization, clarity, coherence, and point of view.

Techniques for revising written texts to achieve clarity and economy of expression

Enhancing Interest:

- Start out with an attention-grabbing introduction. This sets an engaging tone for the entire piece and will be more likely to pull the reader in.
- Use dynamic vocabulary and varied sentence beginnings. Keep the readers on their toes. If they can predict what you are going to say next, "switch it up."
- Avoid using clichés (as cold as ice, the best thing since sliced bread, nip it in the bud). These are easy shortcuts, but they are not interesting, memorable, nor convincing.

Ensuring Understanding:

- Avoid using the words, "clearly," "obviously," and "undoubtedly." Often, things that are clear or obvious to the author are not as apparent to the reader. Instead of using these words, make your point so strongly that it is clear on its own.
- Use the word that best fits the meaning you intend, even if the words are longer or a little less common. Try to find a balance, selecting a familiar yet precise word.
- When in doubt, explain further.

Revision of sentences to eliminate wordiness, ambiguity, and redundancy:

Sometimes this exercise is seen by students as simply catching errors in spelling or word use. Students need to reframe their thinking about revising and editing. Some questions that need to be asked:

- Is the reasoning coherent?
- Is the point established?
- Does the introduction make the reader want to read this discourse?
- What is the thesis? Is it proven?
- What is the purpose? Is it clear? Is it useful, valuable, interesting?
- Is the style of writing so wordy that it exhausts the reader and interferes with engagement?
- Is the writing so spare that it is boring?
- Are the sentences too uniform in structure?

- Are there too many simple sentences?
- Are too many of the complex sentences the same structure?
- Are the compounds truly compounds or are they unbalanced?
- Are parallel structures truly parallel?
- If there are characters, are they believable?
- If there is dialogue, is it natural or stilted?
- Is the title appropriate?
- Does the writing show creativity or is it boring?
- Is the language appropriate? Is it too formal? Too informal? If jargon is used, is it appropriate?

Studies have clearly demonstrated that the most fertile area in teaching writing is this one. If students can learn to revise their own work effectively, they are well on their way to becoming effective, mature writers. Word-processing is an important tool for teaching this stage in the writing process. Microsoft Word has tracking features that make the revision exchanges between teachers and students more effective than ever before.

Skill 11.2 Make revisions that improve the unity and focus of a passage or that improve cohesion and the effective sequence of ideas.

Techniques to Maintain Focus

- **Focus on a main point.** The point should be clear to readers, and all sentences in the paragraph should relate to it.

- **Start the paragraph with a topic sentence.** This should be a general, one-sentence summary of the paragraph's main point, relating both back toward the thesis and toward the content of the paragraph. (A topic sentence is sometimes unnecessary if the paragraph continues a developing idea that was clearly introduced in a preceding paragraph, or if the paragraph appears in a narrative of events where generalizations might interrupt the flow of the story.)

- **Stick to the point.** Eliminate sentences that do not support the topic sentence.

- **Be flexible.** If there is not enough evidence to support the claim your topic sentence is making, do not fall into the trap of wandering or introducing new ideas within the paragraph. Either find more evidence, or adjust the topic sentence to collaborate with the evidence that is available.

Skill 11.3   Improve the clarity and effectiveness of a passage through changes in word choice.

Choose the appropriate word or expression in context

Choose the most effective word or phrase within the context suggested by the sentences.

1)   The defendant was accused of_____money from his employer.

A) stealing
B) embezzling
C) robbing

2)   O.J. Simpson's angry disposition_____ his ex-wife Nicole.

A) mortified
B) intimidated
C) frightened

3)   Many tourists are attracted to Florida because of its_____climate.

A) friendly
B) peaceful
C) balmy

4)   The woman was angry because the tomato juice left an_____stain on her brand-new carpet.

A) unsightly
B) ugly
C) unpleasant

5)   After disobeying orders, the Army private was_____by his superior officer.

A) degraded
B) attacked
C) reprimanded

6)   Sharon's critical evaluation of the student's book report left him feeling _____ , which caused him to want to quit school.

A) surprised
B) depressed
C) discouraged

7)   The life-saving medication created by the scientist had a very_____
       impact on further developments in the treatment of cancer.

       A) beneficial
       B) fortunate
       C) miraculous

8)   *Phantom of The Opera* is one of Andrew Lloyd Webber's most
       successful musicals, largely because of its_____themes.

       A) romantic
       B) melodramatic
       C) imaginary

9)   The massive Fourth of July fireworks display_____the partygoers
       with lots of colored light and sound.

       A) disgusted
       B) captivated
       C) captured .

10)   Many of the residents of Grand Forks, North Dakota, were forced to
       _____their homes because of the flood.

       A) escape
       B) evacuate
       C) exit

ANSWERS : 1.A., 2.C., 3.C., 4.A. ,5.C., 6.C., 7.A., 8.A., 9.B., 10.B.

Choose the sentence that expresses the thought most clearly, most effectively and is structurally correct in grammar and syntax.

1)   A. The movie was three hours in length, featuring interesting characters, and moved at a fast pace.

      B. The movie was three hours long, featured interesting characters, and moved at a fast pace.

      C. Moving at a fast pace, the movie was three hours long and featured interesting characters.

2)   A. We were so offended by the waiter's demeanor that we left the restaurant without paying the check.

      B. The waiter's demeanor offended us so much that without paying the check, we left the restaurant.

      C. We left the restaurant without paying the check because we were offended by the waiter's demeanor.

3)   A. In today's society, information about our lives is provided to us by computers.

      B. We rely on computers in today's society to provide us information about our lives.

      C. In today's society, we rely on computers to provide us with information about our lives.

4)   A. Folding the sides of the tent carefully, Jack made sure to be quiet so none of the other campers would be woken up.

      B. So none of the other campers would be woken up, Jack made sure to be quiet by folding the sides of the tent carefully.

      C. Folding the sides of the tent carefully, so none of the other campers would wake up, Jack made sure to be quiet.

ANSWER KEY

  1) B.
  2) A.
  3) C.
  4) A.

Choose the most effective word or phrase within the context suggested by the sentence(s).

1) The six hundred employees of General Electric were_____by the company due to budgetary cutbacks.

   A) released
   B) terminated
   C) downsized

2) The force of the tornado_____the many residents of the town of Russell, Kansas.

   A) intimidated
   B) repulsed
   C) frightened

3) Even though his new car was a lot easier to drive, Fred_____to walk to work every day because he liked the exercise.

   A) needed
   B) preferred
   C) considered

4) June's parents were very upset over the school board's decision to suspend her from Adams High for a week. Before they filed a lawsuit against the board, they_____with a lawyer to help them make a decision.

   A) consulted
   B) debated
   C) conversed

5) The race car driver's_____in handling the automobile was a key factor in his victory.

   A) patience
   B) precision
   C) determination

6) After impressing the judges with her talent and charm, the beauty contestant_____more popularity by singing an aria from *La Boheme*.

   A) captured
   B) scored
   C) gained

7) The stained-glass window was_____when a large brick flew through it during the riot.

A) damaged
B) cracked
C) shattered

8) The class didn't know what happened to the professor until it was_____ by the principal why he dropped out of school.

A) informed
B) discovered
C) explained

9) The giant penthouse on the top of the building allows the billionaire industrialist_____the citizens on the street.

A) to view from above
B) the chance to see
C) to glance at

10) Sally's parents_____her to attend the dance after she promised to return by midnight.

A) prohibited
B) permitted
C) asked

ANSWERS: 1) C., 2) C., 3) B., 4) A., 5) B., 6) C., 7) C., 8) C., 9) C., 10) B

Skill 11.4 Eliminate or replace unnecessary or imprecise words and phrases.

The main idea of a passage may contain a wide variety of supporting information, but it is important that each sentence be related to the main idea. When a sentence contains information that bears little or no connection to the main idea, it is said to be **irrelevant**. It is important to continually assess whether or not a sentence contributes to the overall task of supporting the main idea. When a sentence is deemed irrelevant, it is best to either omit it from the passage or to make it relevant by one of the following strategies:

1. Adding detail – Sometimes a sentence can seem out of place if it does not contain enough information to link it to the topic. Adding specific information can show how the sentence is related to the main idea.

2. Adding an example – This is especially important in passages in which information is being argued or compared or contrasted. Examples can support the main idea and give the document overall credibility.

3. Using diction effectively – It is important to understand connotation, avoid ambiguity, and steer clear of too much repetition when selecting words.

4. Adding transitions – Transitions are extremely helpful for making sentences relevant because they are specifically designed to connect one idea to another. They can also reduce a paragraph's choppiness.

Skill 11.5 Insert appropriate transitional words or phrases (e.g., however, as a result, consequently) in a passage to convey the structure of the text and to help readers understand the sequence of a writer's ideas.

Even if the sentences that make up a given paragraph or passage are arranged in logical order, the document as a whole can still seem choppy, the various ideas disconnected. **Transitions**, words that signal relationships between ideas, can help improve the flow of a document. Transitions can help achieve clear and effective presentation of information by establishing connections between sentences, paragraphs and sections of a document. With transitions, each sentence builds on the ideas in the last, and each paragraph has clear links to the preceding one. As a result, the reader receives clear directions on how to piece together the writer's ideas in a logically coherent argument. By signaling how to organize, interpret, and react to information, transitions allow writers to effectively and elegantly explain their ideas

Logical Relationship	Transitional Expression
Compare	also, in the same way, just as, so too, likewise, similarly
Exception/Contrast	but, however, in spite of, on the one hand/on the other hand, nevertheless, nonetheless, notwithstanding, in contrast, on the contrary, still, yet
Sequence/Order	first, second, third, next, then, finally
Time	after, afterward, at last, before, currently, during, earlier, immediately, later, meanwhile, now, recently, simultaneously, subsequently, then
Example	for example, for instance, namely, specifically, to illustrate
Emphasis	even, indeed, in fact, of course, truly
Place/Position	above, adjacent, below, beyond, here, in front, in back, nearby, there
Cause and Effect	accordingly, consequently, hence, so, therefore, thus, because
Additional Support or Evidence	additionally, again, also, and, as well, besides, equally important, further, furthermore, in addition, moreover, then
Conclusion/Summary	finally, in a word, in brief, in conclusion, in the end, in the final analysis, on the whole, thus, to conclude, to summarize, in sum, in summary

The following example shows good logical order and transitions

No one really knows how Valentine's Day started. There are several legends, however, which are often told. The first attributes Valentine's Day to a Christian priest who lived in Rome during the third century, under the rule of Emperor Claudius. Rome was at war, and apparently Claudius felt that married men didn't fight as well as bachelors. Consequently, Claudius banned marriage for the duration of the war. But Valentinus, the priest, risked his life to secretly marry couples in violation of Claudius' law. The second legend is even more romantic. In this story, Valentinus is a prisoner, having been condemned to death for refusing to worship pagan deities. While in jail, he fell in love with his jailer's daughter, who happened to be blind. Daily he prayed for her sight to return, and miraculously it did. On February 14, the day that he was condemned to die, he was allowed to write the young woman a note. In this farewell letter, he promised eternal love and signed at the bottom of the page the now famous words, "Your Valentine."

COMPETENCY 12.0 RECOGNIZE SENTENCES AND PARAGRAPHS THAT EFFECTIVELY COMMUNICATE INTENDED MESSAGE

Skill 12.1 **Demonstrate an understanding of unity within paragraphs and apply methods for enhancing paragraph organization and unity.**

See COMPETENCY 11.0.

Skill 12.2 **Recognize effective topic sentences and distinguish between effective and ineffective development of ideas within a paragraph.**

See COMPETENCY 13.0.

Skill 12.3 **Identify sentence fragments and run-on sentences.**

Fragments occur (1) if word groups standing alone are missing either a subject or a verb, and (2) if word groups containing a subject and verb and standing alone are actually made dependent because of the use of subordinating conjunctions or relative pronouns.

Error: The teacher waiting for the class to complete the assignment.

Problem: This sentence is not complete because an *ing* word alone does not function as a verb. When a helping verb is added (for example, *was waiting*), it will become a sentence.

Correction: *The teacher was waiting for the class to complete the assignment.*

Error: Until the last toy was removed from the floor.

Problem: Words such as *until, because, although, when*, and *if* make a clause dependent and thus incapable of standing alone. An independent clause must be added to make the sentence complete.

Correction: *Until the last toy was removed from the floor, the kids could not go outside to play.*

Error: The city will close the public library. Because of a shortage of funds.

Problem: The problem is the same as above. The dependent clause must be joined to the independent clause.

Correction: *The city will close the public library because of a shortage of funds.*

Error: Anyone planning to go on the trip should bring the necessary items. Such as a backpack, boots, a canteen, and bug spray.

Problem: The second word group is a phrase and cannot stand alone because there is neither a subject nor a verb. The fragment can be corrected by adding the phrase to the sentence.

Correction: *Anyone planning to go on the trip should bring the necessary items, such as a backpack, boots, a canteen, and bug spray.*

PRACTICE EXERCISE – FRAGMENTS

Choose the option that corrects the underlined portion(s) of the sentence.
If no error exists, choose "No change is necessary."

1)   Despite the lack of funds in the <u>budget it</u> was necessary to rebuild the roads that were damaged from the recent floods.

A) budget: it
B) budget, it
C) budget; it
D) No change is necessary

2)   After determining that the fire was caused by faulty <u>wiring, the</u> building inspector said the construction company should be fined.

A) wiring. The
B) wiring the
C) wiring; the
D) No change is necessary

3)   Many years after buying a grand <u>piano Henry</u> decided he'd rather play the violin instead.

A) piano: Henry
B) piano, Henry
C) piano; Henry
D) No change is necessary

4)   Computers are being used more and more <u>frequently. because</u> of their capacity to store information.

A) frequently because
B) frequently, because
C) frequently; because
D) No change is necessary

5)   Doug washed the floors <u>every day.to</u> keep them clean for the guests.

A) every day to
B) every day,
C) every day;
D) No change is necessary.

ANSWER KEY: PRACTICE EXERCISE FOR FRAGMENTS

1. B   The clause that begins with *despite* is independent and must be separated with the clause that follows by a comma. Option A is incorrect because a colon is used to set off a list or to emphasize what follows. In Option B, a comma incorrectly suggests that the two clauses are dependent.

2. D   In the test item, a comma correctly separates the dependent clause *After...wiring* at the beginning of the sentence from the independent clause that follows. Option A incorrectly breaks the two clauses into separate sentences, while Options B omits the comma, and Option C incorrectly suggests that the phrase is an independent clause.

3. B   The *phrase Henry decided...instead* must be joined to the independent clause. Option A incorrectly puts a colon before *Henry decided*, and Option C incorrectly separates the phrase as if it were an independent clause.

4. A   The second clause *because...information* is dependent and must be joined to the first independent clause. Option B is incorrect because as the dependent clause comes at the end of the sentence, rather than at the beginning, a comma is not necessary. In Option C, a semi-colon incorrectly suggests that the two clauses are independent.

5. A   The second clause *to keep...guests* is dependent and must be joined to the first independent clause. Option B is incorrect because as the dependent clause comes at the end of the sentence, rather than at the beginning, a comma is not necessary. In Option C, a semi-colon incorrectly suggests that the two clauses are independent.

Run-on sentences and comma splices

Comma splices appear when two sentences are joined by only a comma. Fused sentences appear when two sentences are run together with no punctuation at all.

Error: Dr. Sanders is a brilliant scientist, his research on genetic disorders won him a Nobel Prize.

Problem: A comma alone cannot join two independent clauses (complete sentences). The two clauses can be joined by a semi-colon, or they can be separated by a period.

Correction: *Dr. Sanders is a brilliant scientist; his research on genetic disorders won him a Nobel Prize.*
                            OR
                 Dr. Sanders is a brilliant scientist. His research on genetic disorders won him a Nobel Prize.

Error: Florida is noted for its beaches they are long, sandy, and beautiful.

Problem: The first sentence ends with the word beaches, and the second sentence cannot be joined with the first. The fused sentence error can be corrected in several ways: (1) one clause may be made dependent on another with a subordinating conjunction or a relative pronoun; (2) a semi-colon may be used to combine two equally important ideas; (3) the two independent clauses may be separated by a period.

Correction: *Florida is noted for its beaches, which are long, sandy, and beautiful.*
                            OR
                 Florida is noted for its beaches; they are long, sandy, and beautiful.
                            OR
                 Florida is noted for its beaches. They are long, sandy, and beautiful.

Error: The number of hotels has increased, however, the number of visitors has grown also.

Problem: The first sentence ends with the word increased, and a comma is not strong enough to connect it to the second sentence. The adverbial transition *however* does not function the same way as a coordinating conjunction and cannot be used with commas to link two sentences. Several different corrections are available.

Correction: *The number of hotels has increased; however, the number of visitors has grown also.*
[Two separate but closely related sentences are created with the use of the semicolon.]

OR

The number of hotels has increased. However, the number of visitors has grown also.
[Two separate sentences are created.]

OR

Although the number of hotels have increased, the number of visitors has grown also.
[One idea is made subordinate to the other and separated with a comma.]

OR

The number of hotels have increased, but the number of visitors has grown also.
[The comma before the coordinating conjunction *but* is appropriate. The adverbial transition *however* does not function the same way as the coordinating conjunction *but* does.]

PRACTICE EXERCISE - FUSED SENTENCES AND COMMA SPLICES

Choose the option that corrects an error in the underlined portion(s). If no error exists, choose "No change is necessary".

1)   Scientists are excited at the ability to clone a <u>sheep however,</u> it is not yet known if the same can be done to humans.

    A) sheep, however,
    B) sheep. However,
    C) sheep, however;
    D) No change is necessary

2)   Because of the rising cost of college <u>tuition the</u> federal government now offers special financial assistance, <u>such as loans,</u> to students.

    A) tuition, the
    B) tuition; the
    C) such as loans
    D) No change is necessary

3)   As the number of homeless people continues to <u>rise, the major cities</u> such as <u>New York and Chicago,</u> are now investing millions of dollars in low-income housing.

    A) rise. The major cities
    B) rise; the major cities
    C) New York and Chicago
    D) No change is necessary

4)   Unlike in <u>the 1950s, most</u> households find the husband and wife working full-time to make <u>ends meet in many</u> different career fields.

    A) the 1950s; most
    B) the 1950s most
    C) ends meet, in many
    D) No change is necessary

ANSWER KEY : PRACTICE EXERCISE FOR COMMA SPLICES AND FUSED SENTENCES

1) B   Option B correctly separates two independent clauses. The comma in Option A after the word sheep creates a run-on sentence. The semi-colon in Option C does not separate the two clauses but occurs at an inappropriate point.

2) A   The comma in Option A correctly separates the independent clause and the dependent clause. The semi-colon in Option B is incorrect because one of the clauses is independent. Option C requires a comma to prevent a run-on sentence.

3) C   Option C is correct because a comma creates a run-on. Option A is incorrect because the first clause is dependent. The semi-colon in Option B incorrectly divides the dependent clause from the independent clause.

4) D   Option D correctly separates the two clauses with a comma. Option A incorrectly uses a semi-colon to divide the clauses. The lack of a comma in Option B creates a run-on sentence. Option C puts a comma in an inappropriate place.

Skill 12.4 Recognize wordiness, redundancy, and ineffective repetition in sentences and paragraphs.

Wordiness

These items occur in passages of 45 words or less with five underlined choices. The passages contain irrelevant, repetitive, and/or wordy expressions. This section requires you to choose the word or word group that is unnecessary to the context without affecting the overall meaning of the passage. The other word options all serve a function in the passages.

Choose the underlined portion that is unnecessary within the context of the passage.

1) Some children decide to <u>actively</u> participate in <u>extracurricular</u> activities, such as after-school sports and <u>various</u> clubs. Many teachers and administrators <u>willingly</u> volunteer to supervise the children during their <u>spare</u> time.

    A) actively
    B) extracurricular
    C) various
    D) willingly
    E) spare

2) Our high-school reunion was being held for the first time at the <u>swanky</u> Boca Hilton, known for its elegance and <u>glamor</u>. We arrived in a <u>long</u> stretch limo and prepared to dance and have a good time <u>reminiscing</u> with our <u>dear</u> friends.

    A) swanky
    B) glamour
    C) long
    D) reminiscing
    E) dear

3) Once we reached <u>the top of</u> the mountain, a <u>powerful</u> storm came from <u>out of</u> nowhere, bringing rain and <u>large</u> hailstones from the dark <u>black</u> skies above.

    A) the top of
    B) powerful
    C) out of
    D) large
    E) black

4)   Policemen often undergo a rigorous <u>harsh</u> training period
      to <u>adequately</u> prepare them for the <u>intense</u> dangers and stresses of
      the job. <u>Only</u> the most physically fit candidates are capable of
      handling the challenges of dealing with the <u>criminal</u> elements of
      our society.

      A) harsh
      B) adequately
      C) intense
      D) Only
      E) criminal

5)   The <u>early morning</u> hurricane struck at dawn, knocking out power
      lines and <u>ripping the roofs</u> from buildings <u>all</u> throughout Broward
      County. <u>Massive</u> winds and rain wreaked havoc, as terrified residents
      ran <u>madly</u> for shelter and safety.

      A) early morning
      B) ripping the roofs from
      C) all
      D) Massive
      E) madly

6)   Alan's alcoholism affected the entire family <u>very deeply</u>. When his
      father asked <u>him to</u> stop drinking, he <u>refused and</u> drove off in his
      sister's car, which crashed into a utility pole. <u>Fortunately</u>, Alan
      miraculously survived and now is undergoing intensive treatment
      in a top-notch facility <u>that is well-regarded</u>.

      A) very deeply
      B) him to
      C) refused and
      D) Fortunately
      E) that is well-regarded

7)   Soap operas are popular among <u>many</u> television viewers because
      of their ability to <u>blend</u> real issues such as drug abuse, infidelity, and
      AIDS, <u>with melodramatic plots</u> concerning lust, greed, vanity, and
      revenge. <u>These shows</u> often have very devoted followings among
      viewers, who watch them <u>faithfully</u> every day.

      A) many
      B) blend
      C) with melodramatic plots
      D) These
      E) faithfully

8) Walt Disney World <u>is one of</u> the most visited tourist attractions in the United States. Its success <u>and prosperity</u> can be attributed to the <u>blend of</u> childhood fantasy and adult imagination. The park features rides and <u>attractions</u> that hold considerable appeal for <u>both</u> children and adults.

A) is one of
B) and prosperity
C) blend of
D) attractions
E) both

9) Jason was the best <u>baseball</u> player on the Delray Beach High School baseball team; in fact, he was known as the star <u>of the team</u>. He could play several positions on the field <u>with enthusiasm and skill</u>, but his strength was hitting balls <u>out of the park</u>. When Jason was at the plate, the coach expected him to score a home run <u>every time</u>.

A) baseball
B) of the team
C) with enthusiasm and skill
D) out of the park
E) every time

10) Many of the major cities in the United States are grappling with <u>a variety of</u> problems such as crime, crumbling roadways, a shortage of <u>funding for</u> schools and health care, and a lack of jobs. There are <u>no easy</u> solutions to these problems, but mayors who have <u>strong</u> leadership abilities <u>work to</u> create good ideas to deal with them.

A) a variety of
B) funding for
C) no easy
D) strong
E) work to

ANSWERS: 1) D, 2) A, 3)E, 4) A, 5) A, 6) E, 7) E, 8) B, 9) A, 10) E

Skill 12.5   Recognize inefficiency in sentence and paragraph construction.

Sentence structure

Recognize simple, compound, complex, and compound-complex sentences. Use dependent (subordinate) and independent clauses correctly to create these sentence structures.

Simple – Consists of one independent clause
    Joyce wrote a letter.

Compound – Consists of two or more independent clauses. The two clauses are usually connected by a coordinating conjunction (and, but, or, nor, for, so, yet). Compound sentences are sometimes connected by semicolons.
    Joyce wrote a letter, and Dot drew a picture.

Complex- Consists of an independent clause plus one or more dependent clauses. The dependent clause may precede the independent clause or follow it.
    While Joyce wrote a letter, Dot drew a picture.

Compound/Complex – Consists of one or more dependent clauses plus two or more independent clauses .
    When Mother asked the girls to demonstrate their newfound skills, Joyce wrote a letter, and Dot drew a picture.

Note: Do **not** confuse compound sentence elements with compound sentences.

    Simple sentence with compound subject
        Joyce and Dot wrote letters.
        The girl in row three and the boy next to her were passing notes across the aisle.

    Simple sentence with compound predicate
        Joyce wrote letters and drew pictures.
        The captain of the high school debate team graduated with honors and studied broadcast journalism in college.

    Simple sentence with compound object of preposition
        Colleen graded the students' essays for style and mechanical accuracy.

Types of Clauses

Clauses are connected word groups that are composed of *at least* one subject and one verb. (A subject is the doer of an action or the element that is being joined. A verb conveys either the action or the link.)

Students are waiting for the start of the assembly.
Subject   Verb

At the end of the play, students wait for the curtain to come down.
                              Subject Verb

Clauses can be independent or dependent.

Independent clauses can stand alone or can be joined to other clauses.

Independent clause	for and nor	
Independent clause,	but or yet so	Independent clause
Independent clause	;	Independent clause
Dependent clause	,	Independent clause
Independent clause		Dependent clause

Dependent clauses, by definition, contain at least one subject and one verb. However, they cannot stand alone as a complete sentence. They are structurally dependent on the main clause.

There are two types of dependent clauses: (1) those with a subordinating conjunction, and (2) those with a relative pronoun

Sample coordinating conjunctions:
Although
When
If
Unless
Because

Unless a cure is discovered, many more people will die of the disease.
      Dependent clause   +   Independent clause

Sample relative pronouns:
Who
Whom
Which
That

The White House has an official website, which contains press releases, news updates, and biographies of the President and Vice-President.
(Independent clause + relative pronoun + relative dependent clause)

COMPETENCY 13.0   PREPARE AN ORGANIZED, DEVELOPED COMPOSITION IN EDITED ENGLISH AS USED IN THE UNITED STATES IN RESPONSE TO INSTRUCTIONS REGARDING CONTENT, PURPOSE AND AUDIENCE.

On the Basic Skills Test, you will be expected to compose a unified, focused, and sustained piece of writing on a given topic using language and style appropriate to a specified audience, purpose, and occasion.

You must also:

1. Take a position on a contemporary social or political issue and defend that position with reasoned arguments and supporting examples.

2. Use effective sentence structure and apply the standards of edited English in the United States.

3. Demonstrate the ability to spell, capitalize, and punctuate according to the standards of edited English in the United States.

ESSAY GUIDELINES

Topic Analysis

Even before you select a topic, determine what each prompt is asking you to discuss. This first decision is crucial. If you pick a topic you don't really understand or about which you have little to say, you'll have difficulty developing your essay. So take a few moments to analyze each topic carefully *before* you begin to write.

Topic A: A modern invention that can be considered a wonder of the world

In general, the topic prompts have two parts:
         the *SUBJECT* of the topic and
         an *ASSERTION* about the subject.

The **subject** is *a modern invention*. In this prompt, the word *modern* indicates you should discuss something invented recently, at least in this century. The word *invention* indicated you're to write about something created by humans (not natural phenomena such as mountains or volcanoes). You may discuss an invention that has potential for harm, such as chemical warfare or the atomic bomb; or you may discuss an invention that has the potential for good: the computer, DNA testing, television, antibiotics, and so on.

The **assertion** (a statement of point of view) is that *the invention has such powerful or amazing qualities that it should be considered a wonder of the world*. The assertion states your point of view about the subject, and it limits the range for discussion. In other words, you would discuss particular qualities or uses of the invention, not just discuss how it was invented or whether it should have been invented at all.

Note also that this particular topic encourages you to use examples to show the reader that a particular invention is a modern wonder. Some topic prompts lend themselves to essays with an argumentative edge, one in which you take a stand on a particular issue and persuasively prove your point. Here, you undoubtedly could offer examples or illustrations of the many "wonders" and uses of the particular invention you chose.

Be aware that misreading or misinterpreting the topic prompt can lead to serious problems. Papers that do not address the topic occur when one reads too quickly or only half-understands the topic. This may happen if you misread or misinterpret words. Misreading can also lead to a paper that addresses only part of the topic prompt rather than the entire topic.

To develop a complete essay, spend a few minutes planning. Jot down your ideas and quickly sketch an outline. Although you may feel under pressure to begin writing, you will write more effectively if you plan out your major points.

Prewriting
Before actually writing, you'll need to generate content and to develop a writing plan. Three prewriting techniques that can be helpful are:

Brainstorming

When brainstorming, quickly create a list of words and ideas that are connected to the topic. Let your mind roam free to generate as many relevant ideas as possible in a few minutes. For example, on the topic of computers you may write

> computer- modern invention
> types- personal computers, micro-chips in calculators and watches
> wonder - acts like an electronic brain
> uses - science, medicine, offices, homes, schools
> problems- too much reliance; the machines aren't perfect

This list could help you focus on the topic and states the points you could develop in the body paragraphs. The brainstorming list keeps you on track and is well worth the few minutes it takes to jot down the ideas. While you haven't ordered the ideas, seeing them on paper is an important step.

Questioning

Questioning helps you focus as you mentally ask a series of exploratory questions about the topic. You may use the most basic questions: **who, what, where, when, why, and how.**

"**What** is my subject?"
    [computers]

"**What** types of computers are there?"
    [personal computers, micro-chip computers]

"**Why** have computers been a positive invention?"
    [acts like an electronic brain in machinery and equipment; helps solve complex scientific problems]

"**How** have computers been a positive invention?"
    [used to make improvements in:
- science (space exploration, moon landings)
- medicine (MRIs, CAT scans, surgical tools, research models)
- business (PCs, FAX, telephone equipment)
- education (computer programs for math, languages, science, social studies), and
- personal use (family budgets, tax programs, healthy diet plans)]

"**How** can I show that computers are good?"
    [citing numerous examples]

"**What** problems do I see with computers?"
    [too much reliance; not yet perfect.]

"**What** personal experiences would help me develop examples to respond to this topic?
    [my own experiences using computers]

Of course, you may not have time to write out the questions completely. You might just write the words *who, what, where, why, how* and the major points next to each. An abbreviated list might look as follows:

What — computers/modern wonder/making life better
How — through technological improvements: lasers, calculators, CAT scans, MUs.

Where – in science and space exploration, medicine, schools, offices

In a few moments, your questions should help you to focus on the topic and to generate interesting ideas and points to make in the essay. Later in the writing process, you can look back at the list to be sure you've made the key points you intended.

Clustering

Some visual thinkers find clustering an effective prewriting method. When clustering, you draw a box in the center of your paper and write your topic within that box. Then you draw lines from the center box and connect it to small satellite boxes that contain related ideas. Note the cluster below on computers:

SAMPLE CLUSTER

Writing the Thesis

After focusing on the topic and generating your ideas, form your thesis, the controlling idea of your essay. The thesis is your general statement to the reader that expresses your point of view and guides your essay's purpose and scope. The thesis should allow you either to explain your subject or to take an arguable position about it. A strong thesis statement is neither too narrow nor too broad.

Subject and Assertion of the Thesis

From the analysis of the general topic, you saw the topic in terms of its two parts--*subject* and *assertion*. On the exam, your thesis or viewpoint on a particular topic is stated in two important points:

1.   the *SUBJECT* of the paper
2.   the *ASSERTION* about the subject

The **subject of the thesis** relates directly to the topic prompt but expresses the specific area you have chosen to discuss. (Remember the exam topic will be general and will allow you to choose a particular subject related to the topic.) For example, the computer is one modern invention.

The **assertion of the thesis** is your viewpoint, or opinion, about the subject. The assertion provides the motive or purpose for your essay, and it may be an arguable point or one that explains or illustrates a point of view.

For example, you may present an argument for or against a particular issue. You may contrast two people, objects, or methods to show that one is better than the other. You may analyze a situation in all aspects and make recommendations for improvement. You may assert that a law or policy should be adopted, changed or abandoned. You may also, as in the computer example, explain to your reader that a situation or condition exists; rather than argue a viewpoint, you would use examples to illustrate your assertion about the essay's subject.

Specifically, the **subject** of Topic A is *the computer*. The **assertion** is that *it is a modern wonder that has improved our lives and that we rely upon it*. Now you quickly have created a workable thesis in a few moments:

> *The computer is a modern wonder of the world that has improved our lives and that we have come to rely upon.*

Guidelines for Writing Thesis Statements

The following guidelines are not a formula for writing thesis statements but rather are general strategies for making your thesis statement clearer and more effective.

1.   State a *particular point* of *view* about the topic with both a *subject* and an *assertion*. The thesis should give the essay purpose and scope and thus provide the reader a guide. If the thesis is vague, your essay may be undeveloped because you do not have an idea to assert or a point to explain. Weak thesis statements are often framed as facts, questions or announcements:

   a.   Avoid a fact statement as a thesis. While a fact statement may provide a subject, it generally does not include a point of view about the subject to provide the basis for an extended discussion. Example: *Recycling saved our community over $10,000 last year.* This fact statement provides a detail, *not* a point of view. Such a detail might be found within an essay but it does not state a point of view.

   b.   Avoid framing the thesis as a vague question. In many cases, rhetorical questions do not provide a clear point of view for an extended essay. Example: *How do people recycle?* This question neither asserts a point of view nor helpfully guides the reader to understand the essay's purpose and scope.

   c.   Avoid the "announcer" topic sentence that merely states the topic you will discuss
   Example: I *will discuss ways to recycle.* This sentence states the subject, but the scope of the essay is only suggested. Again, this statement does not assert a viewpoint that guides the essay's purpose. It merely "announces" that the writer will write about the topic.

2.   Start with a workable thesis. You might revise your thesis as you begin writing and discover your own point of view.

3.   If feasible and appropriate, perhaps state the thesis in multi-point form, expressing the scope of the essay. By stating the points in parallel form, you clearly lay out the essay's plan for the reader.
   Example: *To improve the environment, we can recycle our trash, elect politicians who see the environment as a priority, and support lobbying groups who work for environmental protection.*

4.   Because of the exam time limit, place your thesis in the first paragraph to key the reader to the essay's main idea.

Creating a working outline

A good thesis gives structure to your essay and helps focus your thoughts. When forming your thesis, look at your prewriting strategy–clustering, questioning, or brainstorming. Then decide quickly which two or three major areas you'll discuss. Remember you must limit *the scope* of the paper because of the time factor.

The **outline** lists those main areas or points as topics for each paragraph. Looking at the prewriting cluster on computers, you might choose several areas in which computers help us, for example in science and medicine, business, and education. You might also consider people's reliance on this "wonder" and include at least one paragraph about this reliance. A formal outline for this essay might look like the one below:

I. Introduction and thesis
II. Computers used in science and medicine
II. Computers used in business
IV. Computers used in education
V. People's reliance on computers
VI. Conclusion

Under time pressure, however, you may use a shorter organizational plan, such as abbreviated key words in a list. For example:

1. intro: wonders of the computer OR
2. science
3. med
4. schools
5. business
6. conclusion

a. intro: wonders of computers - science
b. in the space industry
c. in medical technology
d. conclusion

Developing the essay

With a working thesis and outline, you can begin writing the essay. The essay should be in three main sections:

1) The **introduction** sets up the essay and leads to the thesis statement.
2) The **body paragraphs** are developed with concrete information leading from the **topic sentences**.
3) The **conclusion** ties the essay together.

Introduction

Put your thesis statement into a clear, coherent opening paragraph. One effective device is to use a funnel approach in which you begin with a brief description of the broader issue and then move to a clearly focused, specific thesis statement.

Consider the following introductions to the essay on computers. The length of each is an obvious difference. Read each and consider the other differences.
Does each introduce the subject generally?
Does each lead to a stated thesis?
Does each relate to the topic prompt?

Introduction 1: *Computers are used every day. They have many uses. Some people who use them are workers, teachers and doctors.*

Analysis: This introduction does give the general topic, computers used every day, but it does not explain what those uses are. This introduction does not offer a point of view in a clearly stated thesis; nor does it convey the idea that computers are a modem wonder.

Introduction 2: *Computers are used just about everywhere these days. I don't think there's an office around that doesn't use computers, and we use them a lot in all kinds of jobs. Computers are great for making life easier and work better. I don't think we'd get along without the computer.*

Analysis: This introduction gives the general topic about computers and mentions one area that uses computers. The thesis states that people couldn't get along without computers, but it does not state the specific areas the essay discusses. Note, too, the meaning is not helped by vague diction such as *a lot* or *great.*

Introduction 3: *Each day we either use computers or see them being used around us. We wake to the sound of a digital alarm operated by a micro-chip. Our cars run by computerized machinery. We use computers to help us learn. We receive phone calls and letters transferred from computers across continents. Our astronauts walked on the moon, and returned safely, all because of computer technology. The computer is a wonderful electronic brain that we have come to rely on that has changed our world through advances in science, business, and education.*

Analysis: This introduction is the most thorough and fluent because it provides interest in the general topic and offers specific information about computers as a modern wonder. It also leads to a thesis that directs the reader to the scope of the discussion--advances in science, business, and education.

Topic Sentences

Just as the essay must have an overall focus reflected in the thesis statement, each paragraph must have a central idea reflected in the topic sentence. A good topic sentence also provides transition from the previous paragraph and relates to the essay's thesis. Good topic sentences, therefore, provide unity throughout the essay.

Consider the following potential topic sentences. Be sure that each provides transition and clearly states the subject of the paragraph.

Topic Sentence 1: *Computers are used in science.*

Analysis: This sentence simply states the topic--computers used in science. It does not relate to the thesis or provide transition from the introduction. The reader still does not know how computers are used.

Topic Sentence 2: *Now I will talk about computers used in science.*

Analysis: Like the faulty "announcer" thesis statement, this "announcer" topic sentence is vague and merely names the topic.

Topic Sentence 3: *First, computers used in science have improved our lives.*

Analysis: The transition word *First* helps link the introduction and this paragraph. It adds unity to the essay. It does not, however, give specifics about the improvement computers have made in our lives.

Topic Sentence 4: *First used in scientific research and spaceflights, computers are now used extensively in the diagnosis and treatment of disease.*

Analysis: This sentence is the most thorough and fluent. It provides specific areas that will be discussed in the paragraph and offers more than an announcement of the topic. The writer gives concrete information about the content of the paragraph that will follow.

Summary Guidelines for Writing Topic Sentences
1. Specifically relate the topic to the thesis statement.
2. State clearly and concretely the subject of the paragraph
3. Provide some transition from the previous paragraph
4. Avoid topic sentences that are facts, questions, or announcers.

Supporting Details

If you have a good thesis and a good outline, you should be able to construct a complete essay. Your paragraphs should contain concrete, interesting information and supporting details to support your point of view. As often as possible, create images in your reader's mind. Fact statements also add weight to your opinions, especially when you are trying to convince the reader of your viewpoint. Because every good thesis has an assertion, you should offer specifics, facts, data, anecdotes, expert opinion, and other details to *show* or *prove* that assertion. While *you* know what you mean, your *reader* does not. On the exam, you must explain and develop ideas as fully as possible in the time allowed.

In the following paragraph, the sentences in **bold print** provide a skeleton of a paragraph on the benefits of recycling. The sentences in bold are generalizations that by themselves do not explain the need to recycle. The sentences in *italics* add details to SHOW the general points in bold. Notice how the supporting details help you understand the necessity for recycling.

While one day recycling may become mandatory in all states, right now it is voluntary in many communities. *Those of us who participate in recycling are amazed by how much material is recycled.* **For many communities, the blue-box recycling program has had an immediate effect.** *By just recycling glass, aluminum cans, and plastic bottles, we have reduced the volume of disposable trash by one-third, thus extending the useful life of local landfills by over a decade. Imagine the difference if those dramatic results were achieved nationwide.* **The amount of reusable items we thoughtlessly dispose of is staggering.** *For example, Americans dispose of enough steel every day to supply Detroit car manufacturers for three months. Additionally, we dispose of enough aluminum annually to rebuild the nation's airfleet. These statistics, available from the Environmental Protection Agency (EPA), should encourage all of us to watch what we throw away.* **Clearly, recycling in our homes and in our communities directly improves the environment.**

Notice how the author's supporting examples enhance the message of the paragraph and relate to the author's thesis noted above. If you only read the bold-face sentences, you have a glimpse of the topic. This paragraph of illustration, however, is developed through numerous details creating specific images: *reduced the volume of disposable trash by one-third; extended the useful life of local landfills by over a decade; enough steel every day to supply Detroit car manufacturers for three months; enough aluminum to rebuild the nation's airfleet.* If the writer had merely written a few general sentences, as those shown in bold face, you would not fully understand the vast amount of trash involved in recycling or the positive results of current recycling efforts.

End your essay with a brief straightforward **concluding paragraph** that ties together the essay's content and leaves the reader with a sense of its completion. The conclusion should reinforce the main points and offer some insight into the topic, provide a sense of unity for the essay by relating it to the thesis, and signal clear closure of the essay.

* * *

On the next page is sample strong response to the prompt:
A problem people recognize and should do something about.

Sample Strong Response

Does the introduction help orient the reader to the topic?

Is there a thesis? Does it clearly state the main idea of the essay?

Does each paragraph have a topic sentence that provides transition and defines the idea?

Do the paragraphs purposefully support the thesis? Do they have interesting details and examples?

Time Magazine, which typically selects a Person of the Year, chose Earth as the Planet of the Year in 1988 to underscore the severe problems facing our planet and, therefore, us. We hear dismal reports every day about the water shortage, the ozone depletion, and the obscene volume of trash generated by our society. Because the problem is global, many people feel powerless to help. Fortunately, by being environmentally aware, we can take steps to alter what seems inevitable. We can recycle our trash and support politicians and lobbying groups who will work for laws to protect the environment.

While one day recycling may be mandatory in all states, right now it is voluntary in many communities. Those of us who participate in recycling are amazed by how much material is recycled. For many communities, the blue box recycling program has had an immediate effect. By just recycling glass, aluminum cans, and plastic bottles, we have reduced the volume of disposable trash by one-third, thus extending the useful life of local landfills by over a decade. Imagine the difference if those dramatic results were achieved nationwide. The amount of reusable items we thoughtlessly dispose of is staggering. For example, Americans dispose of enough steel every day to supply Detroit car manufacturers for three months. Additionally, we dispose of enough aluminum annually to rebuild the nation's air fleet. These statistics, available from the Environmental Protection Agency (EPA), should encourage us to watch what we throw away. Clearly, recycling in our homes and communities directly improves the environment.

Are the paragraphs unified and coherent? Is the material in each paragraph relevant and important?

Moreover, we must be aware of the political issues involved in environmental protection because, unfortunately, the environmental crisis continues despite policies and laws on the books. Enacted in the 1970s, the federal Clean Water Act was intended to clean up polluted waters throughout the nation and to provide safe drinking water for everyone. However, today, with the Clean Water Act still in place, dangerous medical waste has washed onto public beaches in Florida, and recently several people died from the polluted drinking water in Madison, Wisconsin. Additionally, contradictory government policies often work against resource protection. For example, some state welfare agencies give new mothers money only for disposable, not cloth, diapers. In fact, consumer groups found that cloth diapers are cheaper initially and save money over time as we struggle with the crisis of bulging landfills. Clearly, we need consistent government policies and stiffer laws to ensure mandatory enforcement and heavy fines for polluters. We can do this best by electing politicians who will fight for such laws and voting out those who won't.

We can also work to save our planet by supporting organizations that lobby for meaningful, enforceable legal changes. Most of us do not have time to write letters, send telegrams, or study every issue concerning the environment. We can join several organizations that act as watchdogs for us all. For example, organizations such as Greenpeace, the Cousteau Society and the Sierra Club all offer memberships for as low as 15 dollars. By supporting these organizations, we ensure that they have the necessary resources to keep working for all of us and do not have to alter their standards because they must accept funding from special interest groups.

Does the conclusion tie the essay together?

Is the essay edited for grammar and mechanical errors?

Clearly, we all must become environmentally aware. Only through increased awareness can we avoid the tragic consequences of living on a dying planet. We must actively support recycling programs and support those who fight to protect our fragile environment.

Analysis: While not every essay needs to be this thorough in order to pass the exam, this essay shows that with a clear thesis and concept in mind, a writer can produce a literate, interesting piece at one sitting. The introduction creates interest in the general topic and leads to a thesis in the last sentence. The reader has a very clear idea what will be addressed in the essay, and all body paragraphs have topic sentences that relate to the thesis and provide transition. The numerous supporting details and examples are presented in the sophisticated style that reads easily and is enhanced by a college-level vocabulary and word choice. Transition words and phrases add unity to sentences and paragraphs. Grammar and mechanics areas are correct, so errors don't detract from the fine writing. For all these reasons, this essay is a polished piece of writing deserving of an upper-range score

Sample Test I: Language Arts

DIRECTIONS : *The passage below contains many errors. Read the passage. Then answer each test item by choosing the option that corrects an error in the underlined portion(s). No more than one underlined error will appear in each item. If no error exists, choose "No change is necessary."*

Climbing to the top of Mount Everest is an adventure. One which everyone--whether physically fit or not--seems eager to try. The trail stretches for miles, the cold temperatures are usually frigid and brutal.

Climbers must endure several barriers on the way, including other hikers, steep jagged rocks, and lots of snow. Plus, climbers often find the most grueling part of the trip is their climb back down, just when they are feeling greatly exhausted. Climbers who take precautions are likely to find the ascent less arduous than the unprepared. By donning heavy flannel shirts, gloves, and hats, climbers prevented hypothermia, as well as simple frostbite. A pair of rugged boots is also one of the necesities. If climbers are to avoid becoming dehydrated, there is beverages available for them to transport as well.

Once climbers are completely ready to begin their lengthy journey, they can comfortable enjoy the wonderful scenery. Wide rock formations dazzle the observers eyes with shades of gray and white, while the peak forms a triangle that seems to touch the sky. Each of the climbers are reminded of the splendor and magnificence of Gods great Earth.

1. **If climbers are to avoid <u>becoming</u> dehydrated, there <u>is</u> beverages available for <u>them</u> to transport as well.**
    (Easy) (Skill 7.1)

    A. becoming

    B. are

    C. him

    D. No change is necessary

2. **By donning heavy flannel shirts, boots, and <u>hats, climbers</u> <u>prevented</u> hypothermia, as well as simple frostbite.**
    (Average Rigor) (Skill 7.1)

    A. hats climbers

    B. can prevent

    C. hypothermia;

    D. No change is necessary

3. **Plus, climbers often find the most grueling part of the trip is <u>their</u> climb back <u>down, just</u> when they <u>are</u> feeling greatly exhausted.**
(Average Rigor) (Skill 7.1)

A. his

B. down; just

C. were

D. No change is necessary

4. **Each of the climbers <u>are</u> reminded of the splendor and <u>magnificence</u> of <u>God's</u> great Earth.**
(Rigorous) (Skills 7.1, 7.2)

A. is

B. magnifisence

C. Gods

D. No change is necessary

5. **The <u>trail</u> stretches for <u>miles,</u> the cold temperatures are <u>usually</u> frigid and brutal.**
(Rigorous) (Skills 7.1, 7.3, 8.1)

A. trails

B. miles;

C. usual

D. No change is necessary

6. **Climbing to the top of Mount Everest is an <u>adventure. One</u> which everyone <u>—whether</u> physically fit or not—<u>seems</u> eager to try.**
(Rigorous) (Skills 7.1, 8.1)

A. adventure, one

B. people, whether

C. seem

D. No change is necessary

7. **Wide rock formations dazzle the <u>observers eyes</u> with shades of gray and <u>white, while</u> the peak <u>forms</u> a triangle that seems to touch the sky.**
(Rigorous) (Skill 7.2)

A. observers' eyes

B. white; while

C. formed

D. No change is necessary

8. **<u>Climbers who</u> take precautions are likely to find the ascent <u>less difficult than</u> the unprepared.**
(Average Rigor) (Skill 7.3)

A. Climbers, who

B. least difficult

C. then

D. No change is necessary

9. **Once climbers are completely prepared for <u>their</u> lengthy <u>journey, they</u> can <u>comfortable</u> enjoy the wonderful scenery.**
(Easy) (Skill 7.3)

   A. they're

   B. journey; they

   C. comfortably

   D. No change is necessary

10. **Climbers must endure <u>several</u> barriers <u>on the way, including</u> other <u>hikers,</u> steep jagged rocks, and lots of snow.**
(Average Rigor) (Skills 8.1, 12.3)

   A. several

   B. on the way, including

   C. hikers'

   D. No change is necessary

11. **A pair of rugged boots <u>is</u> <u>also one</u> of the <u>necesities</u>.**
(Rigorous) (Skill 10.5)

   A. are

   B. also, one

   C. necessities

   D. No change is necessary

DIRECTIONS: *The passage below contains several errors. Read the passage. Then answer each test item by choosing the option that corrects an error in the underlined portion(s). No more than one underlined error will appear in each item. If no error exists, choose "No change is necessary."*

Every job places different kinds of demands on their employees. For example, whereas such jobs as accounting and bookkeeping require mathematical ability; graphic design requires creative/artistic ability.

Doing good at one job does not usually guarantee success at another. However, one of the elements crucial to all jobs are especially notable: the chance to accomplish a goal.

The accomplishment of the employees varies according to the job. In many jobs the employees become accustom to the accomplishment provided by the work they do every day.

In medicine, for example, every doctor tests him self by treating badly injured or critically ill people. In the operating room, a team of Surgeons, is responsible for operating on many of these patients. In addition to the feeling of accomplishment that the workers achieve, some jobs also give a sense of identity to the employees'. Profesions like law, education, and sales offer huge financial and emotional rewards. Politicians are public servants: who work for the federal and state governments. President bush is basically employed by the American people to make laws and run the country.

Finally; the contributions that employees make to their companies and to the world cannot be taken for granted. Through their work, employees are performing a service for their employers and are contributing something to the world.

12. The <u>accomplishment</u> of the <u>employees</u> <u>varies</u> according to the job.
(Average Rigor) (Skill 7.1)

A. accomplishment,

B. employee's

C. vary

D. No change is necessary

13. Politicians <u>are</u> public <u>servants: who</u> <u>work</u> for the federal and state governments.
(Easy) (Skill 7.1)

A. were

B. servants who

C. worked

D. No change is necessary

14. <u>However,</u> one of the elements crucial to all jobs <u>are</u> especially <u>notable:</u> the accomplishment of a goal.
(Average Rigor) (Skill 7.1)

A. However

B. is

C. notable;

D. No change is necessary

15. In many jobs the employees <u>become</u> <u>accustom</u> to the accomplishment <u>provided</u> by the work they do every day.
(Average Rigor) (Skill 7.1)

A. became

B. accustomed

C. provides

D. No change is necessary

16. In medicine, for example, every doctor <u>tests</u> <u>him self</u> by treating badly injured and critically ill people.
(Average Rigor) (Skill 7.2)

A. test

B. himself

C. critical

D. No change is necessary

17. **Every job <u>places</u> different kinds of demands on <u>their</u> <u>employees</u>.**
(Rigorous) (Skill 7.2)

    A. place

    B. its

    C. employes

    D. No change is necessary

18. **Doing <u>good</u> at one job does not <u>usually</u> guarantee <u>success</u> at another.**
(Rigorous) (Skill 7.3)

    A. well

    B. usualy

    C. succeeding

    D. No change is necessary

19. **<u>For example,</u> <u>whereas</u> such jobs as accounting and bookkeeping require mathematical <u>ability;</u> graphic design requires creative/artistic ability.**
(Average Rigor) (Skill 8.1)

    A. For example

    B. whereas,

    C. ability,

    D. No change is necessary

20. **<u>Finally;</u> the contributions that employees make to <u>their</u> companies and to the world cannot be <u>taken</u> for granted.**
(Average Rigor) (Skill 8.1)

    A. Finally,

    B. their

    C. took

    D. No change is necessary

21. **In the <u>operating room,</u> a team of <u>Surgeons, is</u> responsible for operating on many of <u>these</u> patients.**
(Easy) (Skill 8.2)

    A. operating room:

    B. surgeons is

    C. those

    D. No change is necessary

22. **President <u>bush</u> is basically employed <u>by</u> the American people to <u>make</u> laws and run the country.**
(Easy) (Skill 8.2)

    A. Bush

    B. to

    C. made

    D. No change is necessary

23. In addition to the feeling of accomplishment that the workers <u>achieve</u>, some jobs also <u>give</u> a sense of self-identity to the <u>employees'</u>. *(Average Rigor) (Skill 8.3)*

A. achieve

B. gave

C. employees

D. No change is necessary

24. <u>Profesions</u> like law, <u>education,</u> and sales <u>offer</u> huge financial and emotional rewards. *(Rigorous) (Skill 8.3)*

A. Professions

B. education;

C. offered

D. No change is necessary

DIRECTIONS: *For the underlined sentence(s), choose the option that expresses the meaning with the most fluency and the clearest logic within the context. If the underlined sentence should not be changed, choose Option A, which shows no change.*

25. Selecting members of a President's cabinet can often be an aggravating process. <u>Either there are too many or too few qualified candidates for a certain position, and then they have to be confirmed by the Senate, where there is the possibility of rejection.</u> *(Rigorous) (Skill 11.2)*

A. Either there are too many or too few qualified candidate for a certain position, and then they have to be confirmed by the Senate, where there is the possibility of rejection.

B. Qualified candidates for certain positions face the possibility of rejection, when they have to be confirmed by the Senate.

C. The Senate has to confirm qualified candidates, who face the possibility of rejection.

D. Because the Senate has to confirm qualified candidates; they face the possibility of rejection.

26. **Treating patients for drug and/or alcohol abuse is a sometimes difficult process.** <u>Even though there are a number of different methods for helping the patient overcome a dependency, there is no way of knowing which is best in the long-run.</u>
(Rigorous) (Skill 11.2)

A. Even though there are a number of different methods for helping the patient overcome a dependency, there is no way of knowing which is best in the long-run.

B. Even though different methods can help a patient overcome a dependency, there is no way to know which is best in the long-run.

C. Even though there is no way to know which way is best in the long run, patients can overcome their dependencies when they are helped.

D. There is no way to know which method will help the patient overcome a dependency in the long-run, even though there are many different ones.

27. **Many factors account for the decline in quality of public education.** <u>Overcrowding, budget cutbacks, and societal deterioration which have greatly affected student learning.</u>
(Rigorous) (Skill 11.2)

A. Overcrowding, budget cutbacks, and societal deterioration which have greatly affected student learning.

B. Student learning has been greatly affected by overcrowding, budget cutbacks, and societal deterioration.

C. Due to overcrowding, budget cutbacks, and societal deterioration, student learning has been greatly affected.

D. Overcrowding, budget cutbacks, and societal deterioration have affected students learning greatly.

DIRECTIONS: *Choose the sentence that logically and correctly expresses the comparison.*

(Easy) (Skill 7.3)

28. A. The Empire State Building in New York is taller than buildings in the city.

    B. The Empire State Building in New York is taller than any other building in the city.

    C. The Empire State Building in New York is tallest than other buildings in the city.

DIRECTIONS: *Choose the underlined word or phrase that is unnecessary within the context of the passage.*

29. **Considered by many to be one of the worst terrorist incidents on American soil was the bombing of the Oklahoma City Federal Building which will be remembered for years to come.**
    (Average Rigor) (Skill 11.1)

    A. considered by many to be

    B. terrorist

    C. on American soil

    D. for years to come

30. **The flu epidemic struck most of the respected faculty and students of The Woolbright School , forcing the Boynton Beach School Superintendent to close it down for two weeks.**
    (Average Rigor) (Skill 11.1)

    A. flu

    B. most of

    C. respected

    D. for two weeks

31. **The expanding number of television channels has prompted cable operators to raise their prices, even though many consumers do not want to pay a higher increased amount for their service.**
    (Easy) (Skill 11.1)

    A. expanding

    B. prompted

    C. even though

    D. increased

DIRECTIONS: *Choose the most effective word within the context of the sentence.*

32. **Many of the clubs in Boca Raton are noted for their _____ elegance.**
(Average Rigor) (Skill 11.2)

    A. vulgar

    B. tasteful

    C. ordinary

33. **When a student is expelled from school, the parents are usually _____ in advance.**
(Average Rigor) (Skill 11.2)

    A. rewarded

    B. congratulated

    C. notified

34. **Before appearing in court, the witness was _____ the papers requiring her to show up.**
(Average Rigor) (Skill 11.2)

    A. condemned

    B. served

    C. criticized

DIRECTIONS: *The passage below contains several errors. Read the passage. Then answer each test item by choosing the option that corrects an error in the underlined portion(s). No more than one underlined error will appear in each item. If no error exists, choose "No change is necessary."*

The discovery of a body at Paris Point marina in Boca Raton shocked the residents of Palmetto Pines, a luxury condominium complex located next door to the marina.

The victim is a thirty-five year old woman who had been apparently bludgeoned to death and dumped in the ocean late last night. Many neighbors reported terrible screams, gunshots: as well as the sound of a car backfiring loudly to Boca Raton Police shortly after midnight. The woman had been spotted in the lobby of Palmetto Pines around ten thirty, along with an older man, estimated to be in his fifties, and a younger man, in his late twenties.

"Apparently, the victim had been driven to the complex by the older man, and was seen arguing with him when the younger man intervened", said Sheriff Fred Adams, "all three of them left the building together and walked to the marina, where gunshots rang out an hour later." Deputies found five bullets on the sidewalk and some blood, along with a steel pipe that is assumed to be the murder weapon. Two men were seen fleeing the scene in a red Mercedes short after, rushing toward the Interstate.

The Palm Beach County Coroner, Melvin Watts, said he concluded the victim's skull had been crushed by a blunt tool, which resulted in a brain hemorrhage. As of now, there is no clear motive for the murder.

35. **Deputies found five bullets on the sidewalk and some <u>blood,</u> along with a steel pipe that is <u>assumed to be</u> the murder weapon.**
   (Rigorous) (Skill 7.1)

   A. blood;

   B. assuming

   C. to have been

   D. No change is necessary

36. **The victim <u>is</u> a thirty-five year old who had been apparently <u>bludgeoned</u> to death and dumped in the <u>ocean late</u> last night.**
   (Rigorous) (Skill 7.1)

   A. was

   B. bludgoned

   C. ocean: late

   D. No change is necessary

37. Two men <u>were</u> seen fleeing the scene in a red Mercedes <u>short</u> after, <u>rushing</u> toward the Interstate.
(Easy) (Skill 7.3)

   A. are

   B. shortly

   C. rushed

   D. No change is necessary

38. As of <u>now,</u> <u>there</u> <u>is</u> no clear motive for the murder.
(Rigorous) (Skill 8.1)

   A. now;

   B. their

   C. was

   D. No change is necessary

39. The discovery of a body at Paris Point <u>marina</u> in Boca Raton shocked the <u>residents</u> of Palmetto Pines, a luxury <u>condominium</u> complex located next door to the marina.
(Easy) (Skill 8.2)

   A. Marina

   B. residence

   C. condominium

   D. No change is necessary

40. Many <u>neighbors</u> reported terrible screams, <u>gunshots: as</u> well as the sound of a car backfiring <u>loudly</u> to Boca Raton Police shortly after midnight.
(Average Rigor) (Skill 8.2)

   A. nieghbors

   B. gunshots, as

   C. loud

   D. No change is necessary

41. The woman <u>had</u> been spotted in the lobby of Palmetto Pines around ten <u>thirty,</u> along with an older <u>man, estimated</u> to be in his fifties, and a younger man in his late twenties.
(Rigorous) (Skill 8.2)

   A. has

   B. thirty;

   C. man estimated

   D. No change is necessary

42. **"Apparently, the victim had been driven to the complex by the older man, and was seen arguing with him when the younger man intervened," said <u>Sheriff Fred Adams, "all</u> three of them left the building together and walked to the marina, when gunshots rang out an hour later."**
(Rigorous) (Skill 8.2)

A. sheriff Fred Adams, "all

B. sheriff Fred Adams, "All

C. Sheriff Fred Adams." All

D. No change is necessary

43. **The <u>Palm Beach</u> County <u>Coroner,</u> Kelvin Watts, said he concluded the victim's skull had been crushed by a blunt tool, which resulted in a brain <u>hemorrage</u>.**
(Rigorous) (Skill 8.2)

A. palm beach

B. coroner

C. hemorrhage

D. No change is necessary

Answer Key: Language Arts

1.	B	23.	C
2.	B	24.	~~D~~ A
3.	D	25.	C
4.	A	26.	B
5.	B	27.	B
6.	A	28.	B
7.	A	29.	A
8.	C	30.	C
9.	C	31.	D
10.	B	32.	B
11.	B	33.	C
12.	C	34.	B
13.	B	35.	C
14.	B	36.	A
15.	B	37.	B
16.	B	38.	D
17.	B	39.	A
18.	A	40.	B
19.	C	41.	C
20.	A	42.	C
21.	B	43.	~~D~~ C
22.	A		

Rigor Table: Language Arts

	Easy 20%	Average 40%	Rigorous 40%
Questions (43)	1, 9, 13, 21, 22, 28, 31, 37, 39	2, 3, 8, 10, 12, 14, 15, 16, 19, 20, 23, 29, 30, 32, 33, 34, 40	4, 5, 6, 7, 11, 17, 18, 24, 25, 26, 27, 35, 36, 38, 41, 42, 43
TOTALS	9 (20.9%)	17 (39.5%)	17 (39.5%)

Rationales with Sample Questions: Language Arts

DIRECTIONS : *The passage below contains many errors. Read the passage. Then answer each test item by choosing the option that corrects an error in the underlined portion(s). No more than one underlined error will appear in each item. If no error exists, choose "No change is necessary."*

Climbing to the top of Mount Everest is an adventure. One which everyone--whether physically fit or not--seems eager to try. The trail stretches for miles, the cold temperatures are usually frigid and brutal.

Climbers must endure severel barriers on the way, including other hikers, steep jagged rocks, and lots of snow. Plus, climbers often find the most grueling part of the trip is their climb back down, just when they are feeling greatly exhausted. Climbers who take precautions are likely to find the ascent less arduous then the unprepared. By donning heavy flannel shirts, gloves, and hats, climbers prevented hypothermia, as well as simple frostbite. A pair of rugged boots is also one of the necesities. If climbers are to avoid becoming dehydrated, there is beverages available for them to transport as well.

Once climbers are completely ready to begin their lengthy journey, they can comfortable enjoy the wonderful scenery. Wide rock formations dazzle the observers eyes with shades of gray and white, while the peak forms a triangle that seems to touch the sky. Each of the climbers are reminded of the splendor and magnifisence of Gods great Earth.

1. If climbers are to avoid <u>becoming</u> dehydrated, there <u>is</u> beverages available for <u>them</u> to transport as well.
    (Easy) (Skill 7.1)

    A. becoming

    B. are

    C. him

    D. No change is necessary

Answer B: are

The plural verb *are* must be used with the plural subject *beverages*. Option A is incorrect because *becoming* has only one m. Option C is incorrect because the plural pronoun *them* is needed to agree with the referent *climbers*.

2.   By donning heavy flannel shirts, boots, and <u>hats, climbers</u> <u>prevented</u> hypothermia, as well as simple frostbite.
(Average Rigor) (Skill 7.1)

    A. hats climbers

    B. can prevent

    C. hypothermia;

    D. No change is necessary

Answer B: can prevent

The verb *prevented* is in the past tense and must be changed to the present *can prevent* to be consistent. Option A is incorrect because a comma is needed after a long introductory phrase. Option C is incorrect because the semicolon creates a fragment of the phrase *as well as simple frostbite.*

3.   Plus, climbers often find the most grueling part of the trip is <u>their</u> climb back <u>down, just</u> when they <u>are</u> feeling greatly exhausted.
(Average Rigor) (Skill 7.1)

    A. his

    B. down; just

    C. were

    D. No change is necessary

Answer D: No change is necessary

The present tense must be used consistently throughout, therefore Option C is incorrect. Option A is incorrect because the singular pronoun *his* does not agree with the plural antecedent *climbers*. Option B is incorrect because a comma, not a semicolon, is needed to separate the dependent clause from the main clause.

4.	Each of the climbers <u>are</u> reminded of the splendor and <u>magnificence</u> of <u>God's</u> great Earth.
	(Rigorous) (Skills 7.1, 7.2)

	A.	is

	B.	magnifisence

	C.	Gods

	D.	No change is necessary

Answer A: is

The singular verb *is* agrees with the singular subject *each*. Option B is incorrect because *magnificence* is misspelled. Option C is incorrect because an apostrophe is needed to show possession.

5.	The <u>trail</u> stretches for <u>miles</u>, the cold temperatures are <u>usually</u> frigid and brutal.
	(Rigorous) (Skills 7.1, 7.3, 8.1)

	A.	trails

	B.	miles;

	C.	usual

	D.	No change is necessary

Answer B: miles

A semicolon, not a comma, is needed to separate the first independent clause from the second independent clause. Option A is incorrect because the plural subject *trails* needs the singular verb stretch. Option C is incorrect because the adverb form *usually* is needed to modify the adjective *frigid.*

6. Climbing to the top of Mount Everest is an <u>adventure. One</u> which everyone <u>—whether </u>physically fit or not—<u>seems </u>eager to try. *(Rigorous) (Skills 7.1, 8.1)*

   A. adventure, one

   B. people, whether

   C. seem

   D. No change is necessary

Answer A: adventure, one

A comma is needed between *adventure* and *one* to avoid creating a fragment of the second part. In Option B, a comma after *everyone* would not be appropriate when the dash is used on the other side of *not*. In Option C, the singular verb *seems* is needed to agree with the singular subject *everyone*.

7. Wide rock formations dazzle the <u>observers eyes</u> with shades of gray and <u>white, while</u> the peak <u>forms</u> a triangle that seems to touch the sky. *(Rigorous) (Skill 7.2)*

   A. observers' eyes

   B. white; while

   C. formed

   D. No change is necessary

Answer A: observers' eyes

An apostrophe is needed to show the plural possessive form *observers' eyes*. Option B is incorrect because the semicolon would make the second half of the item seem like an independent clause when the subordinating conjunction *while* makes that clause dependent. Option C is incorrect because *formed* is in the wrong tense.

8.   **<u>Climbers who</u> take precautions are likely to find the ascent <u>less difficult</u> <u>then</u> the unprepared.**
     (Average Rigor) (Skill 7.3)

   A. Climbers, who

   B. least difficult

   C. than

   D. No change is necessary

Answer C: than

Option C is correct because the comparative adverb *than*, not *then*, is needed. Option A is incorrect because a comma would make the phrase *who take precautions* seem less restrictive or less essential to the sentence. Option B is incorrect because *less* is appropriate when two items--the prepared and the unprepared--are compared.

9.   **Once climbers are completely prepared for <u>their</u> lengthy <u>journey,</u> <u>they</u> can <u>comfortable</u> enjoy the wonderful scenery.**
     (Easy) (Skill 7.3)

   A. they're

   B. journey; they

   C. comfortably

   D. No change is necessary

Answer C: comfortably

The adverb form *comfortably* is needed to modify the verb phrase *can enjoy*. Option A is incorrect because the possessive plural pronoun is spelled *their*. Option B is incorrect because a semi-colon would make the first half of the item seem like an independent clause when the subordinating conjunction *once* makes that clause dependent.

10. **Climbers must endure <u>several</u> barriers <u>on the way, including</u> other <u>hikers</u>, steep jagged rocks, and lots of snow.**
    (Average Rigor) (Skills 8.1, 12.3)

    A. several

    B. on the way, including

    C. hikers'

    D. No change is necessary

Answer B: on the way, including

A comma is needed to set off the modifying phrase. Option A is incorrect because the word *several* is already correct in the sentence. Option C is incorrect because no apostrophe is needed after *hikers* since possession is not involved.

11. **A pair of rugged boots <u>is also one</u> of the <u>necesities</u>.**
    (Rigorous) (Skill 10.5)

    A. are

    B. also, one

    C. necessities

    D. No change is necessary

Answer B: also one

Option B is correct because the transition *also* is needed to continue the list of necessary items from the previous sentence. Option A is incorrect because singular verb *is* must agree with the singular noun *pair* (a collective singular). Option C is incorrect because *necessities* is spelled correctly in the text.

DIRECTIONS: *The passage below contains several errors. Read the passage. Then answer each test item by choosing the option that corrects an error in the underlined portion(s). No more than one underlined error will appear in each item. If no error exists, choose "No change is necessary."*

Every job places different kinds of demands on their employees. For example, whereas such jobs as accounting and bookkeeping require mathematical ability; graphic design requires creative/artistic ability.

Doing good at one job does not usually guarantee success at another. However, one of the elements crucial to all jobs are especially notable: the chance to accomplish a goal.

The accomplishment of the employees varies according to the job. In many jobs the employees become accustom to the accomplishment provided by the work they do every day.

In medicine, for example, every doctor tests him self by treating badly injured or critically ill people. In the operating room, a team of Surgeons, is responsible for operating on many of these patients. In addition to the feeling of accomplishment that the workers achieve, some jobs also give a sense of identity to the employees'. Profesions like law, education, and sales offer huge financial and emotional rewards. Politicians are public servants: who work for the federal and state governments. President bush is basically employed by the American people to make laws and run the country.

Finally; the contributions that employees make to their companies and to the world cannot be taken for granted. Through their work, employees are performing a service for their employers and are contributing something to the world.

12. **The <u>accomplishment</u> of the <u>employees</u> <u>varies</u> according to the job.** *(Average Rigor) (Skill 7.1)*

   A. accomplishment,

   B. employee's

   C. vary

   D. No change is necessary

Answer C: vary

The singular verb *vary* is needed to agree with the singular subject *accomplishment*. Option A is incorrect because a comma after *accomplishment* would suggest that the modifying phrase of the employees is additional instead of essential. Option B is incorrect because employees is not possessive.

13. Politicians <u>are</u> public <u>servants: who work</u> for the federal and state governments.
(Easy) (Skill 7.1)

    A. were

    B. servants who

    C. worked

    D. No change is necessary

Answer B: servants who

A colon is not needed to set off the introduction of the sentence. In Option A, *were*, is the incorrect tense of the verb. In Option C, *worked*, is in the wrong tense.

14. <u>However,</u> one of the elements crucial to all jobs <u>are</u> especially <u>notable:</u> the accomplishment of a goal.
(Average Rigor) (Skill 7.1)

    A. However

    B. is

    C. notable;

    D. No change is necessary

Answer B: is

The singular verb *is* is needed to agree with the singular subject *one*. Option A is incorrect because a comma is needed to set off the transitional word *however*. Option C is incorrect because a colon, not a semicolon, is needed to set off an item.

15. **In many jobs the employees <u>become</u> <u>accustom</u> to the accomplishment <u>provided</u> by the work they do every day.**
    (Average Rigor) (Skill 7.1)

   A. became

   B. accustomed

   C. provides

   D. No change is necessary

Answer B: accustomed

The past participle *accustomed* is needed with the verb *become*. Option A is incorrect because the verb tense does not need to change to the past *became*. Option C is incorrect because *provides* is the wrong tense.

16. **In medicine, for example, every doctor <u>tests</u> <u>him self</u> by treating badly injured and critically ill people.**
    (Average Rigor) (Skill 7.2)

   A. test

   B. himself

   C. critical

   D. No change is necessary

Answer B: himself

The reflexive pronoun *himself* is needed. (Him self is nonstandard and never correct.) Option A is incorrect because the singular verb test is needed to agree with the singular subject doctor. Option C is incorrect because the adverb *critically* is needed to modify the verb *ill*.

17.   Every job <u>places</u> different kinds of demands on <u>their employees</u>.
        (Rigorous) (Skill 7.2)

        A. place

        B. its

        C. employes

        D. No change is necessary

Answer B: its

The singular possessive pronoun *its* must agree with its antecedent *job*, which is singular also. Option A is incorrect because *place* is a plural form and the subject, *job*, is singular. Option C is incorrect because the correct spelling of employees is given in the sentence.

18.   Doing <u>good</u> at one job does not <u>usually</u> guarantee <u>success</u> at another.
        (Rigorous) (Skill 7.3)

        A. well

        B. usualy

        C. succeeding

        D. No change is necessary

Answer A: well

The adverb *well* modifies the word *doing*. Option B is incorrect because *usually* is spelled correctly in the sentence. Option C is incorrect because *succeeding* is in the wrong tense.

19. <u>For example,</u> <u>whereas</u> such jobs as accounting and bookkeeping require mathematical <u>ability;</u> graphic design requires creative/artistic ability.
    (Average Rigor) (Skill 8.1)

    A. For example

    B. whereas,

    C. ability,

    D. No change is necessary

Answer C: ability,

An introductory dependent clause is set off with a comma, not a semicolon. Option A is incorrect because the transitional phrase *for example* should be set off with a comma. Option B is incorrect because the adverb *whereas* functions like *while* and does not take a comma after it.

20. <u>Finally;</u> the contributions that employees make to <u>their</u> companies and to the world cannot be <u>taken</u> for granted.
    (Average Rigor) (Skill 8.1)

    A. Finally,

    B. their

    C. took

    D. No change is necessary

Answer A: Finally,

A comma is needed to separate *Finally* from the rest of the sentence. Finally is a preposition which usually heads a dependent sentence, hence a comma is needed. Option B is incorrect because *their* is misspelled. Option C is incorrect because *took* is the wrong form of the verb.

21.   In the <u>operating room,</u> a team of <u>Surgeons, is</u> responsible for operating on many of <u>these</u> patients.
       (Easy) (Skill 8.2)

       A. operating room:

       B. surgeons is

       C. those

       D. No change is necessary

Answer B: surgeons is

Surgeons is not a proper name so it does not need to be capitalized. A comma is not needed to break up a team of surgeons from the rest of the sentence. Option A is incorrect because a comma ,not a colon, is needed to set off an item. Option C is incorrect because *those* is an incorrect pronoun.

22.   President <u>bush</u> is basically employed <u>by</u> the American people to <u>make</u> laws and run the country.
       (Easy) (Skill 8.2)

       A. Bush

       B. to

       C. made

       D. No change is necessary

Answer A: Bush

Bush is a proper name and should be capitalized. Option B, *to*, does not fit with the verb *employed*. Option C uses the wrong form of the verb, *make*.

23. **In addition to the feeling of accomplishment that the workers <u>achieve</u>, some jobs also <u>give</u> a sense of self-identity to the <u>employees'</u>.**
(Average Rigor) (Skill 8.3)

   A. achieve

   B. gave

   C. employees

   D. No change is necessary

Answer C: employees

Option C is correct because *employees* is not possessive. Option A is incorrect because *achieve* is spelled correctly in the sentence. Option B is incorrect because *gave* is the wrong tense.

24. **<u>Profesions</u> like law, <u>education,</u> and sales <u>offer</u> huge financial and emotional rewards.**
(Rigorous) (Skill 8.3)

   A. Professions

   B. education;

   C. offered

   D. No change is necessary

Answer D: No change is necessary

Option A is incorrect because *professions* is spelled correctly in the sentence. Option B is incorrect because a comma is not needed to join compound objects of prepositions. In Option C, *offered*, is in the wrong tense.

DIRECTIONS: *For the underlined sentence(s), choose the option that expresses the meaning with the most fluency and the clearest logic within the context. If the underlined sentence should not be changed, choose Option A, which shows no change.*

25. **Selecting members of a President's cabinet can often be an aggravating process. <u>Either there are too many or too few qualified candidates for a certain position, and then they have to be confirmed by the Senate, where there is the possibility of rejection.</u>**
   (Rigorous) (Skill 11.2)

   A. Either there are too many or too few qualified candidate for a certain position, and then they have to be confirmed by the Senate, where there is the possibility of rejection.

   B. Qualified candidates for certain positions face the possibility of rejection, when they have to be confirmed by the Senate.

   C. The Senate has to confirm qualified candidates, who face the possibility of rejection.

   D. Because the Senate has to confirm qualified candidates; they face the possibility of rejection.

Answer C: The Senate has to confirm qualified candidates, who face the possibility of rejection.

Option C is the most straightforward and concise sentence. Option A is too unwieldy with the wordy *Either...or* phrase at the beginning. Option B doesn't make clear the fact that candidates face rejection by the Senate. Option D illogically implies that candidates face rejection because they have to be confirmed by the Senate.

26.   Treating patients for drug and/or alcohol abuse is a sometimes difficult process. <u>Even though there are a number of different methods for helping the patient overcome a dependency, there is no way of knowing which is best in the long-run.</u>
(Rigorous) (Skill 11.2)

A. Even though there are a number of different methods for helping the patient overcome a dependency, there is no way of knowing which is best in the long-run.

B. Even though different methods can help a patient overcome a dependency, there is no way to know which is best in the long-run.

C. Even though there is no way to know which way is best in the long run, patients can overcome their dependencies when they are helped.

D. There is no way to know which method will help the patient overcome a dependency in the long-run, even though there are many different ones.

Answer B: Even though different methods can help a patient overcome a dependency, there is no way to know which is best in the long-run.

Option B is concise and logical. Option A tends to ramble with the use of *there are* and the verbs *helping* and *knowing*. Option C is awkwardly worded and repetitive in the first part of the sentence, and vague in the second because it never indicates how the patients can be helped. Option D contains the unnecessary phrase *even though there are many different ones.*

27. **Many factors account for the decline in quality of public education. <u>Overcrowding, budget cutbacks, and societal deterioration which have greatly affected student learning</u>.**
(Rigorous) (Skill 11.2)

A. Overcrowding, budget cutbacks, and societal deterioration which have greatly affected student learning.

B. Student learning has been greatly affected by overcrowding, budget cutbacks, and societal deterioration.

C. Due to overcrowding, budget cutbacks, and societal deterioration, student learning has been greatly affected.

D. Overcrowding, budget cutbacks, and societal deterioration have affected students learning greatly.

Answer B: Student learning has been greatly affected by overcrowding, budget cutbacks, and societal deterioration.

Option B is concise and best explains the causes of the decline in student education. The unnecessary use of which in Option A makes the sentence feel incomplete. Option C has weak coordination between the reasons for the decline in public education and the fact that student learning has been affected. Option D incorrectly places the adverb *greatly* after learning, instead of before *affected.*

DIRECTIONS: *Choose the sentence that logically and correctly expresses the comparison.*

(Easy) (Skill 7.3)

28.   A. The Empire State Building in New York is taller than buildings in the city.

   B. The Empire State Building in New York is taller than any other building in the city.

   C. The Empire State Building in New York is tallest than other buildings in the city.

Answer B: The Empire State Building in New York is taller than any other building in the city.

Because the Empire State Building is a building in New York City, the phrase *any other* must be included. Option A is incorrect because the Empire State Building is implicitly compared to itself since it is one of the buildings. Option C is incorrect because *tallest i*s the incorrect form of the adjective.

DIRECTIONS: *Choose the underlined word or phrase that is unnecessary within the context of the passage.*

29.   <u>Considered by many to be</u> one of the worst <u>terrorist</u> incidents <u>on American soil</u> was the bombing of the Oklahoma City Federal Building which will be remembered <u>for years to come</u>.
   (Average Rigor) (Skill 11.1)

   A. considered by many to be

   B. terrorist

   C. on American soil

   D. for years to come

Answer: A. considered by many to be

Considered by many to be is a wordy phrase and unnecessary in the context of the sentence. All other words are necessary within the context of the sentence.

30. The <u>flu</u> epidemic struck <u>most of</u> the <u>respected</u> faculty and students of The Woolbright School, forcing the Boynton Beach School Superintendent to close it down <u>for two weeks.</u>
     (Average Rigor) (Skill 11.1)

     A. flu

     B. most of

     C. respected

     D. for two weeks

Answer C: respected

The fact that the faculty might have been *respected* is not really necessary to mention in the sentence. The other words and phrases are all necessary to complete the meaning of the sentence.

31. The <u>expanding</u> number of television channels has <u>prompted</u> cable operators to raise their prices, <u>even though</u> many consumers do not want to pay a higher <u>increased</u> amount for their service.
     (Easy) (Skill 11.1)

     A. expanding

     B. prompted

     C. even though

     D. increased

Answer D: increased

The word *increased* is redundant with higher and should be removed. All the other words are necessary within the context of the sentence.

DIRECTIONS: *Choose the most effective word within the context of the sentence.*

32. **Many of the clubs in Boca Raton are noted for their _____ elegance.**
    (Average Rigor) (Skill 11.2)

    A. vulgar

    B. tasteful

    C. ordinary

Answer B: tasteful

Tasteful means beautiful or charming, which would correspond to an elegant club. The words *vulgar* and *ordinary* have negative connotations.

33. **When a student is expelled from school, the parents are usually _____ in advance.**
    (Average Rigor) (Skill 11.2)

    A. rewarded

    B. congratulated

    C. notified

Answer C: notified

Notified means informed or told, which fits into the logic of the sentence. The words *rewarded* and *congratulated* are positive actions, which don't make sense regarding someone being expelled from school.

34. **Before appearing in court, the witness was _____ the papers requiring her to show up.**
(Average Rigor) (Skill 11.2)

A. condemned

B. served

C. criticized

Answer: B. served

Served means given, which makes sense in the context of the sentence. *Condemned* and *criticized* do not make sense within the context of the sentence.

DIRECTIONS: *The passage below contains several errors. Read the passage. Then answer each test item by choosing the option that corrects an error in the underlined portion(s). No more than one underlined error will appear in each item. If no error exists, choose "No change is necessary."*

The discovery of a body at Paris Point marina in Boca Raton shocked the residents of Palmetto Pines, a luxury condominium complex located next door to the marina.

The victim is a thirty-five year old woman who had been apparently bludgeoned to death and dumped in the ocean late last night. Many neighbors reported terrible screams, gunshots: as well as the sound of a car backfiring loudly to Boca Raton Police shortly after midnight. The woman had been spotted in the lobby of Palmetto Pines around ten thirty, along with an older man, estimated to be in his fifties, and a younger man, in his late twenties.

"Apparently, the victim had been driven to the complex by the older man, and was seen arguing with him when the younger man intervened", said Sheriff Fred Adams, "all three of them left the building together and walked to the marina, where gunshots rang out an hour later." Deputies found five bullets on the sidewalk and some blood, along with a steel pipe that is assumed to be the murder weapon. Two men were seen fleeing the scene in a red Mercedes short after, rushing toward the Interstate.

The Palm Beach County Coroner, Melvin Watts, said he concluded the victim's skull had been crushed by a blunt tool, which resulted in a brain hemorrhage. As of now, there is no clear motive for the murder.

35. **Deputies found five bullets on the sidewalk and some <u>blood,</u> along with a steel pipe that is <u>assumed</u> <u>to be</u> the murder weapon. (Rigorous) (Skill 7.1)**

    A. blood;

    B. assuming

    C. to have been

    D. No change is necessary

Answer C: to have been

The past tense *to have been* is needed to maintain consistency. Option A incorrectly uses a colon, instead of a comma. Option B uses the wrong form of the verb *assumed*.

36. The victim **is** a thirty-five year old who had been apparently **bludgeoned** to death and dumped in the **ocean late** last night. *(Rigorous) (Skill 7.1)*

    A. was

    B. bludgoned

    C. ocean: late

    D. No change is necessary

Answer A: was

The past tense *was* is needed to maintain consistency. Option B creates a misspelling. Option C incorrectly uses a colon when none is needed.

37. Two men **were** seen fleeing the scene in a red Mercedes **short** after, **rushing** toward the Interstate. *(Easy) (Skill 7.3)*

    A. are

    B. shortly

    C. rushed

    D. No change is necessary

Answer B: shortly

The adverb *shortly* is needed instead of the adjective short. Option A incorrectly uses the present tense *are* instead of the past tense *were*. Option C, *rushed*, is the wrong form of the verb.

38.   As of <u>now,</u> <u>there</u> <u>is</u> no clear motive for the murder.
      (Rigorous) (Skill 8.1)

   A. now;

   B. their

   C. was

   D. No change is necessary

Answer D: No change is necessary

Answer A is incorrect. A semi-colon should not be used with an introductory phrase. Answers B and C show correct subject-verb agreement. Therefore, Answer D: *No change is necessary* is the bext choice.

39.   The discovery of a body at Paris Point <u>marina</u> in Boca Raton shocked the <u>residents</u> of Palmetto Pines, a luxury <u>condominium</u> complex located next door to the marina.
      (Easy) (Skill 8.2)

   A. Marina

   B. residence

   C. condominium

   D. No change is necessary

Answer A: Marina

Marina is a name that needs to be capitalized. Options B and C create misspellings.

40. Many <u>neighbors</u> reported terrible screams, <u>gunshots: as</u> well as the sound of a car backfiring <u>loudly</u> to Boca Raton Police shortly after midnight.
(Average Rigor) (Skill 8.2)

    A. nieghbors

    B. gunshots, as

    C. loud

    D. No change is necessary

Answer B: gunshots, as

Option B correctly uses a comma, not a colon to separate the items. Option A creates a misspelling. Option C incorrectly changes the adverb into an adjective.

41. The woman <u>had</u> been spotted in the lobby of Palmetto Pines around ten <u>thirty,</u> along with an older <u>man, estimated</u> to be in his fifties, and a younger man in his late twenties.
(Rigorous) (Skill 8.2)

    A. has

    B. thirty;

    C. man estimated

    D. No change is necessary

Answer C: man estimated

A comma is not needed to separate the item because an older man estimated to be in his fifties is one complete fragment. Option A incorrectly uses the present tense *has* instead of the past tense *had*. Option B incorrectly uses a colon when a comma is needed.

42. "Apparently, the victim had been driven to the complex by the older man, and was seen arguing with him when the younger man intervened," said <u>Sheriff Fred Adams, "all</u> three of them left the building together and walked to the marina, when gunshots rang out an hour later."
(Rigorous) (Skill 8.2)

   A. sheriff Fred Adams, "all

   B. sheriff Fred Adams, "All

   C. Sheriff Fred Adams." All

   D. No change is necessary

Answer C: Sheriff Fred Adams." All

The quote's source comes in the middle of two independent clauses, so a period should follow *Adams*. Option A is incorrect because titles, when they come before a name, must be capitalized. Punctuation is also faulty. Option B is incorrect because the word *Adams* ends a sentence; a comma is not strong enough to support two sentences.

43. The <u>Palm Beach</u> County <u>Coroner,</u> Kelvin Watts, said he concluded the victim's skull had been crushed by a blunt tool, which resulted in a brain <u>hemorrage</u>.
(Rigorous) (Skill 8.2)

   A. palm beach

   B. coroner

   C. hemorrhage

   D. No change is necessary

Answer D: No change is necessary

Option D is correct. Options A and B is should be capitalized. Option A is a proper noun, and B is part of a title. Option C offers a misspelling of *hemorrhage*.

SUBAREA III MATHEMATICS

COMPETENCY 14.0 SOLVE PROBLEMS INVOLVING INTEGERS, FRACTIONS, DECIMALS AND UNITS OF MEASUREMENT

Skill 14.1 Solve problems involving integers, fractions, and decimals, including percentages.

Rational numbers can be expressed as the ratio of two integers, $\frac{a}{b}$ where $b \neq 0$, for example $\frac{2}{3}$, $-\frac{4}{5}$, $5 = \frac{5}{1}$.

The rational numbers include integers, fractions and mixed numbers, and terminating and repeating decimals. Every rational number can be expressed as a repeating or terminating decimal and can be shown on a number line.

Integers are positive and negative whole numbers and zero.
...-6, -5, -4, -3, -2, -1, 0, 1, 2, 3, 4, 5, 6, ...

Whole numbers are natural numbers and zero.
0, 1, 2, 3, 4 ,5 ,6 ...

Natural numbers are the counting numbers.
1, 2, 3, 4, 5, 6, ...

Irrational numbers are real numbers that cannot be written as the ratio of two integers. These are infinite non-repeating decimals.

<u>Examples</u>: $\sqrt{5} = 2.2360..$, pi $= \prod = 3.1415927...$

A **fraction** is an expression of numbers in the form of x/y, where x is the numerator and y is the denominator, which cannot be zero.

Example: $\dfrac{3}{7}$ 3 is the numerator; 7 is the denominator

If the fraction has common factors for the numerator and denominator, divide both by the common factor to reduce the fraction to its lowest form.

Example:

$$\frac{13}{39} = \frac{1 \times 13}{3 \times 13} = \frac{1}{3}$$ Divide by the common factor 13

A **mixed** number has an integer part and a fractional part.

Example: $2\frac{1}{4},\ ^{-}5\frac{1}{6},\ 7\frac{1}{3}$

Percent = per 100 (written with the symbol %). Thus $10\% = \frac{10}{100} = \frac{1}{10}$.

Decimals = deci = part of ten. To find the decimal equivalent of a fraction, use the denominator to divide the numerator as shown in the following example.

Example: Find the decimal equivalent of $\frac{7}{10}$.

Since 10 cannot divide into 7 evenly

$$\frac{7}{10} = 0.7$$

The **exponent form** is a shortcut method to write repeated multiplication. Basic form: b^n, where b is called the base and n is the exponent. b and n are both real numbers. b^n implies that the base b is multiplied by itself n times.

Examples: $3^4 = 3 \times 3 \times 3 \times 3 = 81$

$2^3 = 2 \times 2 \times 2 = 8$

$(^-2)^4 = (^-2) \times (^-2) \times (^-2) \times (^-2) = 16$

$^-2^4 = ^-(2 \times 2 \times 2 \times 2) = ^-16$

Key exponent rules:

For 'a' nonzero, and 'm' and 'n' real numbers:

1) $a^m \cdot a^n = a^{(m+n)}$ Product rule

2) $\dfrac{a^m}{a^n} = a^{(m-n)}$ Quotient rule

3) $\dfrac{a^{-m}}{a^{-n}} = \dfrac{a^n}{a^m}$

When 10 is raised to any power, the exponent tells the numbers of zeroes in the product.

Example: $10^7 = 10,000,000$

Caution: Unless the negative sign is inside the parentheses and the exponent is outside the parentheses, the sign is not affected by the exponent.

$(^-2)^4$ implies that -2 is multiplied by itself 4 times.

$^-2^4$ implies that 2 is multiplied by itself 4 times, then the answer is negated.

Properties are rules that apply for addition, subtraction, multiplication, or division of real numbers. These properties are:

Commutative: You can change the order of the terms or factors as follows.

For addition: $a + b = b + a$
For multiplication: $ab = ba$

Since addition is the inverse operation of subtraction and multiplication is the inverse operation of division, no separate laws are needed for subtraction and division.

Example: $5 + ^-8 = ^-8 + 5 = ^-3$

Example: $^-2 \times 6 = 6 \times ^-2 = ^-12$

Associative: You can regroup the terms as you like.

For addition: $a + (b + c) = (a + b) + c$
For multiplication: $a(bc) = (ab)c$

This rule does not apply for division and subtraction.

Example: $(^-2 + 7) + 5 = ^-2 + (7 + 5)$
$5 + 5 = ^-2 + 12 = 10$

Example: $(3 \times ^-7) \times 5 = 3 \times (^-7 \times 5)$
$^-21 \times 5 = 3 \times ^-35 = ^-105$

Identity: Finding a number so that when added to a term results in that number (additive identity); finding a number such that when multiplied by a term results in that number (multiplicative identity).

For addition: $a + 0 = a$ (zero is additive identity)
For multiplication: $a \cdot 1 = a$ (one is multiplicative)

Example: $17 + 0 = 17$

Example: $^-34 \times 1 = ^-34$
The product of any number and one is that number.

Inverse: Finding a number such that when added to the number it results in zero; or when multiplied by the number results in 1.

For addition: $a + (-a) = 0$
For multiplication: $a \cdot (1/a) = 1$

$(-a)$ is the additive inverse of a; $(1/a)$, also called the reciprocal, is the multiplicative inverse of a.

Example: $25 + ^-25 = 0$

Example: $5 \times \frac{1}{5} = 1$ The product of any number and its reciprocal is one.

Distributive: This technique allows us to operate on terms within a parentheses without first performing operations within the parentheses. This is especially helpful when terms within the parentheses cannot be combined.

$a (b + c) = ab + ac$

Example: $6 \times (^-4 + 9) = (6 \times ^-4) + (6 \times 9)$
$6 \times 5 = {}^-24 + 54 = 30$

To multiply a sum by a number, multiply each addend by the number, then add the products.

Addition of whole numbers

Example: At the end of a day of shopping, a shopper had $24 remaining in his wallet. He spent $45 on various goods. How much money did the shopper have at the beginning of the day?

The total amount of money the shopper started with is the sum of the amount spent and the amount remaining at the end of the day.

$$\begin{array}{r} 24 \\ +\ \ 45 \\ \hline 69 \end{array}$$ ⟶ The original total was $69.

Example: A race took the winner 1 hr. 58 min. 12 sec. on the first half of the race and 2 hr. 9 min. 57 sec. on the second half of the race. How much time did the entire race take?

```
    1 hr. 58 min. 12 sec.
 + 2 hr.  9 min. 57 sec.      Add these numbers
 3 hr. 67 min. 69 sec.
   + 1 min -60 sec.           Change 60 seconds to 1 min.
   3 hr. 68 min.  9 sec.
 + 1 hr.-60 min.     .        Change 60 minutes to 1 hr.
    4 hr.  8 min.  9 sec.  ←final answer
```

Subtraction of Whole Numbers

Example: At the end of his shift, a cashier has $96 in the cash register. At the beginning of his shift, he had $15. How much money did the cashier collect during his shift?

The total collected is the difference of the ending amount and the starting amount.

$$\begin{array}{r} 96 \\ -\ \ 15 \\ \hline 81 \end{array}$$ ⟶ The total collected was $81.

Multiplication of whole numbers

Multiplication is one of the four basic number operations. In simple terms, multiplication is the addition of a number to itself a certain number of times. For example, 4 multiplied by 3 is the equal to 4 + 4 + 4 or 3 + 3 + 3 +3. Another way of conceptualizing multiplication is to think in terms of groups. For example, if we have 4 groups of 3 students, the total number of students is 4 multiplied by 3. We call the *solution* to a multiplication problem the *product*.

The basic algorithm for whole number multiplication begins with aligning the numbers by place value with the number containing more places on top.

$$\begin{array}{r} 172 \\ \times\ 43 \\ \hline \end{array}$$ ⟶ Note that we placed 122 on top because it has more places than 43 does.

Next, we multiply the ones' place of the second number by each place value of the top number sequentially.

$$\begin{array}{r} (2) \\ 172 \\ \times\ 43 \\ \hline 516 \end{array}$$ ⟶ {3 x 2 = 6, 3 x 7 = 21, 3 x 1 = 3}
Note that we had to carry a 2 to the hundreds' column because 3 x 7 = 21. Note also that we add, not multiply, carried numbers to the product.

Next, we multiply the number in the tens' place of the second number by each place value of the top number sequentially. Because we are multiplying by a number in the tens' place, we place a zero at the end of this product.

$$\begin{array}{r} (2) \\ 172 \\ \times\ 43 \\ \hline 516 \\ 6880 \end{array}$$ ⟶ {4 x 2 = 8, 4 x 7 = 28, 4 x 1 = 4}

Finally, to determine the final product we add the two partial products.

$$\begin{array}{r} 172 \\ \times\ 43 \\ \hline 516 \\ +\ 6880 \\ \hline 7396 \end{array}$$ ⟶ The product of 172 and 43 is 7396.

Example: A student buys 4 boxes of crayons. Each box contains 16 crayons. How many total crayons does the student have?

The total number of crayons is 16 x 4.

$$\begin{array}{r} 16 \\ \times\ 4 \\ \hline 64 \end{array}$$ ⟶ Total number of crayons equals 64.

Division of whole numbers

Division, the inverse of multiplication, is another of the four basic number operations. When we divide one number by another, we determine how many times we can multiply the divisor (number divided by) before we exceed the number we are dividing (dividend). For example, 8 divided by 2 equals 4 because we can multiply 2 four times to reach 8 (2 x 4 = 8 or 2 + 2 + 2 + 2 = 8). Using the grouping conceptualization we used with multiplication, we can divide 8 into 4 groups of 2 or 2 groups of 4. We call the answer to a division problem the *quotient*.

If the divisor does not divide evenly into the dividend, we express the leftover amount either as a remainder or as a fraction with the divisor as the denominator. For example, 9 divided by 2 equals 4 with a remainder of 1 or 4 ½.

The basic algorithm for division is long division. We start by representing the quotient as follows.

$14\overline{)293}$ ⟶ 14 is the divisor and 293 is the dividend.
This represents 293 ÷ 14.

Next, we divide the divisor into the dividend starting from the left.

$14\overline{)293}^{\ \ 2}$ ⟶ 14 divides into 29 two times with a remainder.

Next, we multiply the partial quotient by the divisor, subtract this value from the first digits of the dividend, and bring down the remaining dividend digits to complete the number.

$$\begin{array}{r} 2 \\ 14\overline{)293} \\ -28 \\ \hline 13 \end{array}$$ ⟶ 2 x 14 = 28, 29 – 28 = 1, and bringing down the 3 yields 13.

Finally, we divide again (the divisor into the remaining value) and repeat the preceding process. The number left after the subtraction represents the remainder.

$$
\begin{array}{r}
20 \\
14\overline{)293} \\
-28 \\
\hline
13 \\
-0 \\
\hline
13
\end{array}
$$

→ The final quotient is 20 with a remainder of 13. We can also represent this quotient as 20 13/14.

Example: Each box of apples contains 24 apples. How many boxes must a grocer purchase to supply a group of 252 people with one apple each?

The grocer needs 252 apples. Because he must buy apples in groups of 24, we divide 252 by 24 to determine how many boxes he needs to buy.

$$
\begin{array}{r}
10 \\
24\overline{)252} \\
-24 \\
\hline
12 \\
-0 \\
\hline
12
\end{array}
$$

→ The quotient is 10 with a remainder of 12.

Thus, the grocer needs 10 boxes plus 12 more apples. Therefore, the minimum number of boxes the grocer can purchase is 11.

Example: At his job, John gets paid $20 for every hour he works. If John made $940 in a week, how many hours did he work?

This is a division problem. To determine the number of hours John worked, we divide the total amount made ($940) by the hourly rate of pay ($20). Thus, the number of hours worked equals 940 divided by 20.

$$
\begin{array}{r}
47 \\
20\overline{)940} \\
-80 \\
\hline
140 \\
-140 \\
\hline
0
\end{array}
$$

→ 20 divides into 940, 47 times with no remainder.

John worked 47 hours.

Addition and Subtraction of Decimals

When adding and subtracting decimals, we align the numbers by place value as we do with whole numbers. After adding or subtracting each column, we bring the decimal down, placing it in the same location as in the numbers added or subtracted.

Example:　Find the sum of 152.3 and 36.342.

$$
\begin{array}{r}
152.300 \\
+\ \ 36.342 \\
\hline
188.642
\end{array}
$$

Note that we placed two zeroes after the final place value in 152.3 to clarify the column addition.

Example:　Find the difference of 152.3 and 36.342.

$$
\begin{array}{r}
2\ 9\ 10 \\
152.\cancel{300} \\
-\ \ 36.342 \\
\hline
58
\end{array}
\qquad\longrightarrow\qquad
\begin{array}{r}
(4)11(12) \\
15\cancel{2}.\cancel{300} \\
-\ \ 36.342 \\
\hline
115.958
\end{array}
$$

Note how we borrowed to subtract from the zeroes in the hundredths' and thousandths' place of 152.300.

Multiplication of Decimals

When multiplying decimal numbers, we multiply exactly as with whole numbers and place the decimal moving in from the left the total number of decimal places contained in the two numbers multiplied. For example, when multiplying 1.5 and 2.35, we place the decimal in the product 3 places in from the left (3.525).

Example:　Find the product of 3.52 and 4.1.

$$
\begin{array}{r}
3.52 \\
\times\ \ 4.1 \\
\hline
352 \\
+\ 14080 \\
\hline
14432
\end{array}
$$

Note that there are 3 total decimal places in the two numbers.

We place the decimal 3 places in from the left.

Thus, the final product is 14.432.

Example: A shopper has 5 one-dollar bills, 6 quarters, 3 nickels, and 4 pennies in his pocket. How much money does he have?

$$5 \times \$1.00 = \$5.00 \qquad \begin{array}{c} 3 \\ \$0.25 \\ \underline{\times\ \ 6} \\ \$1.50 \end{array} \qquad \begin{array}{c} \$0.05 \\ \underline{\times\ \ 3} \\ \$0.15 \end{array} \qquad \begin{array}{c} \$0.01 \\ \underline{\times\ \ 4} \\ \$0.04 \end{array}$$

Note the placement of the decimals in the multiplication products. Thus, the total amount of money in the shopper's pocket is:

$$\begin{array}{r} \$5.00 \\ 1.50 \\ 0.15 \\ +\ 0.04 \\ \hline \$6.69 \end{array}$$

Division of Decimals

When dividing decimal numbers, we first remove the decimal in the divisor by moving the decimal in the dividend the same number of spaces to the right. For example, when dividing 1.45 into 5.3 we convert the numbers to 145 and 530 and perform normal whole number division.

Example: Find the quotient of 5.3 divided by 1.45.
Convert to 145 and 530.

Divide.

$$\begin{array}{r} 3 \\ 145\overline{)530} \\ -\,435 \\ \hline 95 \end{array} \longrightarrow \begin{array}{r} 3.65 \\ 145\overline{)530.00} \\ -\,435 \\ \hline 950 \\ -\ 870 \\ \hline 800 \end{array} \longrightarrow$$

Because one of the numbers divided contained one decimal place, we round the quotient to one decimal place. Thus, the final quotient is 3.7.

Operating with Percents

Example: 5 is what percent of 20?

This is the same as converting $\dfrac{5}{20}$ to % form.

$$\frac{5}{20} \times \frac{100}{1} = \frac{5}{1} \times \frac{5}{1} = 25\%$$

Example: There are 64 dogs in the kennel. 48 are collies. What percent are collies?

Restate the problem. 48 is what percent of 64?
Write an equation. $48 = n \times 64$
Solve. $\frac{48}{64} = n$

$n = \frac{3}{4} = 75\%$

75% of the dogs are collies.

Example: The auditorium was filled to 90% capacity. There were 558 seats occupied. What is the capacity of the auditorium?

Restate the problem. 90% of what number is 558?
Write an equation. $0.9n = 558$
Solve. $n = \frac{558}{.9}$
         $n = 620$

The capacity of the auditorium is 620 people.

Example: A pair of shoes costs $42.00. Sales tax is 6%. What is the total cost of the shoes?

Restate the problem. What is 6% of 42?
Write an equation. $n = 0.06 \times 42$
Solve. $n = 2.52$

Add the sales tax to the cost. $42.00 + $2.52 = $44.52

The total cost of the shoes, including sales tax, is $44.52.

Addition and subtraction of fractions

Key Points

1. A common denominator is necessary in order to add and subtract reduced and improper fractions.

    Example: $\dfrac{1}{3} + \dfrac{7}{3} = \dfrac{1+7}{3} = \dfrac{8}{3} = 2\dfrac{2}{3}$

    Example: $\dfrac{4}{12} + \dfrac{6}{12} - \dfrac{3}{12} = \dfrac{4+6-3}{12} = \dfrac{7}{12}$

2. Adding an integer and a fraction of the <u>same</u> sign results directly in a mixed fraction.

    Example: $2 + \dfrac{2}{3} = 2\dfrac{2}{3}$

    Example: $^-2 - \dfrac{3}{4} = {}^- 2\dfrac{3}{4}$

3. Adding an integer and a fraction with different signs involves the following steps.

    -get a common denominator
    -add or subtract as needed
    -change to a mixed fraction if possible

    Example: $2 - \dfrac{1}{3} = \dfrac{2 \times 3 - 1}{3} = \dfrac{6-1}{3} = \dfrac{5}{3} = 1\dfrac{2}{3}$

Example: Add $7\dfrac{3}{8} + 5\dfrac{2}{7}$

        Add the whole numbers; add the fractions and combine the two results:

$$7\dfrac{3}{8} + 5\dfrac{2}{7} = (7 + 5) + \left(\dfrac{3}{8} + \dfrac{2}{7}\right)$$

$$= 12 + \dfrac{(7 \times 3) + (8 \times 2)}{56} \quad \text{(LCM of 8 and 7)}$$

$$= 12 + \dfrac{21 + 16}{56} = 12 + \dfrac{37}{56} = 12\dfrac{37}{56}$$

Example: Perform the operation.

$$\frac{2}{3} - \frac{5}{6}$$

We first find the LCM of 3 and 6 which is 6.

$$\frac{2 \times 2}{3 \times 2} - \frac{5}{6} \rightarrow \frac{4-5}{6} = \frac{^{-}1}{6} \qquad \text{(Using method A)}$$

Example: $\quad ^{-}7\frac{1}{4} + 2\frac{7}{8}$

$$^{-}7\frac{1}{4} + 2\frac{7}{8} = (^{-}7 + 2) + (\frac{^{-}1}{4} + \frac{7}{8})$$

$$= (^{-}5) + \frac{(^{-}2+7)}{8} = (^{-}5) + (\frac{5}{8})$$

$$= (^{-}5) + \frac{5}{8} = \frac{^{-}5 \times 8}{1 \times 8} + \frac{5}{8} = \frac{^{-}40+5}{8}$$

$$= \frac{^{-}35}{8} = ^{-}4\frac{3}{8}$$

Divide 35 by 8 to get 4, remainder 3.

Caution: Common error would be

$$^{-}7\frac{1}{4} + 2\frac{7}{8} = ^{-}7\frac{2}{8} + 2\frac{7}{8} = ^{-}5\frac{9}{8} \qquad \text{Wrong.}$$

It is correct to add -7 and 2 to get -5, but adding $\frac{2}{8} + \frac{7}{8} = \frac{9}{8}$

is wrong. It should have been $\frac{^{-}2}{8} + \frac{7}{8} = \frac{5}{8}$. Then,

$$^{-}5 + \frac{5}{8} = ^{-}4\frac{3}{8} \quad \text{as before.}$$

Multiplication of fractions

Using the following example: $3\dfrac{1}{4} \times \dfrac{5}{6}$

1. Convert each number to an improper fraction.

$$3\frac{1}{4} = \frac{(12+1)}{4} = \frac{13}{4} \qquad\qquad \frac{5}{6} \text{ is already in reduced form.}$$

2. Reduce (cancel) common factors of the numerator and denominator if they exist.

$$\frac{13}{4} \times \frac{5}{6} \qquad \text{No common factors exist.}$$

3. Multiply the numerators by each other and the denominators by each other.

$$\frac{13}{4} \times \frac{5}{6} = \frac{65}{24}$$

4. If possible, reduce the fraction back to its lowest term.

$$\frac{65}{24} \quad \text{Cannot be reduced further.}$$

5. Convert the improper fraction back to a mixed fraction by using long division.

$$\frac{65}{24} = 24\overline{)65} \qquad = 2\frac{17}{24}$$
$$\underline{48}$$
$$17$$

Summary of sign changes for multiplication:

a. $(+) \times (+) = (+)$

b. $(-) \times (+) = (-)$

c. $(+) \times (-) = (-)$

d. $(-) \times (-) = (+)$

Example: $\quad 7\frac{1}{3} \times \frac{5}{11} = \frac{22}{3} \times \frac{5}{11}$ Reduce like terms (22 and 11)

$$= \frac{2}{3} \times \frac{5}{1} = \frac{10}{3} = 3\frac{1}{3}$$

Example: $\quad ^{-}6\frac{1}{4} \times \frac{5}{9} = \frac{^{-}25}{4} \times \frac{5}{9}$

$$= \frac{^{-}125}{36} = ^{-}3\frac{17}{36}$$

Example: $\quad \frac{^{-}1}{4} \times \frac{^{-}3}{7}$ Negative times a negative equals a positive.

$$= \frac{1}{4} \times \frac{3}{7} = \frac{3}{28}$$

Division of fractions:

1. Change mixed fractions to improper fraction.

2. Change the division problem to a multiplication problem by using the reciprocal of the number after the division sign.

3. Find the sign of the final product.

4. Cancel if common factors exist between the numerator and the denominator.

5. Multiply the numerators together and the denominators together.

6. Change the improper fraction to a mixed number.

Example: $\quad 3\frac{1}{5} \div 2\frac{1}{4} = \frac{16}{5} \div \frac{9}{4}$

$$= \frac{16}{5} \times \frac{4}{9} \qquad \text{Reciprocal of } \frac{9}{4} \text{ is } \frac{4}{9}.$$

$$= \frac{64}{45} = 1\frac{19}{45}$$

Example: $7\dfrac{3}{4} \div 11\dfrac{5}{8} = \dfrac{31}{4} \div \dfrac{93}{8}$

$= \dfrac{31}{4} \times \dfrac{8}{93}$ Reduce like terms.

$= \dfrac{1}{1} \times \dfrac{2}{3} = \dfrac{2}{3}$

Example: $\left(-2\dfrac{1}{2}\right) \div 4\dfrac{1}{6} = \dfrac{^-5}{2} \div \dfrac{25}{6}$

$= \dfrac{^-5}{2} \times \dfrac{6}{25}$ Reduce like terms.

$= \dfrac{^-1}{1} \times \dfrac{3}{5} = \dfrac{^-3}{5}$

Example: $\left(-5\dfrac{3}{8}\right) \div \left(\dfrac{^-7}{16}\right) = \dfrac{^-43}{8} \div \dfrac{^-7}{16}$

$= \dfrac{^-43}{8} \times \dfrac{^-16}{7}$ Reduce like terms.

$= \dfrac{43}{1} \times \dfrac{2}{7}$ Negative times a negative equals a positive.

$= \dfrac{86}{7} = 12\dfrac{2}{7}$

Converting decimals, fractions and percents

A **decimal** can be converted to a **percent** by multiplying by 100 or by merely moving the decimal point two places to the right. A **percent** can be converted to a **decimal** by dividing by 100, or moving the decimal point two places to the left.

Examples:
$$0.375 = 37.5\%$$
$$0.7 = 70\%$$
$$0.04 = 4\%$$
$$3.15 = 315\%$$
$$84\% = 0.84$$
$$3\% = 0.03$$
$$60\% = 0.6$$
$$110\% = 1.1$$
$$\tfrac{1}{2}\% = 0.5\% = 0.005$$

A **percent** can be converted to a **fraction** by placing it over 100 and reducing to simplest terms.

Example: Convert 0.056 to a fraction.

Multiplying 0.056 by $\dfrac{1000}{1000}$ to get rid of the decimal point:

$$0.056 \times \frac{1000}{1000} = \frac{56}{1000} = \frac{7}{125}$$

Example: Find 23% of 1000.

$$= \frac{23}{100} \times \frac{1000}{1} = 23 \times 10 = 230$$

Example: Convert 6.25% to a decimal and to a fraction.

$$6.25\% = 0.0625 = 0.0625 \times \frac{10000}{10000} = \frac{625}{10000} = \frac{1}{16}$$

An example of a type of problem involving fractions is the conversion of recipes. For example, if a recipe serves 8 people and we want to make enough to serve only 4, we must determine how much of each ingredient to use. The conversion factor, the number we multiply each ingredient by, is:

$$\text{Conversion Factor} = \frac{\text{Number of Servings Needed}}{\text{Number of Servings in Recipe}}$$

Example: Consider the following recipe.

3 cups flour
½ tsp. baking powder
⅔ cup butter
2 cups sugar
2 eggs

If the above recipe serves 8, how much of each ingredient do we need to serve only 4 people?

First, determine the conversion factor.

Conversion Factor = $\dfrac{4}{8} = \dfrac{1}{2}$

Next, multiply each ingredient by the conversion factor.

3 x ½ =	1 ½ cups flour
½ x ½ =	¼ tsp. baking powder
⅔ x ½ = 2/6 =	⅓ cup butter
2 x ½ =	1 cup sugar
2 x ½ =	1 egg

Skill 14.2   Solve problems involving ratios and proportions.

A **ratio** is a comparison of 2 numbers. If a class had 11 boys and 14 girls, the ratio of boys to girls could be written one of 3 ways:

$$11:14 \quad \text{or} \quad 11 \text{ to } 14 \quad \text{or} \quad \frac{11}{14}$$

The ratio of girls to boys is:

$$14:11, \ 14 \text{ to } 11 \text{ or } \frac{14}{11}$$

Ratios can be reduced when possible. A ratio of 12 cats to 18 dogs would reduce to 2:3, 2 to 3 or $2/3$.

Note: Read ratio questions carefully. Given a group of 6 adults and 5 children, the ratio of children to the entire group would be 5:11.

A **proportion** is an equation in which a fraction is set equal to another. To solve the proportion, multiply each numerator times the other fraction's denominator. Set these two products equal to each other and solve the resulting equation. This is called **cross-multiplying** the proportion.

Example: $\dfrac{4}{15} = \dfrac{x}{60}$ is a proportion.

To solve this, cross multiply.

$(4)(60) = (15)(x)$

$240 = 15x$

$16 = x$

Example: $\dfrac{x+3}{3x+4} = \dfrac{2}{5}$ is a proportion.

To solve, cross multiply.

$5(x + 3) = 2(3x + 4)$

$5x + 15 = 6x + 8$

$7 = x$

Example: $\dfrac{x+2}{8} = \dfrac{2}{x-4}$ is another proportion.

To solve, cross multiply.

$(x+2)(x-4) = 8(2)$

$x^2 - 2x - 8 = 16$

$x^2 - 2x - 24 = 0$

$(x-6)(x+4) = 0$

$x = 6$ or $x = {}^-4$

Proportions can be used to solve word problems whenever relationships are compared. Some situations include scale drawings and maps, similar polygons, speed, time and distance, cost, and comparison shopping.

Example 1: Which is the better buy, 6 items for $1.29 or 8 items for $1.69?

Find the unit price.

$\dfrac{6}{1.29} = \dfrac{1}{x}$ $\qquad\qquad$ $\dfrac{8}{1.69} = \dfrac{1}{x}$

$6x = 1.29$ $\qquad\qquad\qquad$ $8x = 1.69$

$x = 0.215$ $\qquad\qquad\qquad$ $x = 0.21125$

Thus, 6 items for $1.29 is the better buy.

Example: A car travels 125 miles in 2.5 hours.. How far will it go in 6 hours?

Write a proportion comparing the distance and time.

$\dfrac{miles}{hours} \qquad \dfrac{125}{2.5} = \dfrac{x}{6}$

$\qquad\qquad\quad 2.5x = 750$

$\qquad\qquad\quad\ \ x = 300$

Thus, the car can travel 300 miles in 6 hours.

Example: The scale on a map is $\frac{3}{4}$ inch = 6 miles. What is the actual distance between two cities if they are $1\frac{1}{2}$ inches apart on the map?

Write a proportion comparing the scale to the actual distance.

scale   actual

$$\frac{\frac{3}{4}}{1\frac{1}{2}} = \frac{6}{x}$$

$\frac{3}{4}x = 1\frac{1}{2} \times 6$

$\frac{3}{4}x = 9$

$x = 12$

Thus, the actual distance between the cities is 12 miles.

Skill 14.3 **Solve problems involving units of measurement, including U.S. customary and metric measurements, and conversions, including scientific notation (e.g., 6.05 × 108).**

Measurements of length (English system)

12 inches (in)	=	1 foot (ft)
3 feet (ft)	=	1 yard (yd)
1760 yards (yd)	=	1 mile (mi)

Measurements of length (Metric system)

kilometer (km)	=	1000 meters (m)
hectometer (hm)	=	100 meters (m)
decameter (dam)	=	10 meters (m)
meter (m)	=	1 meter (m)
decimeter (dm)	=	1/10 meter (m)
centimeter (cm)	=	1/100 meter (m)
millimeter (mm)	=	1/1000 meter (m)

Conversion of length from English to Metric

1 inch	=	2.54 centimeters
1 foot	≈	30 centimeters
1 yard	≈	0.9 meters
1 mile	≈	1.6 kilometers

Measurements of weight (English system)

28 grams (g)	=	1 ounce (oz)
16 ounces (oz)	=	1 pound (lb)
2000 pounds (lb)	=	1 ton (t) (short ton)
1.1 ton (t)	=	1 ton (t)

Measurements of weight (Metric system)

kilogram (kg)	=	1000 grams (g)
gram (g)	=	1 gram (g)
milligram (mg)	=	1/1000 gram (g)

Conversion of weight from English to metric

1 ounce	≈	28 grams
1 pound	≈	0.45 kilogram
	≈	454 grams

Measurement of volume (English system)

8 fluid ounces (oz)	=	1 cup (c)
2 cups (c)	=	1 pint (pt)
2 pints (pt)	=	1 quart (qt)
4 quarts (qt)	=	1 gallon (gal)

Measurement of volume (Metric system)

kiloliter (kl)	=	1000 liters (l)
liter (l)	=	1 liter (l)
milliliter (ml)	=	1/1000 liters (ml)

Conversion of volume from English to metric

1 teaspoon (tsp)	≈	5 milliliters
1 fluid ounce	≈	15 milliliters
1 cup	≈	0.24 liters
1 pint	≈	0.47 liters
1 quart	≈	0.95 liters
1 gallon	≈	3.8 liters

Measurement of time

1 second	=	
1 minute	=	60 seconds
1 hour	=	60 minutes
1 day	=	24 hours
1 week	=	7 days
1 year	=	365 days
1 century	=	100 years

Note: (') represents feet and (") represents inches.

Square units can be derived with knowledge of basic units of length by squaring the equivalent measurements.

> 1 square foot (sq. ft.) = 144 sq. in.
>
> 1 sq. yd. = 9 sq. ft.
>
> 1 sq. yd. = 1296 sq. in.

<u>Example:</u>

14 sq. yd. = _____ sq. ft.

$14 \times 9 = 126$ sq. ft.

Weight

Example: Kathy has a bag of potatoes that weighs 5 lbs., 10 oz. She uses one-third of the bag to make mashed potatoes. How much does the bag weigh now?

1 lb. = 16 oz.

5(16 oz.) + 10 oz.

= 80 oz + 10 oz = 90 oz.

$90 - (\frac{1}{3})90$ oz.

= 90 oz. − 30 oz.

= 60 oz.

60 ÷ 16 = 3.75 lbs.

.75 = 75%

$75\% = \frac{75}{100} = \frac{3}{4}$

Example: The weight limit of a playground merry-go-round is 1000 pounds.
There are 11 children on the merry-go-round.
3 children weigh 100 pounds.
6 children weigh 75 pounds
2 children weigh 60 pounds

George weighs 80 pounds. Can he get on the merry-go-round?

3(100) + 6(75) + 2(60)

= 300 + 450 + 120

= 870

1000 − 870

= 130

Since 80 is less than 130, George can get on the merry-go-round.

See also Skill 16.5.

Scientific notation is a more convenient method for writing very large and very small numbers. It employs two factors. The first factor is a number between 1 and 10. The second factor is a power of 10. This notation is a "shorthand" for expressing large numbers (such as the weight of 100 elephants) or small numbers (such as the weight of an atom in pounds).

Recall that:

$10^n = (10)^n$ Ten multiplied by itself n times.

$10^0 = 1$ Any nonzero number raised to power of zero is 1.

$10^1 = 10$

$10^2 = 10 \times 10 = 100$

$10^3 = 10 \times 10 \times 10 = 1000$ (kilo)

$10^{-1} = 1/10$ (deci)

$10^{-2} = 1/100$ (centi)

$10^{-3} = 1/1000$ (milli)

$10^{-6} = 1/1,000,000$ (micro)

Example: Write 46,368,000 in scientific notation.

1)   Introduce a decimal point and decimal places.
      46,368,000 = 46,368,000.0000

2)   Make a mark between the two digits that give a number between -9.9 and 9.9.
      4 ∧ 6,368,000 .0000

3)   Count the number of digit places between the decimal point and the ∧ mark. This number is the 'n'-the power of ten.

      So, $46,368,000 = 4.6368 \times 10^7$

Example: Write 0.00397 in scientific notation.

1)   Decimal place is already in place.
2)   Make a mark between 3 and 9 to get a one number between -9.9 and 9.9.
3)   Move decimal place to the mark (3 hops).
      0.003 ∧ 97

      Motion is to the right, so n of 10^n is negative.

      Therefore, $0.00397 = 3.97 \times 10^{-3}$.

Skill 14.4   Use estimation skills to solve problems.

To estimate measurement of familiar objects, it is first necessary to determine the units to be used.

Examples:

Length
1. The coastline of Florida
2. The width of a ribbon
3. The thickness of a book
4. The depth of water in a pool

Weight or mass
1. A bag of sugar
2. A school bus
3. A dime

Capacity or volume
1. Paint to paint a bedroom
2. Glass of milk

Money
1. Cost of a house
2. Cost of a cup of coffee
3. Exchange rate

Perimeter
1. The edge of a backyard
2. The edge of a football field

Area
1. The size of a carpet
2. The size of a state

Example: Estimate the measurements of the following objects:

Length of a dollar bill	6 inches
Weight of a baseball	1 pound
Distance from New York to Florida	1100 km
Volume of water to fill a medicine dropper	1 milliliter
Length of a desk	2 meters
Temperature of water in a swimming pool	80° F

Depending on the degree of accuracy needed, an object may be measured to different units. For example, a pencil may be 6 inches to the nearest inch, or 6 3 8 inches to the nearest eighth of an inch. Similarly, it might be 15 cm to the nearest cm or 154 mm to the nearest mm.

Given a set of objects and their measurements, the use of rounding procedures is helpful when attempting to round to the nearest given unit. When rounding to a given place value, it is necessary to look at the number in the next smaller place. If this number is 5 or more, the number in the place we are rounding to is increased by one, and all numbers to the right are changed to zero. If the number is less than 5, the number in the place we are rounding to stays the same, and all numbers to the right are changed to zero.

One method of rounding measurements can require an additional step. First, the measurement must be converted to a decimal number. Then the rules for rounding applied.

Example: Round the measurements to the given units.

MEASUREMENT	ROUND TO NEAREST	ANSWER
1 foot 7 inches	foot	2 ft
5 pound 6 ounces	pound	5 pounds
5 9/16 inches	inch	6 inches

Convert each measurement to a decimal number. Then apply the rules for rounding.

1 foot 7 inches = $1\frac{7}{12}$ ft = 1.58333 ft, round up to 2 ft

5 pounds 6 ounces = $5\frac{6}{16}$ pounds = 5.375 pound, round to 5 pounds

$5\frac{9}{16}$ inches = 5.5625 inches, round up to 6 inches

Example: Janet goes into a store to purchase a CD on sale for $13.95. While shopping, she sees two pairs of shoes, prices $19.95 and $14.50. She has only $50. Can she purchase everything?

Solve by rounding:

$19.95 ® $20.00
$14.50 ® $15.00
$13.95 ® $14.00
        $49.00   Yes, she can purchase the CD and the shoes.

COMPETENCY 15.0 APPLY MATHEMATICAL REASONING SKILLS TO ANALYZE PATTERNS AND SOLVE PROBLEMS

Skill 15.1   Draw conclusions using inductive reasoning.

A simple statement represents a simple idea that can be described as either "true" or "false", but not both. A simple statement is represented by a small letter of the alphabet.

Example: "Today is Monday." This is a simple statement since it can be determined that this statement is either true or false. We can write p = "Today is Monday".

Example: "John, please be quiet." This is not considered a simple statement in our study of logic since we cannot assign a truth value to it.

Simple statements joined together by **connectives** ("and", "or", "not", "if then", and "if and only if") result in compound statements. Note that compound statements can also be formed using "but", "however", or "never the less". A compound statement can be assigned a truth value.

Conditional statements are frequently written in "if-then" form. The "if" clause of the conditional is known as the **hypothesis**, and the "then" clause is called the **conclusion**. In a proof, the hypothesis is the information that is *assumed* to be true, while the conclusion is what is to be *proven* true. A conditional is considered to be of the form: **If p, then q** where *p* is the hypothesis and *q* is the conclusion.

$p \rightarrow q$ is read "if p then q".
~ (statement) is read "it is not true that (statement)".

Quantifiers are words describing a quantity under discussion. These include words like "all", "none" (or "no"), and "some".

Negation of a Statement- If a statement is true, then its negation must be false (and vice versa).

A Summary of Negation Rules:

statement	negation
(1) q	(1) not q
(2) not q	(2) q
(3) π and s	(3) (not π) or (not s)
(4) π or s	(4) (not π) and (not s)
(5) if p, then q	(5) (p) and (not q)

Example: Select the statement that is the negation of "some winter nights are not cold".

A. All winter nights are not cold.
B. Some winter nights are cold.
C. All winter nights are cold.
D. None of the winter nights are cold.

Negation of "some are" is "none are". So the negation statement is "none of the winter night is cold". So the answer is D.

Example: Select the statement that is the negation of "if it rains, then the beach party will not be held".

A. If it does not rain, then the beach party will be held.
B. If the beach party is held, then it will not rain.
C. It does not rain and the beach party will be held.
D. It rains and the beach party will be held.

Negation of "if p, then q" is "p and (not q)". So the negation of the given statement is "it rains and the beach party will be held". So select D.

Example: Select the negation of the statement "If they get elected, then all politicians go back on election promises".

A. If they get elected, then many politicians go back on election promises.
B. They get elected and some politicians go back on election promises.
C. If they do not get elected, some politicians do not go back on election promises.
D. None of the above statements is the negation of the given statement.

Identify the key words of "if...then" and "all...go back". The negation of the given statement is "they get elected, and none of the politicians go back on election promises." So select response D, since A, B, and C statements are not the negations.

Example: Select the statement that is the negation of "the sun is shining bright and I feel great."

A. If the sun is not shining bright. I do not feel great.
B. The sun is not shining bright and I do not feel great.
C. The sun is not shining bring or I do not feel great.
D. the sun is shining bright and I do not feel great.

The negation of "r and s" is "(not r) or (not s)". So the negation of the given statement is "the sun is not shining bright or I do not feel great." We select response C.

Conditional statements can be diagrammed using a **Venn diagram**. A diagram can be drawn with one circle inside another circle. The inner circle represents the hypothesis. The outer circle represents the conclusion. If the hypothesis is taken to be true, then you are located inside the inner circle. If you are located in the inner circle then you are also inside the outer circle, so that proves the conclusion is true.

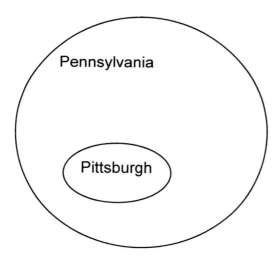

Example: If an angle has a measure of 90 degrees, then it is a right angle.

In this statement "an angle has a measure of 90 degrees" is the hypothesis. In this statement "it is a right angle" is the conclusion.

Example: If you are in Pittsburgh, then you are in Pennsylvania.

In this statement "you are in Pittsburgh" is the hypothesis.
In this statement "you are in Pennsylvania" is the conclusion.

Skill 15.2   Draw conclusions using deductive reasoning.

Deductive reasoning is the process of arriving at a conclusion based on other statements that are all known to be true.

A symbolic argument consists of a set of premises and a conclusion in the format of of *if* [Premise 1 and premise 2] *then* [conclusion].

An argument is **valid** when the conclusion follows necessarily from the premises. An argument is **invalid** or a fallacy when the conclusion does not follow from the premises.

There are 4 standard forms of valid arguments which must be remembered.

1. Law of Detachment	If p, then q p, Therefore, q	(premise 1) (premise 2)
2. Law of Contraposition	If p, then q not q, Therefore not p	
3. Law of Syllogism	If p, then q If q, then r Therefore if p, then r	
4. Disjunctive Syllogism	p or q not p Therefore, q	

Example: Can a conclusion be reached from these two statements?

   A.   All swimmers are athletes.
         All athletes are scholars.

In "if-then" form, these would be:
   If you are a swimmer, then you are an athlete.
   If you are an athlete, then you are a scholar.

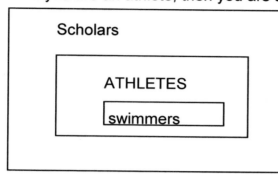

Clearly, if you are a swimmer, then you are also an athlete. This includes you in the group of scholars.

   B.   All swimmers are athletes.
         All wrestlers are athletes.

In "if-then" form, these would be:
   If you are a swimmer, then you are an athlete.
   If you are a wrestler, then you are an athlete.

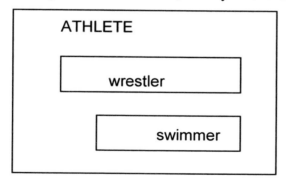

Clearly, if you are a swimmer or a wrestler, then you are also an athlete. This does NOT allow you to come to any other conclusions.

A swimmer may or may NOT also be a wrestler. Therefore, NO CONCLUSION IS POSSIBLE.

Example: Determine whether statement A, B, C, or D can be deduced from the following:

(i)If John drives the big truck, then the shipment will be delivered.

(ii)The shipment will not be delivered.

a.John does not drive the big truck.
b.John drives the big truck.
c.The shipment will not be delivered.
d.None of the above conclusion is true.

Let p: John drives the big truck.
q: The shipment is delivered.

statement (i) gives p → q, statement (ii) gives ~ q. This is the Law of Contraposition.

Therefore, the logical conclusion is ~p or "John does not drive the big truck." So the answer is response A.

Example: Given that:
(i)Peter is a Jet Pilot or Peter is a Navigator.
(ii)Peter is not a Jet Pilot

Determine which conclusion can be logically deduced.

a.Peter is not a Navigator.
b.Peter is a Navigator.
c.Peter is neither a Jet Pilot nor a Navigator.
d.None of the above is true.

Let p: Peter is a Jet Pilot
q: Peter is a Navigator.

So we have p ∨ q from statement (i)
~p   from statement (ii)

So choose response B.

Skill 15.3   Identify errors in mathematical explanations.

The following are some possible types of errors in mathematical explanations:

- Information not appropriate or extraneous to the explanation
- Misuse of mathematical terms
- Inappropriate strategy for solving the problem
- Inappropriate or unexplained diagram
- Incomplete argument
- Incorrect labels or descriptions
- Key elements of the strategy are missing
- Algorithms incorrectly executed
- Words do not reflect the problem
- Process cannot be identified

COMPETENCY 16.0 SOLVE PROBLEMS INVOLVING ALGEBRA AND GEOMETRY

Skill 16.1   Graph numbers or number relationships.

A relationship between two quantities can be shown using a table, graph or rule. In this example, the rule y = 9x describes the relationship between the total amount earned, y, and the total amount of $9 sunglasses sold, x.

A table using this data would appear as:

number of sunglasses sold	1	5	10	15
total dollars earned	9	45	90	135

Each *(x,y)* relationship between a pair of values is called the coordinate pair and can be plotted on a graph. The coordinate pairs *(1,9), (5,45), (10,90),* and *(15,135),* are plotted on the graph below.

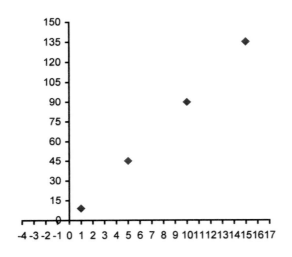

The graph above shows a linear relationship. A linear relationship is one in which two quantities are proportional to each other. Doubling *x* also doubles *y*. On a graph, a straight line depicts a linear relationship.

The function or relationship between two quantities may be analyzed to determine how one quantity depends on the other. For example, the function below shows a relationship between y and x: y=2x+1

The relationship between two or more variables can be analyzed using a table, graph, written description or symbolic rule. The function, y=2x+1, is written as a symbolic rule. The same relationship is also shown in the table below:

x	0	2	3	6	9
y	1	5	7	13	19

A relationship could be written in words by saying the value of y is equal to two times the value of x, plus one. This relationship could be shown on a graph by plotting given points such as the ones shown in the table above.

Another way to describe a function is as a process in which one or more numbers are input into an imaginary machine that produces another number as the output. If 5 is input, (x), into a machine with a process of x +1, the output, (y), will equal 6.

In real situations, relationships can be described mathematically. The function, y=x+1, can be used to describe the idea that people age one year on their birthday. To describe the relationship in which a person's monthly medical costs are 6 times a person's age, we could write y=6x. The monthly cost of medical care could be predicted using this function. A 20-year-old person would spend $120 per month (120=20*6). An 80-year-old person would spend $480 per month (480=80*6). Therefore, one could analyze the relationship to say: As one gets older, medical costs increase $6.00 each year.

*   *   *

A first degree equation has an equation of the form $ax + by = c$. To find the slope of a line, solve the equation for y. This gets the equation into **slope intercept form**, $y = mx + b$. **m is the line's slope.**

The y intercept is the coordinate of the point where a line crosses the y axis. To find the y intercept, substitute 0 for x and solve for y. This is the y intercept. In slope intercept form, $y = mx + b$, b is the y intercept.

To find the x intercept, substitute 0 for y and solve for x. This is the x intercept.

If the equation solves to x = **any number**, then the graph is a **vertical line**. It only has an x intercept. Its slope is **undefined**.

If the equation solves to y = **any number**, then the graph is a **horizontal line**. It only has a y intercept. Its slope is 0 (zero).

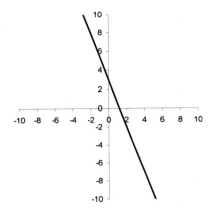

$$5x + 2y = 6$$

$$y = {}^-5/2\,x + 3$$

The equation of a line from its graph can be found by finding its slope (see Skill 3.2 for the slope formula) and its y intercept.

$$Y - y_a = m\left(X - x_a\right)$$

$\left(x_a, y_a\right)$ can be $\left(x_1, y_1\right)$ or $\left(x_2, y_2\right)$ If **m**, the value of the slope, is distributed through the parentheses, the equation can be rewritten into other forms of the equation of a line.

Example: Find the equation of a line through $(9, {}^-6)$ and $({}^-1, 2)$.

$$\text{slope} = \frac{y_2 - y_1}{x_2 - x_1} = \frac{2 - {}^-6}{{}^-1 - 9} = \frac{8}{{}^-10} = \frac{{}^-4}{5}$$

$$Y - y_a = m(X - x_a) \rightarrow Y - 2 = {}^-4/5(X - {}^-1) \rightarrow$$
$$Y - 2 = {}^-4/5(X + 1) \rightarrow Y - 2 = {}^-4/5\,X - 4/5 \rightarrow$$
$$Y = {}^-4/5\;X + 6/5 \quad \text{This is the slope-intercept form.}$$

Multiplying by 5 to eliminate fractions, it is:

$$5Y = {}^-4X + 6 \rightarrow 4X + 5Y = 6 \quad \text{Standard form.}$$

Example: Find the slope and intercepts of $3x + 2y = 14$.

$$3x + 2y = 14$$
$$2y = {}^-3x + 14$$
$$y = {}^-3/2\;x + 7$$

The slope of the line is ${}^-3/2$. The y intercept of the line is 7.

The intercepts can also be found by substituting 0 in place of the other variable in the equation.

To find the y intercept:
let $x = 0$; $3(0) + 2y = 14$
$0 + 2y = 14$
$2y = 14$
$y = 7$
$(0,7)$ is the y intercept.

To find the x intercept:
let $y = 0$; $3x + 2(0) = 14$
$3x + 0 = 14$
$3x = 14$
$x = 14/3$
$(14/3, 0)$ is the x intercept.

Example: Sketch the graph of the line represented by $2x + 3y = 6$.

Let $x = 0 \rightarrow 2(0) + 3y = 6$
$\rightarrow 3y = 6$
$\rightarrow y = 2$
$\rightarrow (0,2)$ is the y intercept.

Let $y = 0 \rightarrow 2x + 3(0) = 6$
$\rightarrow 2x = 6$
$\rightarrow x = 3$
$\rightarrow (3,0)$ is the x intercept.

Let $x = 1 \rightarrow 2(1) + 3y = 6$
$\rightarrow 2 + 3y = 6$
$\rightarrow 3y = 4$
$\rightarrow y = \dfrac{4}{3}$
$\rightarrow \left(1, \dfrac{4}{3}\right)$ is the third point.

Plotting the three points on the coordinate system, we get the following:

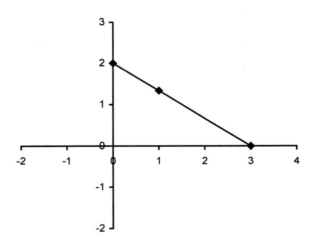

To graph an inequality, solve the inequality for y. This sets up the inequality in **slope intercept form** (for example: $y < mx + b$). The point (0,b) is the y-intercept, and m is the line's slope.

If the inequality solves to $x \geq$ **any number**, then the graph includes a **vertical line**.

If the inequality solves to $y \leq$ **any number**, then the graph includes a **horizontal line**.

When graphing a linear inequality, the line will be dotted if the inequality sign is $<$ or $>$. If the inequality signs are either $\geq$ or $\leq$, the line on the graph will be a solid line. Shade above the line when the inequality sign is $\geq$ or $>$. Shade below the line when the inequality sign is $<$ or $\leq$. For inequalities of the forms $x >$ number, $x \leq$ number, $x <$ number, or $x \geq$ number, draw a vertical line (solid or dotted). Shade to the right for $>$ or $\geq$. Shade to the left for $<$ or $\leq$.

Remember: Dividing or multiplying by a negative number will reverse the direction of the inequality sign.

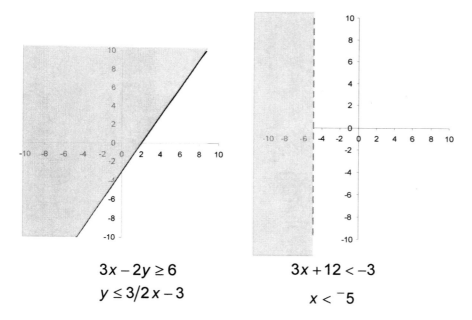

$$3x - 2y \geq 6 \qquad\qquad 3x + 12 < -3$$
$$y \leq 3/2\,x - 3 \qquad\qquad x < {}^-5$$

Example: Solve by graphing:

$$x + y \leq 6$$
$$x - 2y \leq 6$$

Solving the inequalities for y, they become:

$y \leq {}^-x + 6$ (y intercept of 6 and slope = $^-1$)
$y \geq 1/2x - 3$ (y intercept of $^-3$ and slope = $1/2$)

A graph with shading is shown below:

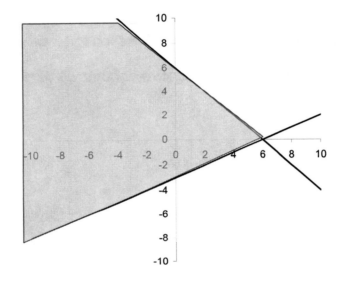

Skill 16.2   Find the value of the unknown in a given one-variable equation.

Procedure for solving algebraic equations

Example: $3(x + 3) = {}^-2x + 4$ Solve for x.

1)   Expand to eliminate all parentheses.

$$3x + 9 = {}^-2x + 4$$

2)   Multiply each term by the LCD to eliminate all denominators.

3)   Combine like terms on each side when possible.

4)   Use the properties to put all variables on one side and all constants on the other side.

$\rightarrow 3x + 9 - 9 = {}^-2x + 4 - 9$ (subtract nine from both sides)

$\rightarrow 3x = {}^-2x - 5$

$\rightarrow 3x + 2x = {}^-2x + 2x - 5$ (add $2x$ to both sides)

$\rightarrow 5x = {}^-5$

$\rightarrow \dfrac{5x}{5} = \dfrac{{}^-5}{5}$ (divide both sides by 5)

$\rightarrow x = {}^-1$

Example: Solve: $3(2x + 5) - 4x = 5(x + 9)$

$$6x + 15 - 4x = 5x + 45$$
$$2x + 15 = 5x + 45$$
$${}^-3x + 15 = 45$$
$${}^-3x = 30$$
$$x = {}^-10$$

Skill 16.3 **Express one variable in terms of a second variable in two-variable equations.**

The solution **set of linear equations** is all the ordered pairs of real numbers that satisfy both equations, thus the intersection of the lines There are two methods for solving linear equations: **linear combinations** and **substitution**.

In the **substitution** method, an equation is solved for either variable. Then, that solution is substituted in the other equation to find the remaining variable.

Example: (1) $2x + 8y = 4$
          (2) $x - 3y = 5$

          (2a) $x = 3y + 5$ Solve equation (2) for x

          (1a) $2(3y + 5) + 8y = 4$ Substitute x in equation (1)
                $6y + 10 + 8y = 4$ Solve.
                $14y = -6$
                $y = \frac{-3}{7}$ Solution

          (2) $x - 3y = 5$
               $x - 3(\frac{-3}{7}) = 5$ Substitute the value of y.
               $x = \frac{26}{7} = 3\frac{5}{7}$ Solution

Thus the solution set of the system of equations is $(3\frac{5}{7}, \frac{-3}{7})$.

In the **linear combinations** method, one or both of the equations are replaced with an equivalent equation in order that the two equations can be combined (added or subtracted) to eliminate one variable.

Example: (1) $4x + 3y = -2$
          (2) $5x - y = 7$

          (1) $4x + 3y = -2$
          (2a) $15x - 3y = 21$ Multiply equation (2) by 3

       $19x = 19$ Combining (1) and (2a)
          $x = 1$ Solve.
To find y, substitute the value of x in equation 1 (or 2).
          (1) $4x + 3y = -2$
              $4(1) + 3y = -2$
                 $4 + 3y = -2$
                    $3y = -2$
                      $y = -2$

Thus the solution is $x = 1$ and $y = -2$ or the order pair (1, -2).

Example: Solve for x and y.

$$4x + 6y = 340$$
$$3x + 8y = 360$$

To solve by addition-subtraction:

Multiply the first equation by 4: $4(4x + 6y = 340)$

Multiply the other equation by $^-3$: $^-3(3x + 8y = 360)$

By doing this, the equations can be added to each other to eliminate one variable and solve for the other variable.

$$16x + 24y = 1360$$
$$\underline{-9x - 24y = {}^-1080}$$
$$7x = 280$$
$$x = 40$$

solving for y, $y = 30$

Skill 16.4   Solve problems involving lines and angles.

A point, a line, and a plane are actually undefined terms since we cannot give a satisfactory definition using simple defined terms. However, their properties and characteristics give a clear understanding of what they are.

A **point** indicates place or position. It has no length, width or thickness.

•   point A
A

A **line** is considered a set of points. Lines may be straight or curved, but the term line commonly denotes a straight line. Lines extend indefinitely.

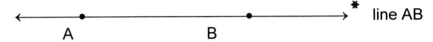

line AB

A **plane** is a set of points composing a flat surface. A plane also has no boundaries.

plane A

A **line segment** has two endpoints.

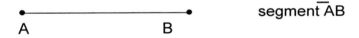

segment $\overline{AB}$

A **ray** has exactly one endpoint. It extends indefinitely in one direction.

ray $\overrightarrow{AB}$

An **angle** is formed by the intersection of two rays.

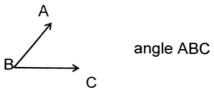

angle ABC

Angles are measured in degrees. $1° = \frac{1}{360}$ of a circle.

A **right angle** measures 90°.

An **acute angle** measures more than 0° and less than 90°.

An **obtuse angle** measures more than 90° and less than 180°.

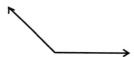

A **straight angle** measures 180°.

A **reflexive angle** measures more than 180° and less than 360°.

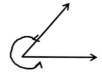

An infinite number of lines can be drawn through any point.

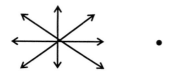

Exactly one line can be drawn through two points.

Intersecting lines share a common point and intersecting planes share a common set of points or line.

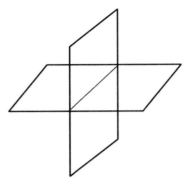

Skew lines do not intersect and do not lie on the same plane.

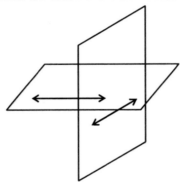

Perpendicular lines or planes form a 90-degree angle to each other. Perpendicular lines have slopes that are negative reciprocals.

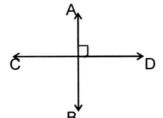

Line AB is perpendicular to line CD.

AB ⊥ CD

Parallel lines or planes do not intersect. Two parallel lines will have the same slope and are everywhere equidistant.

Line AB is parallel to line CD.

A   B

AB || CD

C   D

Skill 16.5   **Solve problems involving two- and three-dimensional geometric figures (e.g., perimeter and area problems, volume and surface area problems).**

Polygons, simple closed **two-dimensional figures** composed of line segments, are named according to the number of sides they have.

A **quadrilateral** is a polygon with four sides.
The sum of the measures of the angles of a quadrilateral is 360°.

A **trapezoid** is a quadrilateral with exactly <u>one</u> pair of parallel sides.

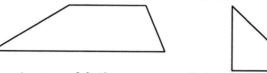

In an **isosceles trapezoid**, the non-parallel sides are congruent.

A **parallelogram** is a quadrilateral with <u>two</u> pairs of parallel sides.

In a parallelogram:
The diagonals bisect each other.
Each diagonal divides the parallelogram into two congruent triangles.
Both pairs of opposite sides are congruent.
Both pairs of opposite angles are congruent.
Two adjacent angles are supplementary.

A **rectangle** is a parallelogram with a right angle.

A **rhombus** is a parallelogram with all sides equal length.

A **square** is a rectangle with all sides equal length.

Example: True or false?
            All squares are rhombuses.   True
            All parallelograms are rectangles.   False - <u>some</u>
                                                            parallelograms are
                                                            rectangles

            All rectangles are parallelograms.   True
            Some rhombuses are squares.   True
            Some rectangles are trapezoids.   False - only <u>one</u> pair of
                                                            parallel
                                                            sides

            All quadrilaterals are parallelograms.   False -some quadrilaterals
                                                            are parallelograms

            Some squares are rectangles.   False - all squares are
                                                            rectangles

            Some parallelograms are rhombuses.   True

A **triangle** is a polygon with three sides.

Triangles can be classified by the types of angles or the lengths of their sides.

An **acute** triangle has exactly three *acute* angles.
A **right** triangle has one *right* angle.
An **obtuse** triangle has one *obtuse* angle.

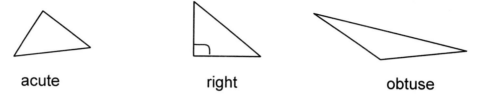

acute   right   obtuse

All *three* sides of an **equilateral** triangle are the same length.
Two sides of an **isosceles** triangle are the same length.
None of the sides of a **scalene** triangle are the same length.

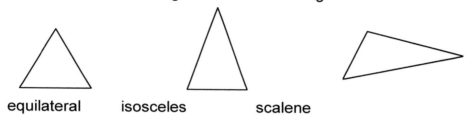

equilateral   isosceles   scalene

Example: Can a triangle have two right angles?
           No. A right angle measures 90°; therefore, the sum of two right
           angles would be 180°, and there could not be third angle.

Example: Can a triangle have two obtuse angles?
           No. Since an obtuse angle measures more than 90°, the sum of
           two obtuse angles would be greater than 180°.

A **cylinder** has two congruent circular bases that are parallel.

A **sphere** is a space figure having all its points the same distance from the center.

A **cone** is a space figure having a circular base and a single vertex.

A **pyramid** is a space figure with a square base and 4 triangle-shaped sides.

A **tetrahedron** is a 4-sided space triangle. Each face is a triangle.

A **prism** is a space figure with two congruent, parallel bases that are polygons.

The **perimeter** of any polygon is the sum of the lengths of the sides.

The **area** of a polygon is the number of square units covered by the figure.

FIGURE	AREA FORMULA	PERIMETER FORMULA
Rectangle	LW	$2(L+W)$
Triangle	$\frac{1}{2}bh$	$a+b+c$
Parallelogram	bh	sum of lengths of sides
Trapezoid	$\frac{1}{2}h(a+b)$	sum of lengths of sides

Perimeter

Example: A farmer has a piece of land shaped as shown below. He wishes to fence this land at an estimated cost of $25 per linear foot. What is the total cost of fencing this property to the nearest foot.

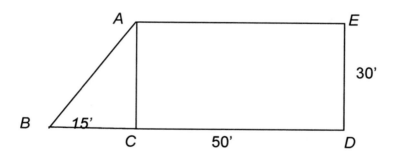

From the right triangle ABC, AC = 30 and BC = 15.

Since $(AB) = (AC)^2 + (BC)^2$
$(AB) = (30)^2 + (15)^2$

So $\sqrt{(AB)^2} = AB = \sqrt{1125} = 33.5410$ feet

To the nearest foot AB = 34 feet.

Perimeter of the piece of land is $= AB + BC + CD + DE + EA$

$= 34 + 15 + 50 + 30 + 50 = 179$ feet

cost of fencing = $25 x 179 = $4, 475.00

Area

Area is the space that a figure occupies. Example:

Example: What will be the cost of carpeting a rectangular office that measures 12 feet by 15 feet if the carpet costs $12.50 per square yard?

12 ft

15 ft

The problem is asking you to determine the area of the office. The area of a rectangle is *length x width = A*
Substitute the given values in the equation $A = lw$

$A = (12 \text{ ft.})(15 \text{ ft.})$

$A = 180 \text{ ft.}^2$

The problem asked you to determine the cost of carpet at $12.50 per square yard.

First, you need to convert 180 ft.^{2} into yards^2.

1 yd. = 3 ft.
    (1 yard)(1 yard) = (3 feet)(3 feet)
  $1 \text{ yd}^2 = 9 \text{ ft } 2$

Hence, $\dfrac{180 \text{ ft}^2}{1} \quad \dfrac{1 \text{ yd}^2}{9 \text{ ft}^2} = \dfrac{20}{1} = 20 \text{ yd}^2$

The carpet cost $12.50 per square yard; thus the cost of carpeting the office described is $12.50 x 20 = $250.00.

Example: Find the area of a parallelogram whose base is 6.5 cm and the height of the altitude to that base is 3.7 cm.

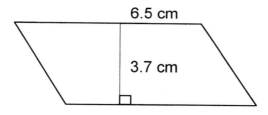

6.5 cm

3.7 cm

A parallelogram = bh

$$= (3.7)(6.5)$$
$$= 24.05 \text{ cm}^2$$

Example: Find the area of this triangle.

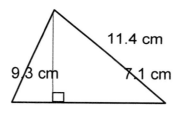

11.4 cm

9.3 cm   7.1 cm

16.8 cm

A triangle = $\frac{1}{2}$bh

$$= 0.5\,(16.8)\,(7.1)$$
$$= 59.64 \text{ cm}^2$$

Example: Find the area of this trapezoid.

17.5 cm

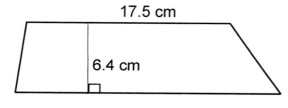

6.4 cm

23.7 cm

The area of a trapezoid equals one-half the sum of the bases times the altitude.

A trapezoid = $\frac{1}{2}$h(b$_1$ + b$_2$)

$$= 0.5\,(6.4)\,(17.5 + 23.7)$$
$$= 131.84 \text{ cm}^2$$

The distance around a circle is the **circumference**. The ratio of the circumference to the diameter is represented by the Greek letter pi. $\Pi \sim 3.14$ $\sim \dfrac{22}{7}$.

The circumference of a circle is found by the formula $C = 2\Pi r$ or $C = \Pi d$ where r is the radius of the circle and d is the diameter.

The **area** of a circle is found by the formula $A = \Pi r^2$.

Example: Find the circumference and area of a circle whose radius is 7 meters.

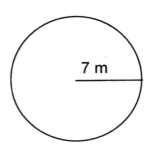

7 m

$C = 2\Pi r$	$A = \Pi r^2$
$= 2(3.14)(7)$	$= 3.14(7)(7)$
$= 43.96$ m	$= 153.86$ m^2

Volume and **Surface area** are computed using the following formulas:

FIGURE	VOLUME	TOTAL SURFACE AREA
Right Cylinder	$\pi r^2 h$	$2\pi rh + 2\pi r^2$
Right Cone	$\dfrac{\pi r^2 h}{3}$	$\pi r \sqrt{r^2 + h^2} + \pi r^2$
Sphere	$\dfrac{4}{3}\pi r^3$	$4\pi r^2$
Rectangular Solid	LWH	$2LW + 2WH + 2LH$

FIGURE	LATERAL AREA	TOTAL AREA	VOLUME
Regular Pyramid	1/2Pl	1/2Pl+B	1/3Bh

P = Perimeter
h = height
B = Area of Base
l = slant height

Example: What is the volume of a shoe box with a length of 35 cms, a width of 20 cms and a height of 15 cms?

Volume of a rectangular solid
= Length x Width x Height
= 35 x 20 x 15
= 10500 cm^3

Example: A water company is trying to decide whether to use traditional cylindrical paper cups or to offer conical paper cups since both cost the same. The traditional cups are 8 cm wide and 14 cm high. The conical cups are 12 cm wide and 19 cm high. The company will use the cup that holds the most water.

Draw and label a sketch of each.

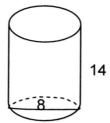

$V = \pi r^2 h$ $V = \dfrac{\pi r^2 h}{3}$ 1. write formula

$V = \pi(4)^2(14)$ $V = \dfrac{1}{3}\pi(6)^2(19)$ 2. substitute

$V = 703.717$ cm^3 $V = 716.283$ cm^3 3. solve

The choice should be the conical cup since its volume is more.

Example: How much material is needed to make a basketball that has a diameter of 15 inches? How much air is needed to fill the basketball?

Draw and label a sketch:

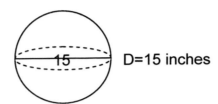

D=15 inches

Total surface area	Volume	
$TSA = 4\pi r^2$	$V = \dfrac{4}{3}\pi r^3$	1. write formula
$= 4\pi(7.5)^2$	$= \dfrac{4}{3}\pi(7.5)^3$	2. substitute
$= 706.858 \text{ in}^2$	$= 1767.1459 \text{ in}^3$	3. solve

COMPETENCY 17.0 UNDERSTAND CONCEPTS AND PROCEDURES RELATED TO DATA ANALYSIS AND STATISTICS

Skill 17.1 Interpret information from tables, line graphs, bar graphs, histograms, pictographs, and pie charts.

To make a **bar graph** or a **pictograph**, determine the scale to be used for the graph. Then determine the length of each bar on the graph or determine the number of pictures needed to represent each item of information. Be sure to include an explanation of the scale in the legend.

Example: A class had the following grades:
4 As, 9 Bs, 8 Cs, 1 D, 3 Fs.
Graph these on a bar graph and a pictograph.

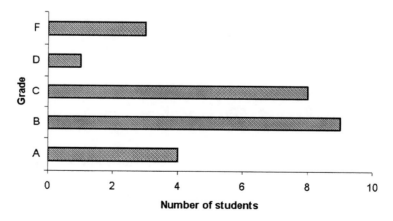

Pictograph

Grade	Number of Students
A	☺☺☺☺
B	☺☺☺☺☺☺☺☺☺
C	☺☺☺☺☺☺☺☺
D	☺
F	☺☺☺

Bar graph

To make a **line graph**, determine appropriate scales for both the vertical and horizontal axes (based on the information to be graphed). Describe what each axis represents and mark the scale periodically on each axis. Graph the individual points of the graph and connect the points on the graph from left to right.

Example: Graph the following information using a line graph.

The number of National Merit finalists/school year

	90-91	91-92	92-93	93-94	94-95	95-96
Central	3	5	1	4	6	8
Wilson	4	2	3	2	3	2

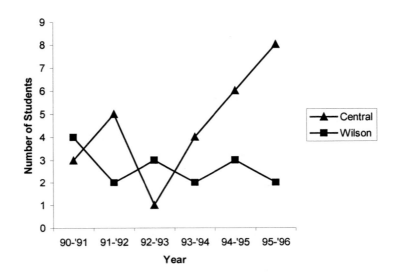

To make a **circle graph**, total all the information that is to be included on the graph. Determine the central angle to be used for each sector of the graph using the following formula:

$$\frac{\text{information}}{\text{total information}} \times 360° = \text{degrees in central} \angle$$

Lay out the central angles to these sizes, label each section and include its percent.

Example: Graph this information on a circle graph:

Monthly expenses:

Rent $400
Food $150
Utilities $75
Clothes $75
Church $100
Misc. $200

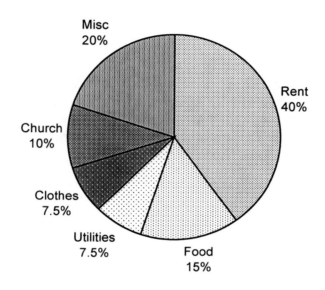

Scatter plots compare two characteristics of the same group of things or people and usually consist of a large body of data. They show how much one variable is affected by another. The relationship between the two variables is their **correlation**. The closer the data points come to making a straight line when plotted, the closer the correlation.

Stem and leaf plots are visually similar to line plots. The **stems** are the digits in the greatest place value of the data values, and the **leaves** are the digits in the next greatest place values. Stem and leaf plots are best suited for small sets of data and are especially useful for comparing two sets of data. The following is an example using test scores:

4	9
5	4 9
6	1 2 3 4 6 7 8 8
7	0 3 4 6 6 6 7 7 7 8 8 8 8
8	3 5 5 7 8
9	0 0 3 4 5
10	0 0

Histograms are used to summarize information from large sets of data that can be naturally grouped into intervals. The vertical axis indicates **frequency** (the number of times any particular data value occurs), and the horizontal axis indicates data values or ranges of data values. The number of data values in any interval is the **frequency of the interval**.

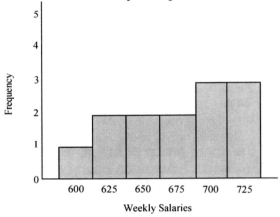

Skill 17.2   Recognize appropriate representations of various data in graphic form (discrete and continuous).

Pictographs can be misleading, especially if drawn to represent 3-dimensional objects. If two or more dimensions are changed in reflecting ratio, the overall visual effect can be misinterpreted. Bar and line graphs can be misleading if the scales are changed. For example, using relatively small scale increments for large numbers will make the comparison differences seem much greater than if larger scale increments are used. Circle graphs, or pie charts, are excellent for comparing relative amounts. However, they cannot be used to represent absolute amounts, and if interpreted as such, they are misleading.

Skill 17.3 **Demonstrate an understanding of fundamental statistical concepts (e.g., mean, correlation, standard deviation).**

The arithmetic **mean** (or average) of a set of numbers is the *sum* of the numbers given, *divided* by the number of items being averaged.

Example: Find the mean. Round to the nearest tenth.
24.6, 57.3, 44.1, 39.8, 64.5
The sum is 230.3 ˜ 5
= 46.06, rounded to 46.1

The **median** of a set is the middle number. To calculate the median, the terms must be arranged in order. If there are an even number of terms, the median is the mean of the two middle terms.

Example: Find the median.

12. 14. 27. 3. 13. 7. 17.   12. 22.   6.   16

Rearrange the terms.
3, 6, 7, 12, 12, 13, 14,   16, 17, 22, 27
Since there are 11 numbers, the middle would be the sixth number or 13.

The **mode** of a set of numbers is the number that occurs with the greatest frequency. A set can have no mode if each term appears exactly one time. Similarly, there can also be more than one mode.

Example: Find the mode.

26, 15, 37, **26,** 35, **26,** 15

15 appears twice, but 26 appears 3 times; therefore, the mode is 26.

The **range** is the difference between the highest and lowest value of data items.

Example: Given the ungrouped data below, calculate the mean and range.

| 15 | 22 | 28 | 25 | 34 | 38 |
| 18 | 25 | 30 | 33 | 19 | 23 |

Mean ($\overline{X}$) = 25.8333333
Range: $38 - 15 = 23$

Skill 17.4 **Interpret graphic and nongraphic representations of frequency distributions, percentiles, central tendency, variability, and correlation.**

Percentiles divide data into 100 equal parts. A person whose score falls in the 65th percentile has outperformed 65 percent of all those who took the test. This does not mean that the score was 65 percent out of 100 nor does it mean that 65 percent of the questions answered were correct. It means that the grade was higher than 65 percent of all those who took the test.

Stanine or "standard nine" scores combine the understandability of percentages with the properties of the normal curve of probability. Stanines divide the bell curve into nine sections, the largest of which stretches from the 40th to the 60th percentile and is the "Fifth Stanine" (the average of taking into account error possibilities).

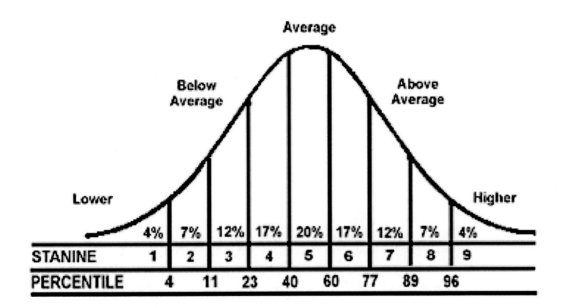

Quartiles divide the data into 4 parts. First find the median of the data set (Q2), then find the median of the upper (Q3) and lower (Q1) halves of the data set. If there is an odd number of values in the data set, include the median value in both halves when finding quartile values. For example, given the data set: {1, 4, 9, 16, 25, 36, 49, 64, 81} first find the median value, which is 25. This is the second quartile. Since there are an odd number of values in the data set (9), we include the median in both halves.

To find the quartile values, we must find the medians of: {1, 4, 9, 16, 25} and {25, 36, 49, 64, 81}. Since each of these subsets has an odd number of elements (5), we use the middle value. Thus the first quartile value is 9, and the third quartile value is 49. If the data set has an even number of elements, average the middle two values. The quartile values are always either one of the data points, or exactly halfway between two data points.

Example: Given the following set of data, find the percentile of the score 104.
70, 72, 82, 83, 84, 87, 100, 104, 108, 109, 110, 115

Find the percentage of scores below 104.

7/12 of the scores are less than 104. This is 58.333%; therefore, the score of 104 is in the 58th percentile.

Example: Find the first, second and third quartile for the data listed.
6, 7, 8, 9, 10, 12, 13, 14, 15, 16, 18, 23, 24, 25, 27, 29, 30, 33, 34, 37

Quartile 1: The 1st Quartile is the median of the lower half of the data set, which is 11.

Quartile 2: The median of the data set is the 2nd Quartile, which is 17.

Quartile 3: The 3rd Quartile is the median of the upper half of the data set, which is 28.

COMPETENCY 18.0 SOLVE APPLIED PROBLEMS USING A COMBINATION OF MATHEMATICAL SKILLS

Skill 18.1 Apply combinations of mathematical skills to solve a series of related problems.

See Competencies 13.0 – 17.0.

Skill 18.2 Identify an equation to solve word problems involving one and two variables.

Example: Mark and Mike are twins. Three times Mark's age plus four equals four times Mike's age minus 14. How old are the boys?

Since the boys are twins, their ages are the same. "Translate" the English into algebra. Let x = their age

$3x + 4 = 4x - 14$

$18 = x$

The boys are each 18 years old.

Example: The YMCA wants to sell raffle tickets to raise $32,000. If they must pay $7,250 in expenses and prizes out of the money collected from the tickets, how many tickets worth $25 each must they sell?

Let x = number of tickets sold
Then $25x$ = total money collected for x tickets

Total money minus expenses is greater than $32,000.

$25x - 7250 = 32,000$
$25x = 39350$
$x = 1570$

If they sell 1,570 tickets, they will raise $32,000.

Example: The Simpsons went out for dinner. All 4 of them ordered the aardvark steak dinner. Bert paid for the 4 meals and included a tip of $12 for a total of $84.60. How much was an aardvark steak dinner?

Let x = the price of one aardvark dinner.
So $4x$ = the price of 4 aardvark dinners.

Some word problems can be solved using a system (group) of equations or inequalities. Watch for words such as *greater than*, *less than*, *at least*, or *no more than*, which indicate the need for inequalities.

Example: Farmer Greenjeans bought 4 cows and 6 sheep for $1700. Mr. Ziffel bought 3 cows and 12 sheep for $2400. If all the cows were the same price and all the sheep were another price, find the price charged for a cow or for a sheep.

Let x = price of a cow
Let y = price of a sheep

Then Farmer Greenjeans' equation would be: $4x + 6y = 1700$
Mr. Ziffel's equation would be: $3x + 12y = 2400$

To solve by **addition-subtraction**:
Multiply the first equation by $^-2$: $^-2(4x + 6y = 1700)$
Keep the other equation the same: $(3x + 12y = 2400)$
By doing this, the equations can be added to each other to eliminate one variable and solve for the other variable.

$$^-8x - 12y = {}^-3400$$
$$\underline{3x + 12y = 2400}$$ Add these equations.
$$^-5x \qquad = {}^-1000$$

$x = 200 \leftarrow$ the price of a cow is $200.
Solving for y, $y = 150 \leftarrow$ the price of a sheep is $150.

To solve by **substitution**:

Solve one of the equations for a variable. (Try to make an equation without fractions if possible.) Substitute this expression into the equation that you have not yet used. Solve the resulting equation for the value of the remaining variable.

$$4x + 6y = 1700$$
$$3x + 12y = 2400 \leftarrow \text{ Solve this equation for } x.$$

It becomes $x = 800 - 4y$. Now substitute $800 - 4y$ in place of x in the OTHER equation. $4x + 6y = 1700$ now becomes:

$$4(800 - 4y) + 6y = 1700$$
$$3200 - 16y + 6y = 1700$$
$$3200 - 10y = 1700$$
$$^{-}10y = ^{-}1500$$
$$y = 150, \text{ or } \$150 \text{ for a sheep.}$$

Substituting 150 back into an equation for y, find x.
$$4x + 6(150) = 1700$$
$$4x + 900 = 1700$$
$$4x = 800 \text{ or } x = 200 \text{ for a cow.}$$

Example: Sharon's Bike Shoppe can assemble a 3-speed bike in 30 minutes or a 10-speed bike in 60 minutes. The profit on each bike sold is $60 for a 3-speed or $75 for a 10-speed bike. How many of each type of bike should they assemble during an 8-hour day (480 minutes) to make the maximum profit? Total daily profit must be at least $300.

Let $x =$ number of 3-speed bikes.
$y =$ number of 10-speed bikes.

Since there are only 480 minutes to use each day,

$30x + 60y \leq 480$ is the first inequality.

Since the total daily profit must be at least $300,

$60x + 75y \geq 300$ is the second inequality.

$32x + 65y \leq 480$ solves to $y \leq 8 - 1/2x$
$60x + 75y \geq 300$ solves to $y \geq 4 - 4/5x$

Graph these 2 inequalities:

$$y \leq 8 - 1/2\,x$$
$$y \geq 4 - 4/5\,x$$

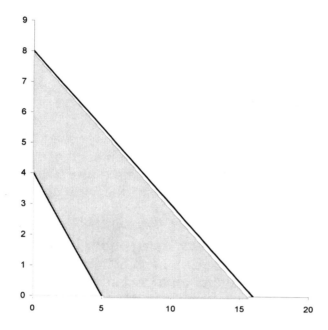

Realize that $x \geq 0$ and $y \geq 0$, since the number of bikes assembled cannot be a negative number. Graph these as additional constraints on the problem. The number of bikes assembled must always be an integer value, so points within the shaded area of the graph must have integer values. The maximum profit will occur at or near a corner of the shaded portion of this graph. Those points occur at (0,4), (0,8), (16,0), or (5,0).

Since profits are $60/3-speed or $75/10-speed, the profit would be :

$$(0,4) \quad 60(0) + 75(4) = 300$$
$$(0,8) \quad 60(0) + 75(8) = 600$$
$$(16,0) \quad 60(16) + 75(0) = 960 \leftarrow \text{Maximum profit}$$
$$(5,0) \quad 60(5) + 75(0) = 300$$

The maximum profit would occur if 16 3-speed bikes are made daily.

Skill 18.3   Apply number concepts and geometric principles to solve practical problems.

See Skill 16.5.

Skill 18.4   Apply statistical principles to analyze patterns and trends in data.

A **trend** line on a line graph shows the correlation between two sets of data. A trend may show positive correlation (both sets of data get bigger together), negative correlation (one set of data gets bigger while the other gets smaller), or no correlation.

An **inference** is a statement which is derived from reasoning. When reading a graph, inferences help with interpretation of the data that is being presented. From this information, a **conclusion** and even **predictions** about what the data actually means is possible.

Example: Katherine and Tom were both doing poorly in math class. Their teacher had a conference with each of them in November. The following graph shows their math test scores during the school year.

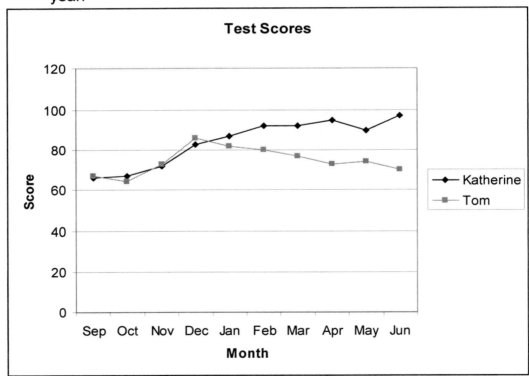

What kind of trend does this graph show?

This graph shows that there is a positive trend in Katherine's test scores and a negative trend in Tom's test scores.

What inferences can you make from this graph?

We can infer that Katherine's test scores rose steadily after November. Tom's test scores spiked in December but then began to fall again and became negatively trended.

What conclusion can you draw based upon this graph?

We can conclude that Katherine took her teacher's meeting seriously and began to study in order to do better on the exams. It seems as though Tom tried harder for a bit, but his test scores eventually slipped back down to the level where he began.

Sample Test: Mathematics

1. $\left(\dfrac{^-4}{9}\right)+\left(\dfrac{^-7}{10}\right)=$

    (Average Rigor) (Skill 14.1)

    A. $\dfrac{23}{90}$

    B. $\dfrac{^-23}{90}$

    C. $\dfrac{103}{90}$

    D. $\dfrac{^-103}{90}$

2. $(5.6)\times\left(^-0.11\right)=$

    (Average Rigor) (Skill 14.1)

    A. $^-0.616$

    B. 0.616

    C. $^-6.110$

    D. 6.110

3. $(3\times9)^4=$

    (Rigorous) (Skill 14.1)

    A. $(3\times9)(3\times9)(27\times27)$

    B. $(3\times9)+(3\times9)$

    C. (12×36)

    D. $(3\times9)+(3\times9)+(3\times9)$
       $+(3\times9)$

4. $4\dfrac{2}{9}\ \times\ \dfrac{7}{10}$

    (Rigorous) (Skill 14.1)

    A. $4\dfrac{9}{10}$

    B. $\dfrac{266}{90}$

    C. $2\dfrac{43}{45}$

    D. $2\dfrac{6}{20}$

5. $0.74=$
    (Easy) (Skill 14.1)

    A. $\dfrac{74}{100}$

    B. 7.4%

    C. $\dfrac{33}{50}$

    D. $\dfrac{74}{10}$

6. $^-9\dfrac{1}{4}\quad\square\quad{}^-8\dfrac{2}{3}$

    (Average Rigor) (Skill 14.1)

    A. $=$

    B. $<$

    C. $>$

    D. $\leq$

7. **303 is what percent of 600?**
(Easy) (Skill 14.1)

   A. 0.505%

   B. 5.05%

   C. 505%

   D. 50.5%

8. **An item that sells for $375 is put on sale at $120. What is the percent of decrease?**
(Average Rigor) (Skill 14.1)

   A. 25%

   B. 28%

   C. 68%

   D. 34%

9. **Two mathematics classes have a total of 410 students. The 8:00 am class has 40 more than the 10:00 am class. How many students are in the 10:00 am class?**
(Rigorous) (Skill 14.1)

   A. 123.3

   B. 370

   C. 185

   D. 330

10. **A restaurant employs 465 people. There are 280 waiters and 185 cooks. If 168 waiters and 85 cooks receive pay raises, what percent of the waiters will receive a pay raise?**
(Average Rigor) (Skill 14.1)

    A. 36.13%

    B. 60%

    C. 60.22%

    D. 40%

11. **Which of the following is an irrational number?**
(Rigorous) (Skill 14.1)

    A. .362626262...

    A. $4\frac{1}{3}$

    B. $\sqrt{5}$

    D. $-\sqrt{16}$

12. Round $1\frac{13}{16}$ of an inch to the nearest quarter of an inch.
(Easy) (Skill 14.1)

A. $1\frac{1}{4}$ inch

B. $1\frac{5}{8}$ inch

C. $1\frac{3}{4}$ inch

D. 2 inches

13. What is the greatest common factor of 16, 28, and 36?
(Easy) (Skill 14.1)

A. 2

B. 4

C. 8

D. 16

14. $\frac{7}{9} + \frac{1}{3} \div \frac{2}{3} =$
(Average Rigor) (Skill 14.1)

A. $\frac{5}{3}$

B. $\frac{3}{2}$

C. 2

D. $\frac{23}{18}$

15. Choose the statement that is true for all real numbers.
(Rigorous) (Skill 14.1)

A. $a = 0, b \neq 0$, then $\frac{b}{a}$ = undefined.

B. $^-(a + (^-a)) = 2a$

C. $2(ab) = {}^-(2a)b$

D. $^-a(b + 1) = ab - a$

16. $(^-2.1 \times 10^4)(4.2 \times 10^{-5}) =$
(Rigorous) (Skill 14.1)

A. 8.82

B. -8.82

C. -0.882

D. 0.882

17. In a sample of 40 full-time employees at a particular company, 35 were also holding down a part-time job requiring at least 10 hours/week. If this proportion holds for the entire company of 25000 employees, how many full-time employees at this company are actually holding down a part-time job of at least 10 hours per week.
(Rigorous) (Skill 14.2)

A. 714

B. 625

C. 21,875

D. 28,571

18. It takes 5 equally skilled people 9 hours to shingle Mr. Joe's roof. Let t be the time required for only 3 of these men to do the same job. Select the correct statement of the given condition.
(Rigorous) (Skill 14.2)

A. $\dfrac{3}{5} = \dfrac{9}{t}$

B. $\dfrac{9}{5} = \dfrac{3}{t}$

C. $\dfrac{5}{9} = \dfrac{3}{t}$

D. $\dfrac{14}{9} = \dfrac{t}{5}$

19. The table below shows the distribution of majors for a group of college students.

• Major	• Proportion of Students
Mathematics	• 0.32
Photography	• 0.26
Journalism	• 0.19
Engineering	• 0.21
Criminal Law	• 0.02

If it is known that a student, chosen at random is not majoring in mathematics or engineering, what is the probability that a student is majoring in journalism?
(Rigorous) (Skill 14.2)

A. 0.19

B. 0.36

C. 0.40

D. 0.81

20. What measure could be used to report the distance traveled in walking around a track?
(Easy) (Skill 14.3)

A. degrees

B. square meters

C. kilometers

D. cubic feet

21. What measure could be used to describe the amount of liquid in a teaspoon?
(Easy) (14.3)

A. Liter

B. Milliliter

C. Centimeter

D. Volume

22. A car gets 25.36 miles per gallon. The car has been driven 83,310 miles. What is a reasonable estimate for the number of gallons of gas used?
(Average Rigor) (Skill 14.4)

A. 2,087 gallons

B. 3,000 gallons

C. 1,800 gallons

D. 164 gallons

23. **Identify the missing term in the following harmonic sequence:**

$$\frac{1}{3}, \frac{1}{6}, \frac{1}{9}, \frac{1}{12}, \frac{1}{15}, ?$$

(Easy) (Skill 15.1)

A. $\frac{1}{16}$

B. $\frac{1}{17}$

C. $\frac{1}{18}$

D. 18

24. **Set A, B, C, and U are related as shown in the diagram.**

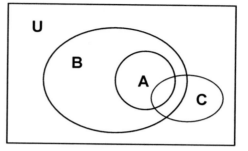

Which of the following is true, assuming not one of the six regions is empty?
(Average Rigor) (Skill 15.2)

A. Any element that is a member of set B is also a member of set A.

B. No element is a member of all three sets A, B, and C.

C. Any element that is a member of set U is also a member of set B.

D. None of the above statements is true.

25. **Given that:**
    i. No athletes are weak.
    ii. All football players are athletes.

    Determine which conclusion can be logically deduced.
    (Average Rigor) (Skill 15.2)

    A. Some football players are weak.

    B. All football players are weak.

    C. No football player is weak.

    D. None of the above is true.

26. **Identify the conditions that correspond to the shaded region of the coordinate plane shown below.**

    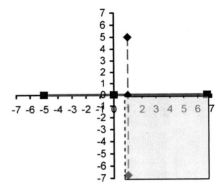

    (Rigorous) (Skill 16.1)

    A. $x \geq 1$ and $y < 0$

    B. $x > 1$ and $y \leq 0$

    C. $x \leq 0$ and $y \geq 1$

    D. $x < 0$ and $y > 1$

27. **Find the equation of a line through (5,6) and (-1,-2) in standard form.**
    (Rigorous) (Skill 16.1)

    A. 3y+4x-2

    B. $-2y = \dfrac{4}{3}x - 1$

    C. 6y + 5x − 1

    D. y = 4x -6

28. Find the value of X.
$3x + 3 = 9$
(Easy) (Skill 16.2)

A. 2

B. 4

C. 9

D. 6

29. For each of the statements below, determine whether $x = \dfrac{1}{6}$ is a solution.

i. $6x \le 4x^2 + 2$
ii. $10x + 1 = 3(4x - 3)$
iii. $|x - 1| = x$
(Rigorous) (Skill 16.2)

A. i, ii, and iii

B. i and iii only

C. i only

D. iii only

30. Solve for x.
$3x - \dfrac{2}{3} = \dfrac{5x}{2} + 2$
(Rigorous) (Skill 16.2)

A. $5\dfrac{1}{3}$

B. $\dfrac{17}{3}$

C. 2

D. $\dfrac{16}{2}$

31. If $4x - (3 - x) = 7(x - 3) + 10$, then
(Average Rigor) (Skill 16.2)

A. $x = 8$

B. $x = -8$

C. $x = 4$

D. $x = -4$

32. Given the formula *d* =*rt*, (where *d* = distance, *r* =rate, and *t* =time), calculate the time required for a vehicle to travel 585 miles at a rate of 65 miles per hour.
(Average Rigor) (Skill 16.2)

A. 8.5 hours

B. 6.5 hours

C. 9.5 hours

D. 9 hours

33. Choose the expression that is not equivalent to 5x + 3y + 15z:
(Average Rigor)(Skill 16.3)

    A. $5(x + 3z) + 3y$

    B. $3(x + y + 5z)$

    C. $3y + 5(x + 3z)$

    D. $5x + 3(y + 5z)$

34. Choose the equation that is equivalent to the following:

    $$\frac{3x}{5} - 5 = 5x$$

    (Rigorous) (Skill 16.3)

    A. $3x - 25 = 25x$

    B. $x - \frac{25}{3} = 25x$

    C. $6x - 50 = 75x$

    D. $x + 25 = 25x$

35. Which is a linear factor of the following expression:

    $$7x^2 + 16x - 15$$
    (Average Rigor) (Skill 16.3)

    A. $(7x + 5)$

    B. $(x - 3)$

    C. $(7x - 5)$

    D. $(2x - 3)$

36. _____ lines do not intersect.
(Rigorous) (Skill 16.4)

    A. Perpendicular

    B. Parallel

    C. Intersecting

    D. Skew

37. Which angle would measure less than 90 degrees?
(Average Rigor) (Skill 16.4)

    A. Acute

    B. Obtuse

    C. Right

    D. Straight

38. The trunk of a tree has a 2.1 meter radius. What is its circumference?
(Rigorous) (Skill 16.5)

    A. 2.1π square meters

    B. 4.2π meters

    C. $2.1\ \pi$ meters

    D. 4.2π square meters

39. **What is the area of a square whose side is 13 feet?**
(Average Rigor) (Skill 16.5)

   A. 169 feet

   B. 169 square feet

   C. 52 feet

   D. 52 square feet

40. **What type of triangle is △ABC?**

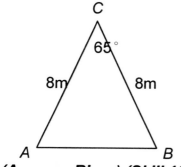

(Average Rigor) (Skill 16.5)

   A. right

   B. equilateral

   C. scalene

   D. isosceles

41. **What unit of measurement would describe the spread of a forest fire in a unit time?**
(Average Rigor) (Skill 16.5)

   A. 10 square yards per second

   B. 10 yards per minute

   C. 10 feet per hour

   D. 10 cubic feet per hour

42. **What is the perimeter of this triangle?**
(Average Rigor) (Skill 16.5)

   A. 7

   B. 21

   C. 37

   D. 49

43. **What is the area of this triangle?**
(Rigorous) (Skill 16.5)

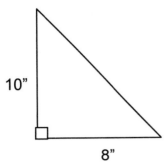

10"

8"

A. 80 square inches

B. 20 square inches

C. 40 square inches

D. 30 square inches

44. **The following chart shows the yearly average number of international tourists visiting Palm Beach for 1990-1994. How may more international tourists visited Palm Beach in 1994 than in 1991?**
(Easy) (Skill 17.1)

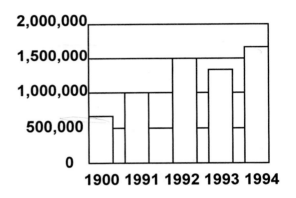

A. 100,000

B. 600,000

C. 1,600,000

D. 8,000,000

45. **What is the mode of the data in the following sample?**

9, 10, 11, 9, 10, 11, 9, 13
(Average Rigor) (Skill 17.3)

A. 9

B. 9.5

C. 10

D. 11

46. Mary did comparison shopping on her favorite brand of coffee. Over half of the stores priced the coffee at $1.70. Most of the remaining stores priced the coffee at $1.80, except for a few who charged $1.90. Which of the following statements is true about the distribution of prices? *(Rigorous) (Skill 17.3)*

A. The mean and the mode are the same.

B. The mean is greater than the mode.

C. The mean is less than the mode.

D. The mean is less than the median.

47. Consider the graph of the distribution of the length of time it took individuals to complete an employment form.

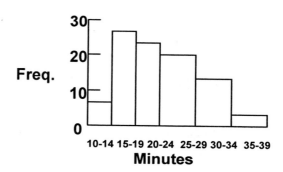

Approximately how many individuals took less than 15 minutes to complete the employment form? *(Average Rigor) (Skill 17.4)*

A. 35

B. 28

C. 7

D. 4

48. Mr. Jones has 15 male students and 13 female students. Mrs. Smith has 10 male students and 17 female students. Who has more students? *(Easy) (Skill 18.1)*

A. They have the same number.

B. Mr. Jone has more.

C. Mrs. Smith has more.

D. Not enough information

49. The owner of a rectangular piece of land 40 yards in length and 30 yards in width wants to divide it into two parts. She plans to join two opposite corners with a fence as shown in the diagram below. The cost of the fence will be approximately $25 per linear foot. What is the estimated cost for the fence needed by the owner?

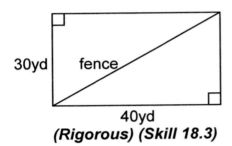

30yd

fence

40yd

(Rigorous) (Skill 18.3)

A. $1,250

B. $62,500

C. $5,250

D. $3,750

50. A student organization is interested in determining how strong the support is among registered voters in the United States for the president's education plan. Which of the following procedures would be most appropriate for selecting a statistically unbiased sample?
(Rigorous) (Skill 18.4)

A. Having viewers call in to a nationally broad-cast talk show and give their opinions.

B. Survey registered voters selected by blind drawing in the three largest states.

C. Select regions of the country by blind drawing and then select people from the voters registration list by blind drawing.

D. Pass out survey forms at the front entrance of schools selected by blind drawing and ask people entering and exiting to fill them in.

Answer Key: Mathematics

1.	D	26.	B
2.	A	27.	A
3.	A	28.	A
4.	C	29.	C
5.	A	30.	A
6.	B	31.	C
7.	D	32.	D
8.	C	33.	B
9.	C	34.	A
10.	B	35.	C
11.	C	36.	B
12.	C	37.	A
13.	B	38.	B
14.	D	39.	B
15.	A	40.	D
16.	C	41.	A
17.	C	42.	B
18.	B	43.	C
19.	C	44.	B
20.	C	45.	A
21.	B	46.	B
22.	B	47.	C
23.	C	48.	B
24.	D	49.	D
25.	C	50.	C

Rigor Table: Mathematics

	Easy 20%	Average 40%	Rigorous 40%
Questions (50)	5, 7, 12, 13, 20, 21, 23, 28, 44, 48	1, 2, 6, 8, 10, 14, 22, 24, 25, 31, 32, 33, 35, 37, 39, 40, 41, 42, 45, 47	3, 4, 9, 11, 15, 16, 17, 18, 19, 26, 27, 29, 30, 34, 36, 38, 43, 46, 49, 50
TOTALS	10 (20%)	20 (40%)	20 (40%)

Rationales with Sample Questions: Mathematics

1. $\left(\dfrac{^-4}{9}\right)+\left(\dfrac{^-7}{10}\right)=$

   (Average Rigor) (Skill 14.1)

   A. $\dfrac{23}{90}$

   B. $\dfrac{^-23}{90}$

   C. $\dfrac{103}{90}$

   D. $\dfrac{^-103}{90}$

Answer D: $\dfrac{^-103}{90}$

Find the LCD of $\dfrac{^-4}{9}$ and $\dfrac{^-7}{10}$. The LCD is 90, so you get $\dfrac{^-40}{90}+\dfrac{^-63}{90}=\dfrac{^-103}{90}$.

2. $(5.6)\times\left(^-0.11\right)=$

   (Average Rigor) (Skill 14.1)

   A. $^-0.616$

   B. 0.616

   C. $^-6.110$

   D. 6.110

Answer A: - 0.616

Simple multiplication. The answer will be negative because a positive times a negative is a negative number. $5.6\times^-0.11=^-0.616$.

3. $(3 \times 9)^4 =$
   (Rigorous) (Skill 14.1)

   A. $(3 \times 9)(3 \times 9)(27 \times 27)$

   B. $(3 \times 9) + (3 \times 9)$

   C. (12×36)

   D. $(3 \times 9) + (3 \times 9) + (3 \times 9)$
      $+ (3 \times 9)$

Answer A: (3 x 9) (3 x 9) (27 x 27)

$(3 \times 9)^4 = (3 \times 9)(3 \times 9)(3 \times 9)(3 \times 9)$, which, when solving two of the parentheses, is $(3 \times 9)(3 \times 9)(27 \times 27)$.

4. $4\frac{2}{9} \times \frac{7}{10}$
   (Rigorous) (Skill 14.1)

   A. $4\frac{9}{10}$

   B. $\frac{266}{90}$

   C. $2\frac{43}{45}$

   D. $2\frac{6}{20}$

Answer C: $2\frac{43}{45}$

Convert any mixed number to an improper fraction: $\frac{38}{9} \times \frac{7}{10}$. Since no common factors of numerators or denominators exist, multiply the numerators and the denominators by each other $= \frac{266}{90}$. Convert back to a mixed number and reduce $2\frac{86}{90} = 2\frac{43}{45}$.

5. **0.74 =**
(Easy) (Skill 14.1)

A. $\dfrac{74}{100}$

B. 7.4%

C. $\dfrac{33}{50}$

D. $\dfrac{74}{10}$

Answer A: $\dfrac{74}{100}$

This is basic conversion of decimals to fractions. 0.74® the 4 is in the hundredths place, so the answer is $\dfrac{74}{100}$.

6. $^-9\dfrac{1}{4}$ ☐ $^-8\dfrac{2}{3}$
(Average Rigor) (Skill 14.1)

A. =

B. <

C. >

D. ≤

Answer B: <

The larger the absolute value of a negative number, the smaller the negative number is. The absolute value of $-9\dfrac{1}{4}$ is $9\dfrac{1}{4}$ which is larger than the absolute value of $-8\dfrac{2}{3}$ is $8\dfrac{2}{3}$. Therefore, the sign should be $-9\dfrac{1}{4} < -8\dfrac{2}{3}$.

7. **303 is what percent of 600?**
   (Easy) (Skill 14.1)

   A. 0.505%

   B. 5.05%

   C. 505%

   D. 50.5%

Answer D: 50.5%

Use x for the percent. $600x = 303$. $\dfrac{600x}{600} = \dfrac{303}{600} \rightarrow x = 0.505 = 50.5\%$.

8. **An item that sells for $375 is put on sale at $120. What is the percent of decrease?**
   (Average Rigor) (Skill 14.1)

   A. 25%

   B. 28%

   C. 68%

   D. 34%

Answer C: 68%

Use $(1 - x)$ as the discount. $375x = 120$.
$375(1 - x) = 120 \rightarrow 375 - 375x = 120 \rightarrow 375x = 255 \rightarrow x = 0.68 = 68\%$.

9. **Two mathematics classes have a total of 410 students. The 8:00 am class has 40 more than the 10:00 am class. How many students are in the 10:00 am class?**
   (Rigorous) (Skill 14.1)

   A. 123.3

   B. 370

   C. 185

   D. 330

Answer C: 185

Let x = # of students in the 8 am class and $x - 40$ = # of student in the 10 am class. $x + (x - 40) = 410 \rightarrow 2x - 40 = 410 \rightarrow 2x = 450 \rightarrow x = 225$. So there are 225 students in the 8 am class, and $225 - 40 = 185$ in the 10 am class.

10. **A restaurant employs 465 people. There are 280 waiters and 185 cooks. If 168 waiters and 85 cooks receive pay raises, what percent of the waiters will receive a pay raise?**
    (Average Rigor) (Skill 14.1)

    A. 36.13%

    B. 60%

    C. 60.22%

    D. 40%

Answer B: 60%

The total number of waiters is 280 and only 168 of them get a pay raise. Divide the number getting a raise by the total number of waiters to get the percent.
$\dfrac{168}{280} = 0.6 = 60\%$.

11. **Which of the following is an irrational number?**
    (Rigorous) (Skill 6.4)

    A. .362626262...

    B. $4\frac{1}{3}$

    C. $\sqrt{5}$

    D. $-\sqrt{16}$

Answer C: $\sqrt{5}$

Irrational numbers are real numbers that cannot be written as the ratio of two integers, such as infinite non-repeating decimals. $\sqrt{5}$ fits this description; the others do not.

12. **Round $1\frac{13}{16}$ of an inch to the nearest quarter of an inch.**
    (Easy) (Skill 14.1)

    A. $1\frac{1}{4}$ inch

    B. $1\frac{5}{8}$ inch

    C. $1\frac{3}{4}$ inch

    D. 2 inches

Answer C: $1\frac{3}{4}$ inch

$1\frac{13}{16}$ inches is approximately $1\frac{12}{16}$, which is also $1\frac{3}{4}$, which is the nearest $\frac{1}{4}$ of an inch, so the answer is C.

13. **What is the greatest common factor of 16, 28, and 36?**
    (Easy) (Skill 14.1)

    A. 2

    B. 4

    C. 8

    D. 16

Answer B: 4

The smallest number in this set is 16; its factors are 1, 2, 4, 8 and 16. 16 in the largest factor, but it does not divide into 28 or 36. Neither does 8. 4 does factor into both 28 and 36. The answer is **B.**

14. $\dfrac{7}{9} + \dfrac{1}{3} \div \dfrac{2}{3} =$

    (Average Rigor) (Skill 14.1)

    A. $\dfrac{5}{3}$

    B. $\dfrac{3}{2}$

    C. 2

    D. $\dfrac{23}{18}$

Answer D: $\dfrac{23}{18}$

First, do the division.
$$\frac{1}{3} \div \frac{2}{3} = \frac{1}{3} \times \frac{3}{2} = \frac{1}{2}$$

Next, add the fractions.
$$\frac{7}{9} + \frac{1}{2} = \frac{14}{18} + \frac{9}{18} = \frac{23}{18}, \text{ which is answer D.}$$

15. **Choose the statement that is true for all real numbers.**
    (Rigorous) (Skill 14.1)

    A. $a = 0, b \neq 0$, then
       $\dfrac{b}{a} =$ undefined.

    B. $^-(a + (^-a)) = 2a$

    C. $2(ab) = ^-(2a)b$

    D. $^-a(b + 1) = ab - a$

Answer A: $a = 0, b \neq 0$, **then** $\dfrac{b}{a} =$ **undefined.**

Any number divided by 0 is undefined.

16. $(^-2.1 \times 10^4)(4.2 \times 10^{^-5}) =$
    (Rigorous) (Skill 14.1)

    A. 8.82

    B. -8.82

    C. -0.882

    D. 0.882

Answer C: -0.882

First, multiply -2.1 and 4.2 to get -8.82. Then, multiply 10^4 by $10^{^-5}$ to get $10^{^-1}$. $^-8.82 \times 10^{^-1} = ^- 0.882$.

17. In a sample of 40 full-time employees at a particular company, 35 were also holding down a part-time job requiring at least 10 hours/week. If this proportion holds for the entire company of 25000 employees, how many full-time employees at this company are actually holding down a part-time job of at least 10 hours per week. *(Rigorous) (Skill 14.2)*

   A. 714

   B. 625

   C. 21,875

   D. 28,571

Answer C: 21,875

$\dfrac{35}{40}$ full time employees have a part time job also. Out of 25,000 full time employees, the number that have a part time job also is

$\dfrac{35}{40} = \dfrac{x}{25000} \rightarrow 40x = 875000 \rightarrow x = 21875$, so 21875 full time employees also have a part time job.

18. It takes 5 equally skilled people 9 hours to shingle Mr. Joe's roof. Let *t* be the time required for only 3 of these men to do the same job. Select the correct statement of the given condition.
(Rigorous) (Skill 14.2)

A. $\dfrac{3}{5} = \dfrac{9}{t}$

B. $\dfrac{9}{5} = \dfrac{3}{t}$

C. $\dfrac{5}{9} = \dfrac{3}{t}$

D. $\dfrac{14}{9} = \dfrac{t}{5}$

Answer B: $\dfrac{9}{5} = \dfrac{3}{t}$

$$\dfrac{9 \text{ hours}}{5 \text{ people}} = \dfrac{3 \text{ people}}{t \text{ hours}}$$

19. The table below shows the distribution of majors for a group of college students.

Major	Proportion of Students
Mathematics	0.32
Photography	0.26
Journalism	0.19
Engineering	0.21
Criminal Law	0.02

If it is known that a student, chosen at random is not majoring in mathematics or engineering, what is the probability that a student is majoring in journalism?
(Rigorous) (Skill 14.2)

A. 0.19

B. 0.36

C. 0.40

D. 0.81

Answer C: 0.40

The proportion of students majoring in math or engineering is 0.32 + 0.21 = 0.53. This means that the proportion of students NOT majoring in math or engineering is 1.00 – 0.53 = 0.47. The proportion of students majoring in journalism out of those not majoring in math or engineering is $\dfrac{0.19}{0.47} = 0.404$.

20. **What measure could be used to report the distance traveled in walking around a track?**
(Easy) (Skill 14.3)

    A. degrees

    B. square meters

    C. kilometers

    D. cubic feet

Answer C: kilometers

Degrees measures angles, square meters measures area, cubic feet measure volume, and kilometers measures length. Kilometers is the only reasonable answer.

21. **What measure could be used to describe the amount of liquid in a teaspoon?**
(Easy) (14.3)

    A. Liter

    B. Milliliter

    C. Centimeter

    D. Volume

Answer B: Milliliter

Liter is a unit that would describe a larger volume such as a soft drink. *Centimeter* is a measure of length. *Volume* is the general term of the amount needed to fill a space. *Milliliter* (B) is the answer.

22. A car gets 25.36 miles per gallon. The car has been driven 83,310 miles. What is a reasonable estimate for the number of gallons of gas used?
   (Average Rigor) (Skill 14.4)

   A. 2,087 gallons

   B. 3,000 gallons

   C. 1,800 gallons

   D. 164 gallons

Answer B: 3,000 gallons

Divide the number of miles by the miles per gallon to determine the approximate number of gallons of gas used. $\dfrac{83310 \text{ miles}}{25.36 \text{ miles per gallon}} = 3285$ gallons. This is approximately 3000 gallons.

23. Identify the missing term in the following harmonic sequence:

   $$\frac{1}{3}, \frac{1}{6}, \frac{1}{9}, \frac{1}{12}, \frac{1}{15}, ?$$
   (Easy) (Skill 15.1)

   A. $\dfrac{1}{16}$

   B. $\dfrac{1}{17}$

   C. $\dfrac{1}{18}$

   D. 18

Answer C: 1/18

The difference between the denominators is 3, so the next term in the progression is $\dfrac{1}{18}$.

24. **Set A, B, C, and U are related as shown in the diagram.**

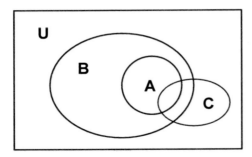

Which of the following is true, assuming not one of the six regions is empty?
(Average Rigor) (Skill 15.2)

A. Any element that is a member of set B is also a member of set A.

B. No element is a member of all three sets A, B, and C.

C. Any element that is a member of set U is also a member of set B.

D. None of the above statements is true.

Answer D: None of the above statements is true.

Answer A is incorrect because not all members of set B are also in set A. Answer B is incorrect because there are elements that are members of all three sets A, B, and C. Answer C is incorrect because not all members of set U is a member of set B. This leaves answer D.

25. **Given that:**
    i. No athletes are weak.
    ii. All football players are
        athletes.

    Determine which conclusion can be logically deduced.
    (Average Rigor) (Skill 15.2)

    A. Some football players are weak.

    B. All football players are weak.

    C. No football player is weak.

    D. None of the above is true.

Answer C: No football player is weak.

Use the Law of Syllogism: If p, then q
                          If q, then r
                          Therefore if p, then r

In "if-then" form this would be, "If you are an athlete, then you are not weak. If you are a football player, then you are an athlete." Clearly, if you are a football player, you are an athlete, which means you are also not weak.

26. **Identify the conditions that correspond to the shaded region of the coordinate plane shown below.**

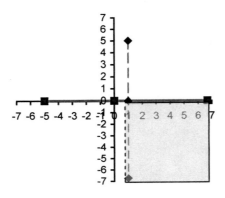

(Rigorous) (Skill 16.1)

A. $x \geq 1$ and $y < 0$

B. $x > 1$ and $y \leq 0$

C. $x \leq 0$ and $y \geq 1$

D. $x < 0$ and $y > 1$

Answer B: $x > 1$ and $y \leq 0$

The line at $x = 1$ is dashed and shaded on the right hand side, so the equation for this line is $x > 1$. The line at $y = 0$ is solid and shaded below, so the equation for this line is $y \leq 0$. So the answer is **B.**

27. **Find the equation of a line through (5,6) and (-1,-2) in standard form. (Rigorous) (Skill 16.1)**

   A. 3y+4x-2

   B. $-2y = \dfrac{4}{3}x - 1$

   C. 6y + 5x – 1

   D. y = 4x -6

Answer A: 3y+4x-2

$$\text{slope} = \frac{y_2 - y_1}{x_2 - x_1} = \frac{-2 - 6}{^-1 - 5} = \frac{-8}{^-6} = \frac{4}{3}$$

$$Y - y_a = m(X - x_a) \rightarrow Y + 2 = \frac{4}{3}(X + 1) \rightarrow$$

$$Y + 2 = \frac{4}{3}x + \frac{4}{3}$$

$$Y = \frac{4}{3}x - \frac{2}{3} \qquad \text{This is the slope-intercept form.}$$

Multiply by 3 to eliminate fractions

$$3y = 4x - 2 \qquad \text{This is the standard form.}$$

The answer is **A.**

28.   **Find the value of X.**
       3x + 3 = 9
       (Easy) (Skill 16.2)

       A. 2

       B. 4

       C. 9

       D. 6

Answer A: 2

3x + 3 = 9
Subtract 3 from each side.
3x = 6
Divide both sides by 3.
X=2

29. For each of the statements below, determine whether $x = \dfrac{1}{6}$ is a solution.

i. $6x \le 4x^2 + 2$
ii. $10x + 1 = 3(4x - 3)$
iii. $|x - 1| = x$

(Rigorous) (Skill 16.2)

A. i, ii, and iii

B. i and iii only

C. i only

D. iii only

Answer C: i only

Substitute $x = \dfrac{1}{6}$ into each equation and solve.

i. $6\left(\dfrac{1}{6}\right) \le 4\left(\dfrac{1}{6}\right)^2 + 2 = 1 \le 4\left(\dfrac{1}{36}\right) + 2 \to 1 \le \dfrac{1}{9} + 2 \to 1 \le 2\dfrac{1}{9}$ True.

ii. $10\left(\dfrac{1}{6}\right) + 1 = 3\left(4\left(\dfrac{1}{6}\right) - 3\right) = 2\dfrac{2}{3} = 3\left(\dfrac{2}{3} - 3\right) \to 2\dfrac{2}{3} = \dfrac{6}{3} - 9 \to 2\dfrac{2}{3} = {}^-7$ False.

iii. $\left|\dfrac{1}{6} - 1\right| = \dfrac{1}{6} \to \left|\dfrac{1}{6} - \dfrac{6}{6}\right| = \dfrac{1}{6} \to \left|\dfrac{{}^-5}{6}\right| = \dfrac{1}{6} \to \dfrac{5}{6} = \dfrac{1}{6}$ False.

So, only (i) is true, which is answer **C**.

30. **Solve for x.**

$$3x - \frac{2}{3} = \frac{5x}{2} + 2$$

(Rigorous) (Skill 16.2)

A. $5\frac{1}{3}$

B. $\frac{17}{3}$

C. 2

D. $\frac{16}{2}$

Answer A: $5\frac{1}{3}$

$$3x(6) - \frac{2}{3}(6) = \frac{5x}{2}(6) + 2(6)$$ 6 is the LCD of 2 and 3

$$18x - 4 = 15x + 12$$

$$18x = 15x + 16$$

$$3x = 16$$

$$x = \frac{16}{3} = 5\frac{1}{3}$$

31.   If $4x - (3 - x) = 7(x - 3) + 10$, then
       (Average Rigor) (Skill 16.2)

       A. $x = 8$

       B. $x = -8$

       C. $x = 4$

       D. $x = -4$

Answer C: x = 4

Solve for x.

$$4x - (3 - x) = 7(x - 3) + 10$$
$$4x - 3 + x = 7x - 21 + 10$$
$$5x - 3 = 7x - 11$$
$$5x = 7x - 11 + 3$$
$$5x - 7x = {}^-8$$
$${}^-2x = {}^-8$$
$$x = 4$$

32.   Given the formula *d = rt*, (where *d* = distance, *r* = rate,
       and *t* = time), calculate the time required for a vehicle
       to travel 585 miles at a rate of 65 miles per hour.
       (Average Rigor) (Skill 16.2)

       A. 8.5 hours

       B. 6.5 hours

       C. 9.5 hours

       D. 9 hours

Answer D: 9 hours

We are given $d = 585$ miles and $r = 65$ miles per hour and *d = rt*. Solve for *t*.
$585 = 65t \rightarrow t = 9$ hours.

33. **Choose the expression that is not equivalent to 5x + 3y + 15z:**
(Average Rigor)(Skill 16.3)

A. 5(x + 3z) + 3y

B. 3(x + y + 5z)

C. 3y + 5(x + 3z)

D. 5x + 3(y + 5z)

Answer B: 3(x + y + 5z)

5x + 3y + 15z = (5x + 15z) + 3y = 5(x + 3z) + 3y   A. is true
       = 5x + (3y + 15z) = 5x + 3(y + 5z)   D. is true
       = 37 + (5x + 15z) = 37 + 5(x + 3z)   C. is true

These can all be solved using the associative property and then factoring.
However, in B. 3(x + y + 5z) by distributive property = 3x + 3y + 15z does not
equal 5x + 37 + 15z.

34. **Choose the equation that is equivalent to the following:**

$$\frac{3x}{5} - 5 = 5x$$

(Rigorous) (Skill 16.3)

A. $3x - 25 = 25x$

B. $x - \dfrac{25}{3} = 25x$

C. $6x - 50 = 75x$

D. $x + 25 = 25x$

Answer A: 3x − 25 = 25x

A is the correct answer because it is the original equation multiplied by 5. The
other choices alter the answer to the original equation.

35.	Which is a linear factor of the following expression:

$7x^2 + 16x - 15$
(Average Rigor) (Skill 16.3)

A.	$(7x + 5)$

B.	$(x - 3)$

C.	$(7x - 5)$

D.	$(2x - 3)$

Answer C: $(7x - 5)$

Factor.
$(\quad - \quad)(\quad + \quad)$
$(7x - 5)(x + 3)$
The answer is **C**.

36.	_____ lines do not intersect.
(Rigorous) (Skill 16.4)

A.	Perpendicular

B.	Parallel

C.	Intersecting

D.	Skew

Answer B: Parallel

Parallel lines continue at equal distance apart indefinitely. The other choices all intersect at some point.

37. **Which angle would measure less than 90 degrees?**
    (Average Rigor) (Skill 16.4)

    A. Acute

    B. Obtuse

    C. Right

    D. Straight

Answer A: Acute

Acute angles measure less than 90 degrees. Obtuse angles measure greater than 90 and less than 180 degrees. Right angles measure 90 degrees, and straight angles measure 180 degrees.

38. **The trunk of a tree has a 2.1 meter radius. What is its circumference?**
    (Rigorous) (Skill 16.5)

    A. 2.1π square meters

    B. 4.2π meters

    C. 2.1π meters

    D. 4.2π square meters

Answer B: 4.2π meters

Circumference is $2\pi r$, where r is the radius. The circumference is $2\pi 2.1 = 4.2\pi$ meters (not square meters because not measuring area).

39. **What is the area of a square whose side is 13 feet?**
   (Average Rigor) (Skill 16.5)

   A. 169 feet

   B. 169 square feet

   C. 52 feet

   D. 52 square feet

Answer B: 169 square feet

Area = length times width (*lw*).
Length = 13 feet
Width = 13 feet (square, so length and width are the same).
Area = $13 \times 13 = 169$ square feet.
Area is measured in square feet, so the answer is B.

40. **What type of triangle is** $\triangle ABC$?

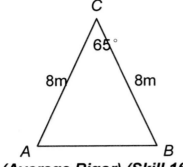

(Average Rigor) (Skill 16.5)

A. right

B. equilateral

C. scalene

D. isosceles

Answer D: isosceles

Two of the sides are the same length, so we know the triangle is either equilateral or isosceles. $\angle CAB$ and $\angle CBA$ are equal, because their sides are. Therefore, $180° = 65° - 2x = \dfrac{115°}{2} = 57.5°$.   Because all three angles are not equal, the triangle is isosceles.

41.　**What unit of measurement would describe the spread of a forest fire in a unit time?**
(Average Rigor) (Skill 16.5)

A.　10 square yards per second

B.　10 yards per minute

C.　10 feet per hour

D.　10 cubic feet per hour

Answer A:　10 square yards per second

The only appropriate answer is one that describes "an area" of forest consumed per unit time. All answers are not units of area measurement except answer A.

42.　**What is the perimeter of this triangle?**
(Average Rigor) (Skill 16.5)

A.　7

B.　21

C.　37

D.　49

Answer B:　21

Perimeter is calculated by adding the measurement of all sides of the figure.

43. **What is the area of this triangle?**
     (Rigorous) (Skill 16.5)

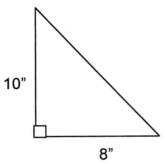

10"

8"

A. 80 square inches

B. 20 square inches

C. 40 square inches

D. 30 square inches

Answer C: 40 square inches

The area of a triangle is $\frac{1}{2}bh$. $\frac{1}{2}x8x10 = 40$ square inches.

44. The following chart shows the yearly average number of international tourists visiting Palm Beach for 1990-1994. How may more international tourists visited Palm Beach in 1994 than in 1991? *(Easy) (Skill 17.1)*

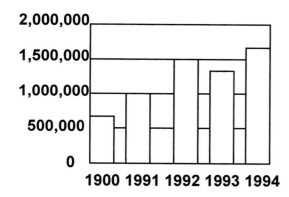

A. 100,000

B. 600,000

C. 1,600,000

D. 8,000,000

Answer B: 600,000

The number of tourists in 1991 was 1,000,000 and the number in 1994 was 1,600,000. Subtract to get a difference of 600,000.

45.   What is the mode of the data in the following sample?

9, 10, 11, 9, 10, 11, 9, 13
(Average Rigor) (Skill 17.3)

A. 9

B. 9.5

C. 10

D. 11

Answer A: 9

The mode is the number that appears most frequently. 9 appears 3 times, which is more than the other numbers.

46.   Mary did comparison shopping on her favorite brand of coffee. Over half of the stores priced the coffee at $1.70. Most of the remaining stores priced the coffee at $1.80, except for a few who charged $1.90. Which of the following statements is true about the distribution of prices?
(Rigorous) (Skill 17.3)

A. The mean and the mode are the same.

B. The mean is greater than the mode.

C. The mean is less than the mode.

D. The mean is less than the median.

Answer B: The mean is greater than the mode.

Over half the stores priced the coffee at $1.70, so this means that this is the mode. The mean would be slightly over $1.70 because other stores priced the coffee at over $1.70.

47. Consider the graph of the distribution of the length of time it took individuals to complete an employment form.

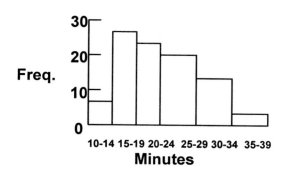

Approximately how many individuals took less than 15 minutes to complete the employment form?
(Average Rigor) (Skill 17.4)

A. 35

B. 28

C. 7

D. 4

Answer C: 7

According to the chart, the number of people who took under 15 minutes is 7.

48. **Mr. Jones has 15 male students and 13 female students. Mrs. Smith has 10 male students and 17 female students. Who has more students?**
(Easy) (Skill 18.1)

A. They have the same number.

B. Mr. Jones has more.

C. Mrs. Smith has more.

D. Not enough information

Answer B: Mr. Jones has more.

Calculate the number of students Mr. Jones has. 15 + 13 = 28
Calculate the number of students Mrs. Smith has. 10 + 17 = 27
Mr. Jones has more students. Answer B.

49.   The owner of a rectangular piece of land 40 yards in length and 30 yards in width wants to divide it into two parts. She plans to join two opposite corners with a fence as shown in the diagram below. The cost of the fence will be approximately $25 per linear foot. What is the estimated cost for the fence needed by the owner?

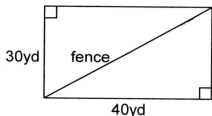

30yd   fence

40yd

(Rigorous) (Skill 18.3)

A. $1,250

B. $62,500

C. $5,250

D. $3,750

Answer D: $3,750

Find the length of the diagonal by using the Pythagorean theorem. Let x be the length of the diagonal.

$$30^2 + 40^2 = x^2 \rightarrow 900 + 1600 = x^2$$
$$2500 = x^2 \rightarrow \sqrt{2500} = \sqrt{x^2}$$

$$x = 50 \text{ yards}$$

Convert to feet. $\dfrac{50 \text{ yards}}{x \text{ feet}} = \dfrac{1 \text{ yard}}{3 \text{ feet}} \rightarrow 150 \text{ feet}$

It cost $25.00 per linear foot, so the cost is (150 ft)($25) = $3,750.

50. **A student organization is interested in determining how strong the support is among registered voters in the United States for the president's education plan. Which of the following procedures would be most appropriate for selecting a statistically unbiased sample? (Rigorous) (Skill 18.4)**

   A. Having viewers call in to a nationally broadcast talk show and give their opinions.

   B. Survey registered voters selected by blind drawing in the three largest states.

   C. Select regions of the country by blind drawing and then select people from the voters registration list by blind drawing.

   D. Pass out survey forms at the front entrance of schools selected by blind drawing and ask people entering and exiting to fill them in.

Answer C: Select regions of the country by blind drawing and then select people from the voters registration list by blind drawing.

C is be the best answer because it is random and it surveys a larger population.

XAMonline, INC. 21 Orient Ave. Melrose, MA 02176

Toll Free number 800-509-4128

TO ORDER Fax 781-662-9268 OR www.XAMonline.com

ILLINOIS TEACHER CERTIFICATION SYSTEM - ICTS - 2008

PO#   Store/School:

Address 1:

Address 2 (Ship to other):

City, State Zip

Credit card number_____-_____-_____-_____   expiration_____

EMAIL _____

PHONE   **FAX**

ISBN	TITLE	Qty	Retail	Tota
978-1-58197-721-9	ICTS Special Education Learning Behavior Specialist I 155		$73.50	
978-1-58197-576-5	ICTS Special Education General Curriculum Test 163		$73.50	
978-1-58197-694-6	ICTS Basic Skills 096		$33.95	
978-1-58197-293-1	ICTS Assessment of Professional Teaching Tests 101-104		$34.95	
978-1-58197-978-7	ICTS Science- Biology 105		$59.95	
978-1-58197-979-4	ICTS Science- Chemistry 106		$59.95	
978-1-58197-673-1	ICTS Science- Earth and Space Science 108		$59.95	
978-1-58197-594-9	ICTS Elementary-Middle Grades 110		$28.95	
978-1-58197-599-4	ICTS Early Childhood Education 107		$73.50	
978-1-58197-722-6	ICTS English Language Arts 111		$59.95	
978-1-58197-982-4	ICTS Social Science- History 114		$59.95	
978-1-58197-643-4	ICTS Mathematics 115		$59.95	
978-1-58197-870-4	ICTS Science: Physics 116		$59.95	
978-1-58197-985-5	ICTS Social Science- Political Science 117		$59.95	
978-1-58197-987-9	ICTS Foreign Language- French Sample Test 127		$15.00	
978-1-58197-988-6	ICTS Foreign Language- Spanish 135		$59.95	
978-1-58197-989-3	ICTS Physical Education 144		$59.95	
978-1-58197-990-9	ICTS Visual Arts Sample Test 145		$15.00	
978-1-58197-992-3	ICTS Library Information Specialist 175		$59.95	
978-1-58197-993-0	ICTS Reading Teacher 177		$59.95	
978-1-58197-994-7	ICTS School Counselor 181		$59.95	
978-1-58197-995-4	ICTS Principal 186		$59.95	
			SUBTOTAL	
			Ship	$8
			TOTAL	

CPSIA information can be obtained
at www.ICGtesting.com
Printed in the USA
FFOW04n0658170816
26903FF